# Rereadings

## Eight Early French Novels

Rereadings

Eight Early French Novels

by Philip Stewart

SUMMA PUBLICATIONS, INC.
Birmingham, Alabama
1984

Printed in the United States of America
Library of Congress Catalog Card Number 83-50520
ISBN 0-917786-00-9

**Pour Anna Faye**

# CONTENTS

# PREFACE

This book is not designed principally to argue a thesis, nor to serve as exemplar for any one critical doctrine. The chapters are discrete essays on a limited number of novels of the seventeenth and eighteenth centuries. Although it is in some ways informed by recent critical insights of linguistic, structural, or semiotic inspiration, and borrows sometimes from those analytical terminologies, these studies do not represent an exercise in a specific methodology, nor offer a theory of interpretation as such. The essay form has been adopted for its flexibility in weaving the interconnections of various aspects of the reading, and also for its freedom from rigid subdivisions which might suggest mechanical application of a system. It is hoped the result will prove accessible even to those who are encountering the novels themselves for the first time.

I am of course much in debt not only to the newer schools but to the numerous valuable studies of the last two decades which have brought so much light to our understanding of literary history. Thanks to them, a reading of these early novels can now be less encumbered by previous oversimplifications and ingrained critical prejudices (in particular, the persistent tendency to rate them in terms of their progress toward "realism"). No attempt is being made here, however, to amass a compendium of such scholarship, which will be cited only in cases where it is immediately relevant to my own readings.

But since it is desirable to be as explicit as possible about one's procedure, I shall attempt in the next few pages to define some of the critical assumptions at work here. What I am attempting is a practical demonstration which I shall call textual reading, to emphasize that what is under discussion is indeed the text itself and not its historical context. The literary text is approached as a relatively autonomous unit capable of being illuminated through discovery of verbal patterns, and ultimately through recognition of the operations which it in effect performs upon itself.

Textual reading chooses to emphasize that literature is a kind of use that is made of language; it looks rather for the meaning-generating functions of the literary discourse in particular works than, as in other forms of literary study, the broader laws controlling literary production, or the relationship between the text and the author's life and thought or other extrinsic data—influences, the genesis of the work, its psychoanalytic structure, and so forth. The purpose is less to interpret than to illustrate through a heightening of the text's plural values why interpretation is required. Which is not to say that this book can pretend to steer a perfectly straight course innocent of any interpretive bent. Without denying the need for symbolic interpretation, which may of course be elicited or even authorized by the text itself, this study is oriented towards elements which are present in the text; interpretation, on the other hand, considers the text primarily in terms of its symbolic relation with other texts, literary or otherwise.

A perspective of this kind imposes, in particular, considerable limits on any tendency to valorize the novel's referential function with regard to the outside world. Literature does not exist principally to celebrate the real; on the contrary, it opposes to it its own "reality." And, as I shall argue directly in the first chapter and imply thereafter, the ways in which the text calls attention to its own literariness undermine the traditional claims of what is too often, and too absent-mindedly, called "realism." The difference between life and the life of fiction is not that the latter is frozen like the fossilized image of life past, but that its mode of life is determined by laws proper to its own narrative nature. No number of words and sentences can make a novel unless they are related among themselves according to certain more or less well-determined expectations. The life of a narrative text is "still" life insofar as it must await the reanimating power of reading, but it is not inert for it can never be read twice the same way.

Such a stance in no way entails a supposition that the work lives in a vacuum. Discourse is *allusive*, and intertextuality exists because different works, whether of the same or different periods, necessarily share some common references. To treat the novels in a manner which intends to be exclusively literary rather than as documents is not to render them, as one historical critic has somewhat maliciously put it, "sans passé, sans histoire, sans contenu."[1] Whether it is appropriate, in terms of efficiency of exposition, to stress those links in the discussion of individual texts is a matter not of doctrine but of judgment in each instance; relative strategy indeed almost always determines choices of emphasis in literary criticism.

It is possible to think of literary creations as objects whose primary purpose is an opening out onto the world, holding the mirror up to nature and so forth. Such a universalizing dimension is being purposefully left aside here in order to grant fuller consideration of the ways in which, in a reverse movement, the text doubles back upon itself, underscoring in the process the fundamental narrativity which (in the case of the novel) is the mode of its own being. This self-reinforcing, autoreferential capacity is more generally acknowledged as an attribute of poetry than of prose fiction: many highly explicit examples can be cited of poems which are about themselves, or about poetry. But it is no less true, in fact, of other literary genres, even if for various reasons we have been less accustomed to perceiving it that way.

One interesting aspect of the "literariness" of these novels, the more pronounced perhaps in that they are closer to the genre's historical beginnings, is that the circle of literary referentiality on which they depend encompasses not just other novels but in large proportion other literary denominations as well, epic and comedy in particular. The novel tends to situate itself discursively in relation to them. Thus, although the developmental assimilations involving various genres can be shown through a pure historical study, they can quite well be discovered as well with the individual text. Although, in varying degrees of explicitness, these novels are found to be "about" themselves, they also participate in this way in a dynamic continuum which makes them equally "about" literary qualities and types more generally, the discourse of fiction, and ultimately literature.

The reflexive function of the text is most evident in its overt self-commentary, but it also possesses subtler means of eliciting or soliciting its own textual and literary presence. These manifestations vary from one work to another, but practice seems to indicate that tropes, and particularly metaphors, are one function through which the text can be fruitfully approached in a large number of cases. The attention which will be focused on them from time to time has nothing to do with the traditional taxonomy of metaphors by virtue of their comparors: animal metaphors, flower metaphors, and the like, all of which categories can of course be subsequently sub-divided. Such an operation provides in fact little information about the function of the metaphor within a linguistic and rhetorical system.[2] What is of interest here is the text as system, or, in Henri Meschonnic's useful formulation, "le sens de la forme." Tropes prove profound, not considered as formal ensembles or stylistic arabesques, but as *figures of reading*. Their virtue lies not in their substitutive, coded value, but in their organic correlation with the other aspects of the textual system: the work "figures" itself.[3] I will be looking for figuration, however, not with exclusive regard to metaphorical constructions in the formal sense, but also to functions of narrative rhetoric; these include conventional pretexts founding the speech act that the text embodies, modulation of different voices in the narrative process, pretensions of objectivity, and the irony or self-parody of the fictional discourse.

These various dimensions will be invoked with flexibiliity as they appear most viable. The narrative structure, for example, seems to me to assume a greater meaning-bearing function in some cases than in others. Sometimes scrutiny brought to bear on a narrative's chronological organization will yield interesting results, especially where it is complex; at other times, it appears patent and unrewarding. Frequently, but not always, systematic analysis of the characters' relations to each other, or to the overall social structure represented, seems to lie close to the heart of the meaning. Rhetoric, both narrowly construed as tropes and broadly construed as persuasive strategies of the discourse, will often be treated at some length. And all of these, as well as other categories such as plot structures and reference codes, will be related in various ways to the kinds of repetitions of verbal patterns and clusters which, viewed from the aspect of the signified, we call themes.

Indeed one of my major purposes is to do justice to the ways in which various themes complement each other, or, to put the argument more strongly, the ways in which they are variations of each other—an avatar of the structuralist premise. Few novels can be said to function in terms of a single, overriding metaphor; and when they do, they are likely to be perceived as allegories. Instead, the richest reading is usually to be found in a nexus of thematic associations and progressions. Thus, however useful and enlightening may be interpretations arising from one privileged and explicit perspective, there is another strategy of reading which is mine here, gravitating instead towards the crossroads of meaning. It is desirable, to that end, to seek the means of integrating in the discussion factors which are usually considered separable—the formal or technical categories which organize the narration, and the most insistent verbal patterns—so that they become coextensive and covalent conceptual components in the meaning. In other words, the themes are then seen as echoes of the formal constituents and figurative make-up, and vice-versa.

These are the means whereby a literary text in effect structures and informs itself, within a framework supplied by the notion of genre and the nature of narrative in general. It orients, to more or less explicit degrees, its own reading. But emphasis on complementarity among the text's devices should not lead us to overlook the sometimes subtle ways in which the text subverts itself, giving the lie to its own pretensions and revealing its own facticity: the reflexive functions of the literary text not only harmonize and make it cohere but problematize and render it complex.

All of these intentions entail an option virtually to eliminate certain topics traditional to literary criticism. One is the broad humanitarian theme, whereby works are thought of as explorations of the human heart if not soul. Another is the psychology of characters, insofar as it involves the projection of an imaginary psyche of which the text displays only selected symptoms. By the same token, no attempt is made to adduce evidence, either from other works by the same author, including his comments about the text under discussion, or from any other contemporary source, with respect to intentions. It makes no difference from the point of view of semantics whether any element of a text was "intended" or not; a word or a phrase has neither more nor less meaning for having been "consciously" applied. Or, to be more exact, intention is of interest only to the extent that it can be deduced directly from the text itself. But it is, in this case, a matter of semantics and not of facts, and the term intention can be quite well done without. The sender, in literature and some other kinds of written discourse, does not occupy the same positive communicative relationship to the message as in everyday speech acts; he is eclipsed by the medium. His is a message enclosed in a bottle and thrown to the sea, which must be deciphered almost exclusively by the aid of its own contents.

To insist on what is *in* the text also implies playing down its "effects," the subjective reactions which take place in the reader rather than designating facts in and of the written object. *Semantic* effects are another matter, since no reading can be effected without the process of linguistic decoding by a receptor. But it is one thing to say that a text signifies, which all discourse does; and another to say that it inspires, frightens, revolts, and the like. One's reactions, whether of antipathy, affection, or humor, to the characters and events, or one's intuitions about their meaning, have no bearing on the status of the text. Except, that is, to the extent that they can be pegged to specific syntagms within the text, which evoke them—but we then have a matter of semantics again, and not of feeling. The text itself controls and dictates the nature of the reader's perceptions to a far greater degree than is usually acknowledged.

The textual reading thus refuses to "read between the lines" in order to tease out from behind the text an essential truth which the text in some way obscures. The text itself may indeed be probed, but it alone, and not some projected complement of it. Reading only the lines does not signify— far from it—a reversion to some illusory notion of literalism, but on the contrary a willingness to recognize the great complexity of what constitutes a literary discourse.

There is no pretension that such purposes, even if worthily fulfilled, exhaust the text or aspire, for that matter, to any other form of completeness; they simply further understanding of the workings of individual texts, and by extension of texts in general. A personal element—the eyes and brain of a particular critic—cannot be eliminated as a prerequisite, and what emerges is in no sense a univocal or single, preferred truth of the text. Any such closure, were it only conceived asymptotically, would run counter to the whole nature of the chosen discourse. Hopefully, the process tends rather to give relief to the text's plurality, its inherent resistance to any and every reductionism which would seek to identify the key, the principal meaning of the work.

If this book is, then, determined by a certain idea of what a textual reading might achieve, it is none the less determined by the novels themselves. It is surely not intended as a book about itself, but as a book about early French novels. Most of the ones chosen for treatment here have been rather thoroughly studied already from the standpoint of literary history, but have not, to my mind, been well enough attended to as autonomous texts. Needless to say, I am implicitly dependent upon the accessibility of reliably established texts, as qualified by criteria and methods which themselves are not all, or are only accessorily, internal: comparisons of editions and manuscripts according to accepted standards. But these are not called upon to guide the reading itself, and are brought up only when particular problems concerning them are inescapably involved.

My list of novels constitutes no sort of canon, although I believe that, for sundry reasons, all have a right to a certain status. Others might have been included in place of these, and some practical considerations, such as the overall balance of the volume, have been taken into account. I have tried to approach each text with the same integrity of reading procedure irrespective of the relative hierarchy in which the critic might rank them by esthetic or whatever other criteria.

Nor will there be, as I stated at the outset, any emphasis on cumulative changes in the novel. Doubtless it is not inappropriate to speak of progression in a genre, so long as the valorization of "progress" in itself is eschewed. As a corpus of technical means and social uses, the novel obviously evolves over time and, like any other genre, has a history. This does not mean, though, that its "early" manifestations have necessarily any less claim to artistic status than, or should be read as "precursors" of, that form at its "height." Without falling back into the historically interesting but utterly futile quarrel of the Ancients and the Moderns, one can maintain that these works should not be approached, as they most generally were in the first half of this century, as symptoms of the long throes of the Realist novel struggling to be born. Just to remove them from such tendencious and debilitating categories is to render them some kind of modest service.

Finally, I should like gratefully to acknowledge here the assistance received in the preparation of this book by fellowships from the National Endowment for the Humanities and the Camargo Foundation.

## NOTES

[1]Frédéric Deloffre, introduction to Marivaux, *La Vie de Marianne* (Paris: Garnier, 1963), p. ii.

[2]"Il ne s'agit pas de collectionner des types, mais de connaître le mode de discursivité d'une oeuvre, sa *pente* métaphorique" (Henri Meschonnic, *Pour la poétique* [Paris: Seuil, 1970. p. 134).

[3]Meschonnic again has aptly coined phrasings for this critical attitude: "Le propre des oeuvres fortes est la transfiguration des figures"; the goal is not to show the figure in the work, but "l'oeuvre dans la figure" (ibid., pp. 21, 134).

# Chapter 1

## Le Roman comique

To the twentieth-century reader it is not immediately obvious that the alliance of the noun *roman* with the adjective *comique* was bold and willful. For *roman* ordinarily called forth entirely different associations, pastoral love idylls like *Astrée* (1607-1624) or heroic adventures such as *Polexandre* (1637) or *Le Grand Cyrus* (1649). But just as comedy was born to parody tragedy, there arose a tradition of *anti-romans*, the first of which, by Jean de Lannel, bore a title similar to Scarron's: *Le Roman satirique* (1624). Charles Sorel was the most irrepressible contributor to this sub-genre, with his *Vraie Histoire comique de Francion* (1623), *Le Berger extravagant* (1627), and *Polyandre* (1648). They bear much good humor but also some aggressive intent. *Le Berger extravagant* is written, as its preface states, "pour faire haïr les mauvaises choses," and its hero, Sorel later wrote, "n'a de l'extravagance que pour se moquer de celle de ces autres bergers et de tous les personnages de nos romans."[1] And like comedy, it justified its mordant verve with an adaptation of the Aristotelian theory of catharsis: ridicule of vice can contribute to its correction. Thinking perhaps of the comic slogan *castigat ridendo mores*, Sorel wrote: "la vraie histoire comique selon tous les meilleurs auteurs, ne doit être qu'une peinture naïve de toutes les diverses humeurs des hommes, avec des censures vives de la plupart de leurs défauts, sous la simple apparence de choses joyeuses";[2] Scarron compares his book to a drunk who is at once entertaining and instructive (pp. 51-52). The vice attacked in this case is a literary vice, and *Le Roman comique* along with other books of its kind was a way of saying that something about the conventional *roman* of its day was incongruous and even unacceptable.

The title is also appropriate because of the multiple suggestions contained in the word *comique*. First, the work is comic in the sense already mentioned, by being unheroic, contemporary, and built around lower-class characters. Further, these characters are specifically a group of actors, or *comédiens* as they were (and still frequently are) called in France. And finally, it is funny: it is itself a *comédie*. (The polysemic *comique* of Corneille's title *L'Illusion comique* was doubtless the source of Scarron's own usage here.)

The book's lack of a clear, formal unity—that is to say, of a classical, hierarchical construction—has led to much misunderstanding by modern critics, as has the narrator's insistence on the "truth" of his fiction. "Le récit va au hasard," comments for example Henri Coulet; "épisodes et personnages se multiplient sans qu'on sache au juste où est le centre de l'intérêt."[3] There is an entirely deliberate diffusion of the plot lines away from a linear axis; there is juxtaposition of genres and mixture of tone;[4] and, while it is reasonable to clarify the sense of their interplay, it would be antithetical to the work's manifest nature to pretend that it possesses a secretly rigorous structure. A novel written implicitly against novels is in a dialectical position, participating in that which it satirizes, illustrating nothing unequivocally. It now parodies, now imitates the novel, and is burlesque with a certain classical grace. This one has elements of Cervantes and even of Rabelais, but the Rabelais it incarnates is paradoxically polite—a Rabelais, as it were, become *honnête homme*.

It behooves us also to avoid here the popular conceit that lauds early novels most when they are thought to contain forward-looking "realism," which purports to be visible with increasing clarity as the characters descend the social scale. *Le Roman comique* contains much that is inelegant; yet it is often just as highly improbable as is lofty romance. Such earthy substances as blood and urine have in truth no privileged power to represent the reality of experience; and high adventures—which this work also includes—are not "really" more outlandish than getting one's foot stuck in a chamber pot, falling through the floor, or being butted in the head by a goat. Vulgarity in a comic novel can be a form of protest or at least reaction against the affected refinement of heroic novels. Both of these poles here influence meaning, but not as functions of any such presupposition that one is truer than the other. Despite the return to the real world which Scarron seems to be advocating in fiction, his subject here is not so much "reality" as it is fiction itself, or more exactly, *le romanesque*.

Comedy is both a part of life and a "play" within it, and Scarron exploits this double nature of the players. To begin with, the literal and the symbolic are combined in their names—"real" stage names that also have designative value. *Le Destin* suggests with some irony that the hero is master of his own destiny, or else, more romantically, that he suffers it under the influence of his *Etoile*. *La Rancune* and *Angélique* are transparent labels for the grumpy old pro and the alluring if saucy young actress. *La Caverne* is risible whether taken as an unusual name of the type derived from nature (as La Montagne, La Vallée, La Rose, ou L'Epine, p. 5), or as a grotesquely equivocal metaphor which is quite transparent even to the inhabitants of Le Mans; still she has nothing of the corpulence or man-eating qualities of Mme *Bouvillon* ('steer'). *Olive* and *Roquebrune* would seem to be rather neutral (the latter, from Provençal geography, could be a family name), but *Léandre* derives from the pastoral and is a conventional name for the swain in comedy.

Other names in the work which are not stage names are similarly suggestive, as the Bouvillon already mentioned. *La Rappinière* evokes both the *rapière* of the *lieutenant de prévôt* and the *rapinerie* ('rapine') of his criminal past (p. 221); and *Doguin* (= diminutive perhaps of *dogue*) makes for the former an appropriate second. *Ragotin* is a diminutive of *ragot* ('squat person') which is his only significant physical trait; *Giflot* (p. 263), the irascible priest, might be construed as *gifle* + *flot*; the pompous name of the Breton senator *La Garouffière* combines such possibilities as *garou* ('werewolf'), *fier*, and a deliberately Angevin suffix (p. 197) -*iere*. Much as in Dickens, the names help label the typical reflexes which give the different ones their distinct personality; each has not so much his own "character" as his own logic to which he is faithful. In most of the other cases Scarron resorts to familiar (especially national) name conventions and is less imaginative.

An itinerant troupe had to be small but also versatile. We have the most detail on the parts played by La Rancune (p. 13), who, in the old manner typified here by the plays of Hardy, sang tenor in trios and played aged women by dint of mask and falsetto, but now plays confidants, ambassadors, *recors* and farcical roles. La Caverne also plays in farces, and otherwise ordinarily is the queen or mother. We know that l'Etoile and Angélique occupy the "premiers rôles" (p. 23), and can conjecture that their male counterparts are Le Destin, always the lead, and Olive. The three men's apprentice-valets also "récitent" in supporting roles, and Roquebrune, who gets only "les derniers rôles," must come even after them. The family troupe described by La Caverne is similar but smaller, apparently eight in all of which three are women: "Notre troupe était composée de notre famille [mother, father, daughter, son] et de trois comédiens, dont l'un était marié avec une comédienne qui jouait les seconds rôles" (p. 167). The only specific play they are said to have performed (p. 169) is Garnier's

*Bradamante* (1582), which has three female and ten male roles, plus extras.

Scarron was of course a theatrical writer, and understood such a practical operation. If we look at the plays they purport to perform within the novel, we shall see that they make sense for a troupe of such composition. Before the accident at Tours, the characters were costumed for Mairet's *Soliman* (p. 52), Le Destin presumably in the title role (the text is somewhat ambiguous about this, but he plays other principal roles). By looking at the play itself, we can see that the troupe is able to cast it nicely with the following approximate distribution:

| | |
|---|---|
| Soliman, sultán | Le Destin |
| Mustapha, crown prince | Olive |
| Bajazet, Soliman's faithful friend | |
| Acmat, counselor to Soliman } | three valets |
| Rustan, grand vizier | |
| Alvante, Despine's governor | La Rancune |
| Osman | Roquebrune |
| ———— | |
| Roxelane, sultan's wife | L'Etoile |
| Hermine, Roxelane's confidante | La Caverne |
| Despine, amazon | Angélique |

Since tragedies had rather spare casts, a small troupe could thus suffice; and since the tragicomedies which called for larger casts also had less rigid staging conventions, the troupe could still fill them by duplication of roles and quick costume changes. In fact, all the plays mentioned are either tragedies or tragicomedies; the actors might have performed comedies as well, but we must remember that this was not necessarily suggested by the appellation *comédiens*.

Now *Marianne*, staged by a bedragled crew of three at Le Mans (p. 7), is a special challenge consisting precisely of overcoming major technical difficulties in the name of entertainment. Since we are told that La Caverne plays the two leading women—Marianne and Salomé—and Le Destin is Hérode, this apparently leaves La Rancune to fill the ten remaining roles—including the female part of Dina—in addition to that of Pherore, which is mentioned (p. 8). In other words, his situation is close to the kind of tour de force he had just himself described:

J'ai joué une pièce moi seul, dit la Rancune, et ai fait en même temps le roi, la reine et l'ambassadeur. Je parlais en fausset quand je faisais la reine; je parlais du nez pour l'ambassadeur, et me tournais vers ma couronne que je posais sur une chaise; et pour le roi, je reprenais mon siège, ma couronne et ma gravité, et grossissais un peu ma voix. [p. 6]

In characterizing such demands on the itinerant actor's virtuosity, La Rancune probably is exaggerating but little.

When the full troupe plays *Le Cid*,[5] Le Destin would doubtless figure Rodrigue opposite l'Etoile as Chimène; the remaining six men can cover all the male roles and, with Angélique as the Infante, La Caverne would simply double as the two *gouvernantes. Dom Japhet d'Arménie* (p. 268), Scarron's own play of 1653, has three female roles and five principal male roles; there are six minor ones which would be filled by combinations of the two extras and others doubling while offstage from their primary roles. And *Nicomède*, finally (p. 271), they could perform without any duplication of personnel. All this serves to show that there is nothing arbitrary in the mechanics of the comic troupe at the novel's center.

Those who play heroes on stage are also the heroes, in another sense, of the novel, and heroes who moreover are made to appear unheroic ("ces très véritables et très peu héroïques aventures" [p. 52]). The role of the narrator is itself a comic "act." The openings of both Part I and Part II set a mock-heroic tone by use of extended epic metaphors upon which Scarron builds puns either by confusing figurative and literal (the procedure common to the numerous "travestis" or parodied classics of the period), or by exaggerating the metaphor to the point of tautology:

Le soleil avait achevé plus de la moitié de sa course et son char, ayant attrapé le penchant du monde, roulait plus vite qu'il ne voulait . . . [p. 3]

Le soleil donnait à plomb sur nos antipodes et ne prêtait à sa soeur qu'autant de lumière qu'il lui en fallait pour se conduire dans une nuit fort obscure. [p. 159]

Against this background of disparaged grandiloquence the narrator pointedly situates his tale in a more familiar world: ". . . Pour parler plus humainement et plus intelligiblement, il était entre cinq et six quand une charrette entra dans les halles du Mans" (p. 3). The same reaction against a certain literary tradition is cited to justify telling the story of a *group*, which will necessarily disperse the interest normally concentrated in romance on the idealized hero: "puisqu'il n'y a rien de plus parfait qu'un héros de livre, demi-douzaine de héros ou soi-disant tels feront plus d'honneur au mien qu'un seul qui serait peut-être celui dont on parlerait le moins, comme il n'y a qu'heur et malheur en ce monde" (pp. 12-13). Lest there be any doubt about what he has in mind, Scarron evokes the type of "roman en cinq parties, chacune de dix volumes," and names a few: *Cassandre, Cléopâtre, Polexandre, L'Illustre Bassa*, and above all the much-derided *Grand Cyrus* of Mlle de Scudéry, qualified elsewhere as "le livre du monde le mieux meublé" (pp. 130, 34). This is an elegant pun because the context in fact concerns furniture; but what such novels are "furnished" with is illustrated in another passage:

> Je ne vous dirai point exactement s'il avait soupé, et s'il se coucha sans manger, comme font quelques faiseurs de romans qui réglant toutes les heures du jour de leurs héros, les font lever de bon matin, conter leur histoire jusqu'à l'heure du dîner, dîner fort légèrement et après dîner reprendre leur histoire ou s'enfoncer dans un bois pour y parler tout seul, si ce n'est quand ils ont quelque chose à dire aux arbres et aux rochers; à l'heure du souper, se trouver à point nommé dans le lieu où l'on mange, où ils soupirent et rêvent au lieu de manger, et puis s'en vont faire des châteaux en Espagne sur quelque terrasse qui regarde la mer . . . [pp. 29-30]

Such a passage seems tedious to us, because the thing satirized is too distant to be familiar. But it is well to realize that Scarron was mocking not some antique, moth-eaten style but the avidly read fictions of his day.[6] They are characterized by *excess*—of detail, sentiment, and abstraction—a surfeit suggested in this example by the novelists' usual failure to allow for the fact that experience includes uneventful spaces, lapses of *insignificant* time. "Ne disons point, si vous voulez, ce qu'il fit jusqu'au dîner . . ." (p. 35); "Je ne sais si la nuit fut longue à venir; car, comme je vous ai déjà dit, je ne prends plus la peine de remarquer ni le temps ni les heures; vous saurez seulement qu'elle vint . . ." (p. 40). What this narrator really hates is verbiage.

Yet one must be cautious in assessing Scarron's contempt for the fiction he mocks; it is far from unequivocal. Le Destin speaks with no apparent irony of "les Astrées et les autres beaux romans que l'on a faits depuis, par lesquels les Francais ont fait voir, aussi bien que par mille autres choses, que, s'ils n'inventent pas tant que les autres nations, ils perfectionnent davantage" (pp. 62-63). We could rationalize his admiration for *Astrée* by its poetic qualities, but what are we to make of "les autres beaux romans"? One answer would be to take it as ironic evidence of Le Destin's bad taste, except that he contrasts his appreciation for these works with his juvenile taste for *Amadis de Gaule*. The spirit behind parody is not invariably caustic, and sometimes is difficult to define. Are we to suppose that Scarron contemns Virgil because he wrote a *Virgile travesti*? The wit of satire may make it seem sharp, but as a medium of criticism it is a dull instrument.

Although I may refer to "Scarron's" novel, it is important here—as in all fictions, but especially those having what has been called a "self-conscious narrator"—not to confuse the author who is its arbiter (outside the text) with the narrator as *conteur* (a character in the text, but quite possibly unknown to the other characters). The novel-reader's dealings are only with the second, although he is a creation of the first. He can be conversationally intrusive ("moi qui vous parle" [p. 26]); and at others posture as the "fidèle et exact historien" (p. 257) who, scrupulously limiting himself to what is attested ("Ils se dirent encore cent belles choses, que je ne vous dirai point, parce que je ne les sais pas et que je n'ai garde de vous en composer d'autres" [p. 27]), is subject to default of memory ("je ne me souviens plus lequel" [p. 39]), but will on occasion conjecture on the basis of odd bits of supposed information ("je crois qu'il se lava la bouche, car j'ai su qu'il avait grand soin de ses dents" [p. 35]). Of course his pretended scruples are merely a game, being often a great display of conscientiousness over decidedly insignificant detail: "son pied droit ou gauche, je n'ai pas su lequel" (p. 195). He sometimes manipulates his relationship with the characters; for example, although it is Ragotin who says "je m'en vais conter une histoire" (p. 25), it is really the primary narrator who is going to tell it, and who thereby preëmpts the narrative function which had begun within the plot: "Ce n'est pas Ragotin qui parle, c'est moi." The frequent "je ne sais pas" has been seen as an aspect of Scarron's respect for the "real," and it is true that the narrator never claims omniscience in *Le Roman comique*; but we should be as wary of taking this stance at face value as we are of everything else. Such clauses impart a conventional semblance of objectivity, but serve equally to impose the constant presence of the narrator, whose *je* always calls attention to him. The phrase "cette véritable histoire" (p. 250) is after all just for laughs; indeed "véritable" is a characteristic adjective in comic titles (later in the century, *histoire véritable* seems to lose its comic connotations) and has little connection with *vraisemblance*. In the realm of events, for instance, the great coincidence of the four *brancards* is carefully developed, then undercut as "une rencontre qui ne s'était peut-être jamais faite" (p. 75).[7]

Scarron plays considerably upon the conventional disjunction of the narrated from the act of narration, usually marked by contrast of the preterite "then" of the story told and the present "now" of whatever narrator is relating it.[8] A chronological paradox such as: "Nous le laisserons reposer dans sa chambre, et verrons dans le suivant chapitre ce qui se passait en celle des comédiens" (p. 23), being a device for backtracking in order to combine simultaneous scenes,[9] can be encountered in any fiction where a *conteur* is present (as first person) in the text. But at other times Scarron manipulates the tenses to create a factitious juxtaposition of two levels. The normally preterite narrated: "Je ne m'amuserai point à vous dire les caresses que ces jeunes amants se *firent*..." can be shifted to the present tense (as is frequently done in French narration for dramatic emphasis): "... dom Fernand qui *frappe* à la porte..." and seem all at once, by virtue of that tense, to intrude upon the narration itself: "... ne *m'*en *laisse* pas le temps." Once the trick has done its humorous service, the preterite resumes its rightful place: "Victoria alla lui ouvrir" (p. 49, italics added).

More amusing because even less normal—indeed wholly incongruous— is the sudden projection of the narrator back into the narrated preterite: "[Le charretier] accepta l'offre qu'elle lui fit, et cependant que ses bêtes *mangèrent*, l'auteur se *reposa* quelque temps et se *mit* à songer à ce qu'il *dirait* dans le second chapitre" (p. 5). Had the verbs *manger, reposer* and *mettre* simply been in the present tense and *dire* in the future, the passage would parallel the example from page 23 cited above. But the procedure here has made the act of narration an event in the narrated, suggesting that in fiction what "happens" (or "happened") and the telling of it are one and the same. All these shadings will be much imitated by Diderot a century later in *Jacques le fataliste;* in both works the narrated becomes a metaphor for the narration, just as suspense on the level of the plot becomes a metaphor for the vagaries of literary creation: "What happened next?" is the parallel within the narrated of "Whence goes my story now?" In Scarron, for instance, there are passages like the following where the narrated (Le Destin is watching out the window for a valet's return) brings us almost without transition back into the act of narration: "Mais, quand on attend quelqu'un avec impatience, les plus sages sont assez sots pour regarder souvent du côté qu'il doit venir, et je finirai par là mon sixième chapitre" (p. 187). The dove-tailing of one (diegetic) level with another (narrational) is carried yet further on another occasion where the narrator tells us that he has derived some information from someone who had read the printer's proofs before publication.[10] The proofs are then a variant written text of the narration-narrated, at once itself and other, containing, while narrating it, its own past. This forms a feedback loop whereby the text discourses upon itself once more, much as the whole constitutes a novel discoursing upon the novel.

The narrator also makes his own style enter into the anti-heroic game (his humor concerning his own function, says Sorel in *La Bibliothèque française*, is what properly characterizes the burlesque), as when he follows a grotesque metaphor with an insolent rejoinder:

Parce qu'il se courbait un peu en marchant, on l'eût pris de loin pour une grosse tortue qui marchait sur les jambes de derrière. Quelque critique murmurera de la comparaison, à cause du peu de proportion qu'il y a d'une tortue à un homme; mais j'entends parler des grandes tortues qui se trouvent dans les Indes et, de plus, je m'en sers de ma seule autorité. [p. 4]

He seems like Hugo to be declaring: "Guerre à la rhétorique et paix à la syntaxe." Part of his assault on grandiose diction lies in an abundance of banal proverbs and phrases drawn from popular expression, and they tend to concentrate in droves: "le diable s'en mêle," "rimer richement en Dieu" [= curse], "assassiner à coups de langue," "vivre de Turc à Maure" [= cutthroat] (p. 7); "faire de nécessité vertu," "reculer pour mieux sauter" (pp. 192, 194). Once a cliché in the narrative is both commented upon by the narrator and then reinforced with another on the diegetic level: "La Rappinière lui fit cent questions sur la comédie, et *de fil en aiguille* (il me semble que ce proverbe est ici fort bien appliqué), lui demanda depuis quand ils avaient Le Destin dans leur troupe et ajouta qu'il était excellent comédien. *Ce qui reluit n'est pas d'or*, repartit la Rancune . . ." (p. 14, italics added). On the other hand there are semi-precious periphrases like "aller où les rois ne peuvent aller qu'en personne" (p. 11 ), "ne répondre que ce que l'on met à fin des lettres" [i.e., "*serviteur*"] (p. 68), "le siège de la raison" (p. 43). Such expressions as the latter can lend themselves to epithetic extension, as in "le vaste siège de son étroite raison" (p. 194). One could cite many more examples.

Comedy in general and burlesque in particular call for combinations of disparate registers. Many simple expressions exploit this mechanism, for instance: "payer en Arabe [= stingily] deux Anglais" (p. 196). Thus it is in the most farcical situations that we are likely to find, and often in proximity to the *mot cru*, the *mot savant* (astronomical, in this example): "son adversaire . . . lui donna un coup de pied, au haut de la tête, qui le fit aller choir sur le *cul* au pied des comédiennes, après une *rétrogradation* fort précipitée" (p. 43, italics added). Ragotin stumbling into beehives brings forth "ces petits éléphants ailés [ mock-precious metaphor], pourvus de proboscides et armés d'aiguillons" (p. 264). Situational humor, which has been overemphasized in discussions of *Le Roman comique*, is not more dominant than is verbal humor, which often comes in the form of learned touches or subtle witticisms such as one might encounter in a literary salon. "La farce divertit encore plus que la comédie," says La Caverne—except in Paris (p. 171); and Scarron, who knows literary triumphs must be won in the capital, does not expect to win by gross effects alone. The finer ones too he often extends, or repeats farther along in the text. "Le concert était ainsi déconcerté" (p. 104) is a fairly evident though clever pun, like the expressive tautology of "la femme du meunier, pitoyable comme une femme" (p. 265). It takes a little schooling, on the other hand, to catch the sense of "animaux imberbes" ('beardless animals'—a euphemism for eunuchs [p. 105]), or note the geometrical metaphor of "je me suis souvent demandé depuis comment on avait pu faire par hasard une si haute pyramide de viande sur si peu de base qu'est le cul d'une assiette" (p. 199). An ironic gloss on one metaphor—"Elle lui sauta aux yeux, furieuse comme une lionne à qui on a ravi ses petits (j'ai peur que la comparaison ne soit ici trop magnifique)"—is soon followed up by another, where word-play is yet more reflexive: "l'hôtesse reçut un coup de poing dans son petit oeil qui lui fit voir cent mille chandelles (c'est un nombre certain pour un incertain) et la mit hors de combat" (p. 192). The *petit* of "petit oeil" in the preceding is itself a development of the *grand/petit* contrast in her portrait traced a few pages earlier:

> Le visage de cette nymphe tavernière était le plus *petit* et son ventre était le plus *grand* du Maine, quoique cette province abonde en personnes *ventrues*. Je laisse aux naturalistes le soin d'en chercher la raison aussi bien que de la *graisse* des chapons du pays. Pour revenir à cette *grosse petite* femme . . .[p. 184, italics added]

The introduction of Ragotin in the story was, in contrast to this one, univocal, but just as effective:

> Il y avait entre autres un *petit* homme veuf, avocat de profession, qui avait une *petite* charge dans une *petite* juridiction voisine. Depuis la mort de sa *petite* femme, il avait menacé les femmes de la ville de se remarier....C'était le plus *grand petit* fou qui ait couru les champs depuis Roland. [p. 25, italics added]

The *petit* which becomes his epithet in quasiclassical fashion is an element of humor in its own right, but does not take on its full value until a concrete example later on effectively points up just how *petit* he really is: "Ragotin . . . se jeta tout furieux sur le premier auteur de sa confusion et lui donna quelques coups de poing dans le ventre et dans les cuisses, ne pouvant pas aller plus haut" (p. 43). Such careful preparation of a phrase which is then left aside awhile only to be recalled in pointedly ironic circumstances is a traditional and effective comic device—witness Figaro's "God-damn!" and "Il y a de l'écho ici." Then there are instances in which an absurd literalism emerges where a metaphor was expected: "Elle n'était pas laide, quoique si maigre et si sèche qu'elle n'avait jamais mouché de chandelle avec les doigts que le feu n'y prît" (p. 10).

One more example will illustrate Scarron's astuteness and creativity with words—this time concerning wine, about which, goodness knows, many jokes have been made. La Rancune takes Ragotin to a cabaret and plies him with unconscionable flattery; "Ragotin avalait cela doux comme lait, conjointement avec plusieurs verres de vin" (p. 48). The way the verb *avaler* passes from the metaphorical to the literal, thanks to the "fluid" transition of the milk comparison, calls attention to how both the flattery and the drink are going to his head. Two pages later, this effect is complemented by: "Enfin, à force d'avaler, ils s'emplirent." Had the author written: "à force de boire, ils s'enivrèrent," the effect would have been much less striking; the meaning is the same, but Scarron's version gives the notion of liquid capacity a humourously graphic form.

In order to discuss some of the formal aspects of the narrative, it will help to begin by codifying its elements—not with the pretension of making simple that which is not, but to facilitate perception of its essential components. This process also serves to reveal that the structures are less incoherent than is usually supposed, and from there we may better understand the extraordinarily rich shifting and echoing of meanings from one stratum to another.

We will call *primary narrative* (P) that one which concerns the movements of the theatrical troupe and others in and about Le Mans. It is picaresque in general type but quite unpicaresque in its precision, covering almost exactly two weeks which can be summarized as in the following table. J (*journée*) designates each day in the chronological sequence. The placement of intercalated narrations in the primary chronology is indicated by H if they are generically *histoires* (a character in P narrating in the first person his own experiences), and N if they are *nouvelles* (stories read or told by characters in P but involving none of its own characters):

J 1    (I. i-v) Arrival in Le Mans of Le Destin, La Rancune, La Caverne (the actors declare their intention of remaining in Le Mans four to five days [p. 6]); first performance and brawl.

J 2    (v-vi) Troupe based in La Rappinière's home; La Rancune goes to an inn: *pot de chambre* trick (night J2/J3).

J 3    (vi-xiii) Doguin's death; incident of the four *brancards*; arrival of remainder of troupe; N 1; Ragotin's hat incident; inn brawl; beginning of H 1 (this is textually the longest day—pp. 19-74)—and ends at 2:00 AM).

J 4    (xiv-xv) Curé de Domfront kidnapped; H 1 continued; serenade.

J 5    (xvi-xviii) Theater opens; end of H 1.

J 6    (I. xix-xxiii + II. i-iii) Loves of La Rappinière, Ragotin, Roquebrune, La Rancune; trip to outskirts of Le Mans; Ragotin's disgrace on horseback; N 2; kidnapping of Angélique; H 2.

J 7    (II. ii + iv-vii) La Rancune's boots (night J6/J7); Le Destin finds Léandre; H 3; Olive, Ragotin, La Rancune arrive; corpse incident (night J7/J8). (Meanwhile La Caverne and l'Etoile have returned to Le Mans [p. 176].)

J 8   (vii-viii) Brawl; Ragotin's *pot de chambre* incident; wedding party of La Garouffière arrives at inn; dinner.

J 9   (ix-xii) Ragotin's clothes foreshortened; La Bouvillon's seduction scene; Angélique returned; H 4 (includes kidnapping of l'Etoile); Le Destin goes to see Verville.

J 10  (xii-xiii) Le Destin and Verville find Saldagne; Etoile rescued (J10/J11); La Rancune, Olive, Ragotin return to Le Mans.

J 11  (xiii-xvi) N 3; La Rappinière summoned, makes restitution; Ragotin's drunken adventure.

J 12  (xvii) Return to Le Mans; project for series of performances.

J 13? (xvii) Performance of *Dom Japhet*; episode of Ragotin and Braguenodière.

J 14  (xviii-xx) Peformance of *Nicomède*; N 4; ram episode.

This, it can be seen, is perfectly orderly; the jumps in time which blur its neatness for the reader result from the interpolations which irregularly require that he readjust his clock. Only towards the end is there any uncertainty: between J 12 and J 13?—between the decision to remain in Le Mans another fortnight for performances, and the first of these performances—there could be another or several days.[11] The point is not that the reader can see this order with his mind's eye, which he cannot, but that it is in fact there, in the text. The primary narration of *Le Roman comique* even has, as earlier commentators have observed, a semblance of the essential classical dramatic unities: place (Le Mans and environs), time (short span of a fortnight), and action (limited and centralized group of related actions).

It should also be noted that the events are clearly contemporaneous to the novel's publication, despite a long presumption among critics that they are to be situated a decade or so earlier.[12] Mentioned in Le Destin's and Verville's past are wars of 1645 and 1649;[13] Léonore's father is known to have served the English king (Charles I) against Parliament, that is, between 1642 and 1645 (p. 121); recent literary works (1647, 1649) as well as the death of Rotrou (in 1650, p. 24) are mentioned in Part I, and in Part II the troupe performs plays dating from 1647 and 1651. This chronological and geographical proximity with its subjects is another trait which *Le Roman comique* has in common with comedy as a theatrical genre.

Chronology is much less tightly controlled in the histoires and nouvelles, most of which take in a greater time span than does the primary narrative: this in conformity with the procedure of the epic, which is ostensibly being imitated.

Here are first the histoires,[14] with the agent or narrator of each, and the auditors'[15] names indicated in brackets:

H 1   Le Destin [La Caverne, Angélique, L'Etoile] (pp. 57-74, 81-103, 111-21

H 2   La Caverne [L'Etoile] (pp. 166-75).

————————————

H 3   Léandre [Le Destin] (pp. 179-81).

H 4   Angélique [Le Destin, Léandre] (pp. 209-211).

H 5   L'Etoile [Le Destin] (pp. 218-19).

H 1 is by far the longest of the interpolations, comprising, in its three installments, one-sixth of the novel. H 2 is incomplete; it is impossible to tell whether the promise to continue it was forgotten or was reserved for an eventual sequel. The last three belong really in a separate category, being far too short to constitute histoires in the usual sense (and of them only H 3 retraces events preceding J 1); they also differ fundamentally from the first two in that they concern and complement events already current in the primary narrative, whereas H 1 and H 2 are pure flashbacks, in no way chronologically coextensive with the primary narrative. It can be noted too that all H agents are members of the inner circle of characters (the troupe), and furthermore that they reaffirm its centrality (especially that of Le Destin) and solidarity by narrating *only to each other*. This more intimate contact afforded with their inner lives sets them apart from the other actors of the troupe whom we might call non-H: La Rancune, Roquebrune, and Olive.

The nouvelles have their own separate titles, and one (N 3) contains its own subsidiary histoires. They are in fact all *nouvelles espagnoles*, both in that Scarron adapted them from a Spanish source (Solorzano), and in that in the context of P they are all explicitly attributed to Spanish origins.

They are listed with the names of their agents in P:

N 1    Ragotin: "Histoire de l'amante invisible" (pp. 26-42).

N 2    Inézille: "A trompeur, trompeur et demi" (pp. 132-51).

N 3    Garouffière (reads): "Le Juge de sa propre cause" (pp. 222-53).

$N_3H_1$ Sophie (pp. 225-38).

$N_3H_2$ Claudia (pp. 231-35).

$N_3H_3$ Carlos (pp. 243-46).

N 4    Inézille (reads): "Les Deux Frères rivaux" (pp. 273-97).

Nouvelles, unlike histoires, are recited in the presence of groups extending to the entire cast of primary narrative P, and by such staging participate in the novel's overall theatrical motif. Inézille has only two functions in the novel, one active and one passive: she is twice an N agent, and twice (for La Rancune and Roquebrune) an object of desire. A nouvelle is less firmly bound to its agent than an histoire, by reason of the agent's lack of relationship to its characters (this is what Genette calls an extradiegetic narrative). There is moreover no duplication between H and N agents. The possibility of giving a title to a nouvelle distinguishes its special status apart as a *conte*, allowing the narrator or *je* of the primary narrative (nP) some latitude which he does not take with histoires: in two cases (N 1 and N 2), nP interposes himself as *conteur* in such a way that the text does not emanate directly from the agent (nN). In the first instance this is explicit, although nP maintains his posture as historian:

Vous allez voir cette histoire dans le suivant chapitre, non telle que la conta Ragotin, mais comme je la pourrai conter d'après un des auditeurs qui me l'a apprise. Ce n'est donc pas Ragotin qui parle, c'est moi. [N 1, p. 26]

Then nP can also reassert himself in the course of N1 itself ("mon livre," p. 26). There is no such explicit affirmation in the case of N 2, but there is no trace either, in the text, of the admixture of French, Spanish, and Italian in which Inézille is supposed to have "agreeably" but awkwardly related it (p. 151).

There were abundant nouvelles in picaresque novels and *Don Quijote*; they belong to the same "open" narrative structure to be found in *Gil Blas* or the novels of Prévost, and which Diderot willfully exploits in *Jacques le fataliste*.[16] Such works could usually be continued almost indefinitely and were endemically prone to remain incompleted, as was the case with *Le Roman comique*. The function of nouvelles and histoires is similar in that they expand temporally, and can thematically reinforce, the primary narrative; but after a beginning *in medias res* the H function is more organically necessary to P, although perhaps not to its thematic development. The fortnight of P is a narrow chronological chassis on which a wider structure comprised of N + H is cantilevered. Nouvelles, again, are freer in this respect; indeed N 3 goes back to before 1535 (Charles V's siege of Tunis, p. 240). An histoire, on the other hand, cannot antedate J 1 by more than a generation unless the teller goes into his parents' lives preceding his own birth (there is a short sample of this procedure in H 1, pp. 57-60), in which case the histoire tends toward nouvelle because it cannot be eyewitness narrative. The various inns in *Le Roman comique* are eminently picaresque locations and are the geographical pivots for nouvelle and histoire intercalations.

It requires no acute powers to observe the great variety introduced into the novel by means of these N/H functions; the real question is whether the interpolations (nouvelles particularly) are mere distractions, valid only autonomously, or whether they can be read as part of an artful design. The modern reader, who has largely lost the habit of this kind of reading, must often be sorely tempted to skip over them and get on with "the" story (P). Indeed a counterpoint can be seen in the generally more romantic quality of N/H over against "comic" P, and yet this separation even is not exclusive: there is much humour in H 1 and H 2, and some romance in P where H 3, 4, 5 dovetail into it. No doubt the inherent independence of nouvelles permits a greater degree of abstraction and thus glamorizes the love interest (the chivalric conventions of N 1, notably), and lends special relief to the burlesque elsewhere in the novel:

The tales are privileged to portray a world whose inhabitants
have no other business but love, and where they can pursue this
exclusive business without interruption from the usual contingencies
of life. . . . This situation is the exact reversal of Ragotin's
predicament, where the love quest is continually frustrated by
an endless series of petty contingencies.[17]

At times it can be persuasively argued too that the nouvelle or histoire
carries an implicit message which derives from its relation to its immediate
context; for example, Garouffiére's story after the kidnapping of L'Etoile
(N 3) might serve

> to point out that justice must be retributive in this disorderly
> world but that it can be attained. Through no fault of their own
> Dom Carlos and Sophie find themselves unjustly separated,
> which is the plight of Destin and Etoile when she is kidnapped.
> . . . Justice is not prevalent, but it can be gained by effort.[18]

An attempt to explain all the interpolations in a similar way, though, is in my
view rather strained, and the substantial interconnections are better
perceived on other levels. There is a strong, even a masterly, coherence to
*Le Roman comique*; it can be sensed but is not easily conceptualized
because it is not to be found quite where we habitually look for one. As
Henri Coulet has remarked, referring specifically to the plot, "tout
s'enchaîne, mais l'enchaînement n'est pas celui du simple bon sens"
(Coulet, p. 207). The real richness of the work is less in its architectonics
than in its textual density, the harmonies of word patterns and the extensive
echoing of one thematic or metaphoric level by others.

Before we come to that, however, the structural components need to
be somewhat further described. The suspense elements critical to the plot of
P are introduced and resolved by degrees of some complexity. They are
codified below. (E = enigma; a, b, etc., are sequential elements of a
predominant E [analogous to Barthes's "code hereméneutique" in *S/Z*];
X = the explanation or resolution of the given E series; and arrows show
linkages in the plot.)

E 1    a—Le Destin's disguise (*emplâtre*): why? (pp. 3, 7, 11)
       aX—He is hiding from an "ancien persécuteur" (p. 53) ⟶ E 2b

E 2
    a—Who are Le Destin and Etoile? (pp. 14, 52-53)
    b—Who is the "persécuteur"? (p. 53)
    aX—H 1; Etoile = Léonore (p. 116)
    bX—H 1; "persécuteur" = Saldagne (pp. 91, 119, 121)


E 3
    a—Why are La Rappinière and Doguin "troubled"? (p. 14)
    b—What is the secret Doguin tells Le Destin? (p. 20)
    abX—H 1, Pont Neuf episode (p. 121; cf. p. 255)


E 4
    $a_1$—(J 3) Who are the two men looking for? (p. 21)
    $a_2$--Who are the men?
    $a_1$X--They want Etoile➤ E2a (p. 22)
    $a_2$X--(implicitly)➤ E2b (p. 121)
    b–(J 4) Why is the curé de Domfront kidnapped? (pp. 75-77)
    bX--It is an error (p. 77)
    c--Who is the prisoner Le Destin recognizes? (p. 80)➤E2a or E2b
    d--Why does the prisoner ask to see Le Destin? (p. 109)

E 5
    a--(J 6) Why is Angélique kidnapped? (p. 152)
    [aX--(false)--Léandre's letter (pp. 181-82)]
    aX--Angélique was taken for Etoile and is recovered (J 9) (pp.
                208-11) ➤ E4a (p. 212) ➤ E6a

E 6
    a--Where is Etoile? (p. 211)➤E4a
    b--What role did Le Destin's valet play? (p. 218)
    aX--Saldagne holds her (p. 219)
    bX—La Rappinière's plot (p. 221)

The several instances in which explanations come long after the problems are raised bear witness to Scarron's deftness in maintaining interest, in resolving things only partially, in bringing about some surprises in the resolutions. Only in E 4 does he seem guilty of leaving loose ends, having planted a clue which leads nowhere (and probably could not have led anywhere even in a sequel). E 3 concerns the somewhat mysterious relationship between Le Destin and La Rancune (cf. pp. 13, 121) as well as the character of La Rappinière. All of the other suspense elements relate to the same complex, the Le Destin-L'Etoile axis, and thus all, although they are part of P, rejoin H 1; yet this is not accomplished fully until E 6 aX, when Saldagne finally emerges from H 1 into P and the whole Saldagne cycle is put to rest. E 6bX is of course a deliberate anticlimax, a surprise X for E 6, but one which is not totally unprepared.[19]

It is not merely because Part Three was never written that this novel is uncompleted; more likely the reverse is true. Trailing off without resolution is an aspect of its immanent structure. For the characteristic pattern of events within is the endless chain which resolves itself only in confusion:

> La Rappinière le prit en queue et se mit à travailler sur lui en coups de poing . . .; un parent de son adversaire prit la Rappinière de la même façon. Ce parent fut investi par un ami de la Rappinière pour faire diversion; celui-ci le fut d'un autre et celui-là d'un autre; enfin tout le monde prit parti dans la chambre. L'un jurait, l'autre injuriait, tous s'entre-battaient. [p. 8].

> [Ragotin] voulant passer outre . . . poussa si rudement le révérend père Giflot, qu'il le fit choir dans l'eau. Le bon prêtre entraîna avec lui le cocher, le cocher le paysan. [p. 263]

The same domino effect in the action is reflected in the cadence and acceleration of the style, which thus itself mirrors the overall model of the action:

> Il se voulut reculer et il tomba à la renverse sur un homme qui était derrière lui et le renversa, lui et son siège, sur le malheureux Ragotin, qui fut renversé sur un autre, qui fut renversé sur un autre, qui fut aussi renversé sur un autre, et ainsi de même jusqu'où finissaient les sièges, dont une file entière fut renversée comme des quilles. Le bruit des tombants, des dames foulées, de celles qui avaient peur, des enfants qui criaient, des gens qui parlaient, de ceux qui riaient, de ceux qui se plaignaient et de ceux qui battaient des mains fit une rumeur infernale. [p. 269]

Indefinite linkage characterizes too the manner in which one chapter leads to another, as is explicitly pointed out when the narrator notifies the reader he must ever expect more of the same:

> Si, par ce qu'il a déjà vu, il a de la peine à se douter de ce qu'il verra, peut-être que j'en suis logé là aussi bien que lui, qu'un chapitre attire l'autre et que je fais dans mon livre comme ceux qui mettent la bride sur le col de leurs chevaux et les laissent aller sur leur bonne foi. [p. 51]

Its failure to exhibit the clear hierarchical design of a proper *roman* is thus basic to the character of the entire *Roman comique*. Its effects are in no way calculated for concentration, but are, on the contrary, scattered: "Il y a bien d'autres choses à dire sur ce sujet; mais il faut les ménager, et les placer en divers endroits de mon livre pour diversifier" (p. 25).

Le Destin, in the middle of a brawl, becomes the instrument of blind chance: "il se mit à jouer des mains et fit un moulinet de ses deux bras, qui maltraita plus d'une mâchoire" (p. 55); likewise La Rancune in another episode "donnait la plupart de ses coups en faisant la demi-pirouette, et tel soufflet tira trois sons différents de trois différentes mâchoires" (p. 192). The object of such flailing--that is, who owns the *mâchoires?*--is indefinite. The narrator gives of himself an impression parallel to that of his characters. The plot line manifests a similar kind of thrashing, and no amount of charitable intent can make it appear tidily assembled. "Finissons la digression" (pp. 198, 267) is a provocation of the reader who is quite aware how much the primary narrative has been hacked up by H/N functions.

It seems every *récit*, primary included, is vulnerable to interruption: discontinuity is the basic rhythm of the text. Le Destin's H 1 is interrupted by a brawl before it can even get under way (p. 54), and halted twice in mid-course, once by the serenade (p. 103); in addition, H 1 tells of an uncompleted letter to Léonore and gives the text of another (pp. 68, 70). La Rancune's tale is interrupted at its inception (pp. 107-8), never to reappear, like La Caverne's which is halted for good by strange noises in her chamber. Léandre's H 3 is not suspended but the conversation following it is (p. 183), just as Bouvillon's attempt upon Le Destin aborts when Ragotin knocks at the door (p. 207). Almost anyone setting out on a journey can expect to be attacked by someone (pp. 21, 75, 167), or, failing that, to be halted by such accidents as a broken axle (p. 203). The chapter titles, as in *Don Quijote*,[20] reinforce this apparent narrative nonchalance, particularly when they say "Qui contient ce que vous verrez, si vous prenez la peine de le lire" (I.xi) or "Qui peut-être ne sera pas trouvé fort divertissant" (I.xxi). Any possibility of a unified, linear, heroic action, or of a steady progression towards any kind of resolution, is inherently ruled out. The end, or non-end, is in the beginning and the totality. Or stated otherwise, the event is a figure having the same structure as the whole.

High drama is quickly brought down to earth and deflated, as in H 2 where a supposed ghost interrupts the story and causes a fright, but turns out to be merely a dog. Any soaring toward tragedy finishes on the level of that first performance in the *tripot*, "non pas par la mort de Marianne et par les désespoirs d'Hérode, mais par mille coups de poing, autant de soufflets, un nombre effroyable de coups de pied, des jurements qui ne se peuvent compter" (p. 7). Invocation of the heroic turns immediately into mock-heroic. "Petit" Ragotin is compared to Roland, and the grandiose diction of "foulant l'étain d'un pied superbe" is applied to him for comic effect precisely when his foot is stuck in a metal champer pot (p. 187). The narrator likes to invoke epic abstractions such as *l'amour* and *la Discorde* (pp. 122, 194) as the forces explaining banal human actions, and makes use of the romantic term *aventure* particularly in burlesque contexts such as the chapter headings "L'Aventure du pot de chambre" (I.vi) and "Aventure du corps mort" (II.vii). Likewise the "prowess" of the heroes is associated not with swords and armor but with low-style fisticuffs: "Le comédien Destin fit des prouesses à coups de poing, dont l'on parle encore dans la ville du Mans" (p. 9); "il faudrait une meilleure plume que la mienne pour bien représenter les beaux coups de poing qui s'y donnèrent" (p. 193). Although l'Etoile is "modeste et douce," "une beauté de roman" (p. 116), beside her is Angélique who, belying her name, knows how to defend herself with "un coup de pied dans l'os des jambes, un soufflet ou un coup de dent" (p. 24); if Le Destin represents true love, he is flanked by two mock-lovers (Roquebrune and Ragotin) and two lechers (La Rancune and La Rappinière), the four amorous R's, all of whom indeed discover their passion simultaneously (pp. 122-23). For all his aspirations Ragotin is of course the antithesis of a love hero, able only to ape the gestures of a higher kind of being which is much beyond his ken.[21] Even two of the idyllic *nouvelles* are gently reduced to human proportions by narrator comments at the end.[22] The sentence following upon the marriage of N 1--"On dit qu'ils se levèrent bien tard le lendemain" (p. 42)--hints of the carnal after the more ethereal (comedy, and even more so farce, is never far away from the flesh; this novel is almost devoid of eroticism, but there is a touch of the lubricious in the role of Bouvillon). And the happily-ever-after clause often attendant on such resolutions in fiction is replaced at the end of N 4 with the dry reflection, "tout y alla bien de part et d'autre, et même longtemps, ce qui est à considérer" (p. 297).

All the same, there is a great deal of romance here that is neither parody nor tongue-in-cheek; although at the extremes tragedy turns to comedy, there are also elements of tragi-comedy. No single tone is allowed to establish its domain, whether heroic or comic. Le Destin is the habitual romantic saver of lives (pp. 10, 85) and savior of damsels, but also vulnerable to something approaching panic (p. 160); even his histoire, announced pathetically as "le récit de leurs malheurs" (p. 54), begins with most unsolemn portraits of his parents--just as La Caverne cannot help laughing over parts of her story (with tragic consequences, indeed), even though it is told while bemoaning the kidnapping of Angélique. The quality of Le Destin's love, on the other hand, is never doubted, and it is presented in traditional terms as soul sickness (p. 66) and a wound: "Avec tant de blessures et tant d'amour, je ne fus pas longtemps sans avoir une fièvre très violente" (p. 69). He suffers like the romantic hero: "Je pleurai comme un enfant, et je m'ennuyai partout où je ne fus pas seul" (p. 84). And he is high-minded (if not noble-born in fact), with a distaste for peasant mentality: he disdains "vrais discours de servante" (pp. 87, 90)--which Madelon precisely does *not* display, because she too is really not a servant (p. 98). While disparaging as a shopworn convention of heroic fantasy princes in humble disguises (p. 30), Scarron presents us with aristocrats disguised as mere actors. L'Etoile (Léonore de la Boissière) creates an immediate impression of *fille de condition* (p. 53). Or take Léandre, who is indeed noble and who invokes romantic clichés about "le bonheur de toute sa vie" (p. 178) and so forth, not to mention his elopement--among the most hackneyed of the old fictional devices. In Léandre's declarations, these elements even emerge clearly from the H/N level into the primary narrative. And it is possible to conjecture that once the ever-lurking menace of Saldagne has been put to rest and the dominant romantic interest in Le Destin-L'Etoile is resolved, Scarron knows or senses that his story has, a fortiori, nowhere really to go.

It is not that Scarron discounts what is exalted in man, or denies that his idealism informs his real behavior. The question of *mesure* is fundamental, and in this his antiheroic protest was classical. The narrator's irony seems sometimes to reject sentiment: "Ils se dirent mille choses si tendres que j'en ai les larmes aux yeux toutes les fois que j'y pense" (p. 41). And his role does serve to control the tone and restrain any tendency in a maudlin direction. He will have none of bathos. But the satire of sentiment seems to relate principally to its excesses not as passion but *as expression*: "ils se dirent des choses si pitoyables que sa soeur, sa parente et le bon religieux, qui en furent témoins, en pleurèrent et en ont toujours pleuré depuis toutes les fois qu'ils y ont songé" (p. 284). Scarron's reply to the love idyll is not a novel devoid of love, but one which restrains effusions. Léandre is dreamily adrift in love, but as soon as he is alone with Angélique the doors close--not because *they* have a right to that, although this is the ironic pretext, but because *we* do, narrator and reader. Their outpourings are dispatched with a clause so we can get on to the next chapter (pp. 212-13). Scarron has rejected part and parcel not *le romanesque* but *un certain romanesque*. His central characters are in some ways ideal heroes, and they alone in the novel romantically bear witness to the possibility of unselfish love: this is why Le Destin tells Léandre that if he really wants Angélique to wife, and none other, he should not leave the troupe (p. 182). Women, it should be noted, are always treated delicately and almost never associated directly with the grosser burlesque.

The only sustained architectural development in the novel depends upon the Le Destin-L'Etoile axis; but aside from this macroplot level there is a continuous weave of other motifs, more picturesque than Le Destin and L'Etoile, which are important factors in its unity. Among them is what I have called the logic of individual characters, most obviously that of the accident-prone Ragotin. He not only manifests his own mechanism, but also pulls along in his wake a farcical fatality which works against him. The style of his antics and disasters is consistent and marked by strong functional (and in keeping with the carnal spirit of farce, anatomical) parallels: his head inextricably stuck into his ludicrous "coiffure" (hat) so that it must be snipped from his head (p. 44) is repeated in the foot wedged in a chamber pot which also has to be cut away (p. 196); and he stumbles denuded into the chamber pot exactly as he will later into six beehives (p. 264). Ragotin is more than a caricature, he is, in Coulet's words, a natural phenomenon (op. cit., p. 204). Since sympathy is inimical to laughter (*dixit* Bergson), his rotten luck is necessarily compounded by character defects which exacerbate it:

> En vérité, quand la fortune a commencé de persécuter un misérable, elle le persécute toujours. . . . Il ne se passait guère de jour qu'il ne s'attirât quelque affaire, à quoi sa mauvaise gloire et son esprit violent et présomptueux contribuaient autant que sa mauvaise fortune qui jusqu'alors ne lui avait point fait de quartier. [pp. 270-71]

Ragotin draws to himself much of the fun poked at the provincial spirit of Le Mans, and links it to the visual dynamism of theatrical slapstick.[23] He is very nearly the embodiment of the spirit of farce. This function, however, does not negate elsewhere the spirit of romance; by counterpoint Ragotin serves to highlight the strengths of the more heroic characters.[24]

Another less obvious but important and organic unifier, a highly enigmatic force, is La Rancune. He is introduced negatively as the one who never laughs, apparently a spirit of anti-comedy (though comedy needs its grumpy figures), "malicieux comme un vieil singe," a sad actor who "n'était plus supporté dans la troupe, qu'à cause qu'il avait vieilli dans le métier" (p. 13). Yet he is a master of "straight" humor, an irrepressible if morbid perpetrator of practical jokes which generate farce: it is he who knows everyone (e.g., the *opérateur*, the gypsies [pp. 80, 258]) and connects them to the story, and has in particular brought Le Destin and L'Etoile into the troupe (p. 120); he is in fact the glue that bonds them all together. Even if La Rancune tortures a merchant with no apparent motive but his misanthropy (pp. 17-19) and "persecutes" the likes of the poet (p. 107), he treats women properly; and Le Destin is able to bring out the humanity in him, symptoms of great emotion and self-sacrifice (pp. 120-21).

In order to identify what Montesquieu called the "chaîne secrète et en quelque facon inconnue"[25] which makes an informally constructed novel cohere, we must largely overlook the evident differences between the P and H/N levels and appreciate how much the thematic resonances proceed in fact from both of these territories. Histoires and nouvelles have their own autonomous internal sinews. For example, Le Destin (H 1) compares his relationship to Glaris with that of Jacob to Esau (Destin: Glaris:: Jacob: Esau), and this analogy is extended, though unspoken, in the pair Saint-Far/Verville (Destin:Glaris::*Jacob:Esau*::Verville:Saint-Far),[26] thus yielding a balanced group with a pivotal Biblical metaphor; in addition, Le Destin's savior is named M. de Saint-Sauveur. But beyond such motifs there are numerous reverberations between the H/N and P levels. Sigognac, in the primary narrative, is functionally as well as orthographically reminiscent of Saldagne, in H 1; moreover Saldagne--and Verville as well--finally surfaces from H to be actualized in P (p. 212). These are important evidence of themes which transcend formal narrative segments.

That motif which more than any other cuts across the apparent divisions to assure thematic stability or at least texture is itself quintessentially theatrical: the mask. Its first manifestation is Le Destin's *emplâtre*, and it returns in every sector of the novel, as the listings below show. One form of mask is the veil worn by so many of the women characters:

| | | | |
|---|---|---|---|
| a. | "L'amante invisible" | N1 | pp. 26 ss. |
| b. | Two women | N1 | 32 |
| c. | Four men and several women-in-waiting | N1 | 33, 35 |
| d. | Porcia | N1 | 36 |
| e. | Léonore | N1 | 64, 73, 120 |

| f. | Domfort's niece | P | 77 |
|---|---|---|---|
| g. | Mlle de Léri | H1 | 88 |
| h. | Claudia and Sophie | N3$_{H1}$ | 235 |
| i. | Giflot's nuns | P | 263 |
| j. | Dorothée | N 4 | 276 |

Invisibility, of course, is what N 1 is all about. Mlle de Léri(g) is veiled only by darkness, but her face is not the less unseen. The veil is a conventional adjunct of Spanish and Italian settings, but what about (f), which is in France? Here as elsewhere the veil serves to heighten the mystery of woman.

Then there is a whole series of disguises, sometimes intended to prevent recognition only, other times benefitting from the special advantages incumbent upon playing a role that is merely adopted; such a role is identified below in parentheses when it is explicit in the text:

| a. | Le Destin | P | pp. 3 |
|---|---|---|---|
| b. | Bandits | P | 21 |
| c. | Saldagne | P | 53 |
| d. | Mlle de Léri (as Madelon) | H1 | 98 |
| e. | Victoria (as duegna) | N2 | 136 |
| f. | Squire (as Rodrigue Santillane) and Béatrix (as wife) | N2 | 136 |
| g. | Léandre (as valet) | H3 | 180 |
| h. | Claudia (as Claudio) | N3$_{H1}$ | 230 |
| i. | Sophie and Dorothée (as men) | N3 | 239-40 ss. |
| j. | Carlos (assumed name) | N3 | 242 |
| k. | Sanche | N4 | 279 |
| l. | Diegue (as pauper) | N4 | 283 |
| m. | Sanche | N4 | 284 |
| n. | Sanche (as fisherman) | N4 | 286 |

There are several instances of transvestism, common also in theatrical comedy. As in theater too, the various forms of mask frequently give rise to the *méprise*. The latter can be either tragic or comic according to treatment, and is often owing to obscuring factors other than masks: Domfort's niece and Angélique (P) are each kidnapped by mistake; in the darkness Mlle de Léri is taken for Mlle de Saldagne (H 1, p. 93), and Juan and Sanche for each other (N 4, p. 292) in very similar fashion.

At the same time the mask can subsume other dimensions of the novel, as a metaphor for the pretentiousness of a Ragotin, who wants to be something he is not, or for the social fakery of an era when "tout le monde se marquise" (p. 31); Victoria's taking a disguise is a direct function of the way that she, being a person who lives in the public eye, defines herself only as she is perceived by others: "Que dira-t-on de moi dans Tolède et que dira-t-on dans toute l'Espagne?" (p. 135)--this, more than a quest for personal happiness, is what motivates her. But most important, the mask brings us back to the dominant theme of comedy, and to its problematic relationship with both the ideal and the world. The comedian performs, of course, *trevesti* (p. 7); and the more romantic of our troupe (Le Destin, L'Etoile, Léandre) are doubly so, being aristocrats disguised as comedians (another reminiscence of Corneille's *Illusion comique*). And yet it is *true* that they are comedians. The arrival of the trio in Le Mans in chapter one is a "comic" entrance in the literal sense that they are clothed as actors. H 2 is absent from the preceding two tables only because it is the story of a family of comedians, to whom, it goes without saying, the mask is by nature paramount.

For the pervasive underlying theme of the *roman comique* is really *comedy* itself, above all in its theatrical sense. There are numerous stock situations from the comic repertory, to which Scarron's reader would have been much more alert than most of us are now. To take the most significant example, Le Destin tells how his father was persuaded to secrete in his home the bastard son of "une fille de fort bonne maison et fort riche," and that as a result he was disfavored: "Je fus mis en nourrice et l'étranger fut mis en la place du fils de la maison" (p. 60). But supposing that Le Destin were himself that noble child, and Glaris instead the poor boy whose parents' cunning thus assured him of a fortune? The father is after all not a father to him but "un très fâcheux vieillard" (p. 85). Any contemporary of Scarron's would have recognized this situation as a *substitution d'enfant*, setting up an eventual *reconnaissance* whereby the hero's intrinsic nobility is officially certified and the gates of favor opened to him.[27] (Scarron has further arranged for Le Destin to be brought up conjointly with Verville, so that he will think and behave like a gentleman.)

There is also a recognition scene of two long-lost brothers in N 4 (p. 297). Saldagne fills the role of vilain, the traditional comic obstacle to the lovers' fulfillment. To what has already been said about Scarron's narrative verve we can add dialogical comic devices, for instance ironic repetition, as in the "Je ne dis pas cela" (p. 206) which, as Molière demonstrated (in *Le Misanthrope*), transfers perfectly to the stage. Most comedies end in marriages, as do all four nouvelles here, and not infrequently in double marriages like the one closing the Verville-St-Far episode in H 1 (p. 102); there is even a triple marriage (N 4, p. 297) to cap things off. H 1 and H 3 presumably too, in some ideal extension, would lead to wedding feasts. In fact there is one of sorts (p. 199), almost rabelaisian, or at the least highly farcical. A second grand comic tableau, comparable to the entrance in chapter one, is described by Le Destin in H 1: the parade into Orléans (pp. 116-17). And, to be sure, farces--usually indelicate, as farces were wont to be--too numerous to mention.

That first vision of the main characters, as comedians, is deftly developed. The narrator does not say who they are, he only suggests it little by little: "Il portait des chausses troussées à bas d'attaches, comme celles des comédiens quand ils représentent un héros de l'antiquité" (p. 4). The literalness of this picturesque note quite escapes us at first, for the characters are indeed in theatrical garb; and not at all because they are actors--who can dress like anyone else--but because they are, by accident, actors in performance regalia, ready to mount the stage in the play that never came off. This sense of the title is confirmed when they are referred to as "trois personnes comiques" (p. 8). *Roman comique* thus means, first of all, *roman des comédiens* or *roman de la comédie*.

The actors are imbued with theater: La Caverne was born backstage; La Rancune is an inveterate performer, even if he is better offstage than on. Even the newcomers, at least Le Destin and Léandre, were first spectators of comedy--"je n'allai plus au collège et ne manquai pas un jour d'aller à la comédie"(p. 180)--and this fact, as Le Destin underscores, is not incidental: "J'allais à la comédie: ce qui est cause peut-être de ce que je suis passable comédien" (p. 86). They have in the novel no names but their stage names, and demand no others. And, just as there is little narrative irony about their loves, there is also little about their quality as actors.[28] Nor is there, on the other hand, any glamorizing of the life of an itinerant actor, which is fraught with dangers: there is mention of Le Destin's valet killed at the theater door by schoolboys (p. 180), of another *portier* who may have suffered the same fate after killing someone himself(p. 6), and the murder of

La Caverne's actor-father--not to mention all the brawls. These actors, some noble themselves, have noble souls although we see them in common surroundings, and are better, one could say, than their profession; one critic has depicted Le Destin as representing a new breed, the actor-*honnête homme*.[29] *Déclassés* themselves, they typify the actor's quest for a tenable and acceptable social role. Scarron thus renders dignity to the comedian, painting him as socially adept and desirable,[30] as had Corneille in *L'Illusion comique*, though his optimism is more guarded: "De nos jours on a rendu en quelque façon justice à leur profession et on les estime plus que l'on ne faisait autrefois" (p. 197).

Ultimately the theatrical dimension is indissociable from the literary. The mention of the play *Dom Japhet* which the troupe performs is unusual not so much because it is Scarron's own, such literary games not being infrequent, as because it is in a different artistic medium from *Le Roman comique*; it serves a self-referent function which brings us full circle, back to the artist who created the novel and the comedy. Comedy derives its breadth of meaning here from being an analog, not so much of "real life" as has too often been repeated, but of the tale, the story--in short the *roman*-- and vice versa.[31]

## NOTES

Paul Scarron (1610-1660), *Le Roman comique*, Part I, 1651; Part II, 1657. Edition: Classiques Garnier(ed. Emile Magne), nouvelle édition, 1973. (Some modern editions, like the original, spell the noun in the title *romant*.) The Part III included even in most present editions is not by Scarron and will not be considered here.

[1]*Bibliothèque des romans* (Paris, 1664), p. 167. The term *anti-roman* in fact comes from this same passage.

[2]Preface of *Polyandre* (Paris, 1648); cf. preface of Lannel: "Les livres sont des miroirs où nous pouvons voir les souillures de notre âme pour les nettoyer" (*Le Roman satirique*, 1624, quoted by Moses Ratner, *Theory and Criticism of the Novel in France from L'Astrée to 1750* [n.p., 1938], p. 26.)

[3]*Le Roman jusqu'à la Révolution* (Paris: Armand Colin, 1967), I, 207.

[4]"Quant au ton de l'ouvrage, on sait qu'il se meut sur trois registres, burlesque, réaliste et romanesque, toujours distincts: on les discerne parfaitement, épisode par épisode, le plus souvent chapitre par chapitre" (Jacques Truchet, "Le *Roman comique* de Scarron et l'univers théâtral," in Jean Jacquot, ed., *Dramaturgie et société* [Paris: CNRS, 1968], p. 259). As an example, Truchet cites, in Part I, the titles of ch. i as realist, ch. ii as burlesque, and ch. xxiii as romanesque: I will argue that these levels are not so discrete as Truchet contends.

[5]If this what is meant by the mention of L'Etoile playing "Ximene" (p. 123): the Garnier edition without clear justification has this changed to "Chimène." Because of this and similar intrusions elsewhere, I will sometimes, while retaining the Garnier edition for convenience of reference, correct the text of quoted passages by means of more reliable editions.

[6]Cf. Northrop Frye: "When the novel was established in the eighteenth century, it came to a reading public familiar with the formulas of prose romance. It is clear that the novel was a realistic displacement of romance, and had few structural features peculiar to itself. . . . This displacement gave the novel's relation to romance . . . a strong element of parody" (*The Secular Scripture* [Cambridge: Harvard, 1976], pp. 38-39). However, the time reference and the ordering of these events are mistaken: parody first enters the novel tradition explicitly, and later becomes more muted by admixing with other elements.

[7]"L'interventionnisme impénitent de Scarron est à double entente: il nie d'un côté ce qu'il affirme de l'autre, il compromet la crédibilité d'une fiction dont il prétend garantir la réalité, il étale l'activité de l'auteur quand celui-ci déclare son désir de disparaître. Ce faisant, il reflète les difficultés et les tensions d'une esthétique romanesque qui se cherche entre l'imaginaire et le réel. Il prend place dans une tradition de romanciers qui réfléchissent sur le roman dans le roman lui-même" (Jean Rousset, "Insertions et interventions dans le *Roman comique*," [*L'Esprit Créateur*, 11, No. 2 (1971), pp. 141-53], p. 153).

[8]*Temps raconté* and *temps racontant* in Rousset's analysis. Rousset divides the role of the primary narrator into four distinct functions which seem to me of doubtful value and are not followed here.

[9]In the technical language of Genette, such an intrusion of the extradiegetic narrator in any diegetic world is called a metalepsis: cf. *Figures III* (Paris: Seuil, 1972), p. 244.

[10]This wrinkle obviates, however, the one problem in the novel (p. 260) posed by a passage that had appeared "omniscient," in that the narrator relates things he could not, through acknowledged channels, have known.

[11]The only hesitation on Scarron's part that I detect is a detail of J 5 (p. 110) where an event in J 3 is situated "quelques jours auparavant." More often, precisions which the reader might be inclined to doubt, like a "deux jours devant" (p. 220) in J 11, turn out to be exactly right.

[12]Principally the influence of Henri Chardon, who notes for instance the presence of the plague around Alençon in 1638 (*Scarron inconnu* [Paris, 1903-1904], II, 225-26); but he must allow too that the plague was more or less constant in the region.

[13]See Marcel Simon's remarks to this effect in his introduction to the Garnier ed., p. xiii.

[14]A mixed case is introduced but quickly aborted in La Rancune's attempt (pp. 107-8), called both *histoire* and *conte*, to relate "la vie toute entière" of Roquebrune. Several elements of my analysis here are borrowed from Jean Rousset's article.

[15]The function of the person to whom a narration is made is often styled the *destinataire, récepteur* or *narrataire* in recent French criticism.

[16]Diderot's novel imitates *Roman comique* more than has usually been realized, both in theme and in specific devices. The story of Victoria de Portocarrero (N 2), for example, very much anticipates the deliberate vengeance of Mme de la Pommeraye, though it is not so cruel.

[17]Ernest Simon, "The Function of the Spanish Stories in Scarron's *Roman comique*," in *L'Esprit Créateur*, 3 (1963), 134.

[18]Frederick A. de Armas, *Paul Scarron* (New York: Twayne, 1972), pp. 88-89. The title of N 3 too suggests a circuit by which one's own virtues immanently procure a just reward.

[19]The chapter title is "Méchante action du sieur de la Rappinière." One could of course go into similar analyses for the H/N components, but

this would overwhelm us with detail. The data here could doubtless be encoded differently, too; no exclusive claims are made for my particular procedure, which is empirical.

[20]One critic has pointed out too the similarity between Le Mans and La Mancha (de Armas, p. 73).

[21]De Armas has pointed out one thematic similarity between the fumbling Ragotin on the one hand and the gallant Dom Carlos in the story he tells (N 1): each is preconditioned (but unvectored) to love, the object of which is then supplied by an outside revelation: Porcia's advances, the oracle of La Rancune (op. cit., p. 82).

[22]See de Armas, p. 78.

[23]Ragotin "exists somewhere between small-town ridiculousness and traditional stage buffoonery" (Benjamin Boyce, introduction to Scarron, *The Comical Romance* [New York and London: Benjamin Blom, 1968], p. xvi).

[24]Cf. de Armas, p. 68.

[25]"Quelques réflexions sur les *Lettres persanes*," written for the 1754 reedition.

[26]Just as Esau was identified with the hunt and Jacob with the flock, Le Destin says of Saint-Far: "Ses divertissements étaient différents des nôtres. Il n'aimait que la chasse et haïssait fort l'étude" (p. 62). If the analogy is rigorous, then Le Destin should be, like Jacob and Saint-Far, the *younger* of the two, i.e. the real Glaris, just as the circumstances of his birth suggest.

[27]These devices were common also in romance and in tragi-comedies, which Sorel calls "romans faits pour la représentation"--a transfer which suggests another parallel between comic novel and comedy (*Connaissance des bons livres*, p. 133).

[28]Cf. Truchet, p. 259.

[29]Giovanna Mariani, *La Condizione dell'uomo di teatro nel "Roman comique" di Scarron* (Florence: Nuova Italia, 1973).

[30]" S'il ravale d'un côté ses héros dans une condition tenue pour inférieure, il réévalue de l'autre cette condition en la faisant vivre sans répugnance à des personnages dont il nous garantit de toutes manières, en particulier par le biais de leur confession personnelle, la dignité d'origine et les qualités morales" (Rousset, p. 146).

[31] Mention should be made here of a study which I encountered only after this chapter was written: Joan E. DeJean's *Scarron's "Roman comique: A Comedy of the Novel, A Novel of Comedy* (Bern, Frankfurt, Las Vegas: Peter Lang, 1977). Many aspects of DeJean's approach to the text are similar to my own, and her work will be usefully consulted for complementary commentary.

# Chapter 2

## Le Roman bourgeois

Fifteen years after *Le Roman comique* began, the grand heroic novels were over, Mme de Lafayette had published *La Princesse de Montpensier*, the first of Mme de Villedieu's works had appeared, and even Mlle de Scudéry was down to works of a single volume. They were still fair game for satire, to be sure, and a combination of antithetical terms make this title *Roman bourgeois* just as aggressive as was *Roman comique*, for the word *bourgeois* attached to *roman* could only seem, to a contemporary reader, an alliance of the ridiculous with the sublime. To underscore their disparity, Furetière begins like Scarron in mock-epic fashion with a burlesque parody of the *Aeneid*, perhaps deliberately adopting for ironic purposes the notion that the novel descended from the epic: "Je chante les amours et les aventures de plusieurs bourgeois de Paris" (p. 903). In contrast with Virgil's hero, necessarily in the singular and at once defined by his exploits of arms (*Arma virumque cano*), the idea of a *roman* with several heroes, not to mention that of *amours bourgeoises* and *aventures bourgeoises*, was ludicrous, the degradation of a literary ideal by contamination with the petty. The muses and all that are just further embroidery on this introit. *Le Roman bourgeois* is quite in the comic novel tradition (its subtitle is *ouvrage comique*) but with a significant innovation in subject matter. In that, it reflects the prominence of the bourgeois as comic figure in the theater, notably that of Molière.

Certainly it is difficult--this I will not deny--for a modern reader to find very much of literary value in *Le Roman bourgeois*. To begin with, this particular quarrel over genres no longer interests us, who rarely read the old romances anyway outside of literature courses where they are prescribed. And for another thing, we have lost the habit of reading this kind of text, fragmented by numerous subplots and interlarded with variously tangential or unrelated tales, and we are frustrated by not being allowed to carry through on a dominant plot. This is a matter of generic conditioning, and even well-structured works which also manifest this characteristic, such as *Don Quixote* and *Gil Blas*, to some extent offend our novel-reading expectations and require an effort of mental readaptation. And *Le Roman bourgeois* just does not have the artistic stature of those works nor of *Le Roman comique*. Still I find it true that the reader who can abide it is reasonably well rewarded both by the verve of Furetière and by some aspects of his originality, not to mention a certain documentary interest in his depiction of social types--although that too is an enterprise largely literary in nature (closely related to the *caractère* or *portrait* in the manner of La Bruyère) and is not so vividly "real" as has often been pretended. Though *Le Roman bourgeois* is not a prime candidate for rehabilitation, I can agree with Henri Coulet in finding it an "oeuvre marquante dans l'histoire du genre romanesque, . . . oeuvre instructive par son échec même."[1]

Although Furetière's strategy is different from Scarron's, it is just as clear that here the conventional novel, with its high-flown sentiments and rhetoric, is the basic target. He chooses to situate most of the action around the Place Maubert precisely because it is the most bourgeois neighborhood in town, and is unimposing: an ordinary novelist, it is suggested, would nonetheless elevate it to comparison with the monumental Place Royal (a humorous juxtaposition since the latter is a square and the former a triangle) or someplace grander still (p. 904). There are throughout numerous allusions to the tired clichés of which are constructed the plots of novels (p. 939), and deliberate rejection of *combat de passions*, which to some readers, the narrator allows, will mean the absence of fiction's greatest beauties, tantamount in his view to well-known refrains which one can afford to skip over with an "etc." like a hurried priest reading his breviary (p. 1018). Examples are named: *Amadis de Gaule, Astrée, Le Grand Cyrus*--"toujours la même chose," as anyone can easily discover by opening one at random (p. 936). Furetière's characters, like his setting, being unexceptional, will represent a reversal of the conventions--some wise and some foolish (mostly the latter)--of novels; with their freckles and smallpox scars, they will not sit for idealized portraits (pp. 904, 906-7).

Still it would be a mistake to take certain of the narrator's comments literally, and be absent-mindedly deluded into believing that his novel is devoted to depiction of the strictly real, or that its narrative technique is unexampled. Like Scarron, Furetière addresses himself less to the real than to the nature of fiction. His "realism" must not be taken too seriously, although it usually has been; the moment we look to the whole of the text, it is revealed to be a fictional game which repeatedly transgresses the rules of verisimilitude it argues. He imitates many of Scarron's narrative postures, notably that of the scrupulous historian who is denied omniscience and refuses to overstep his sources: "on ne sait rien de tout cela, parce que la chose se passa en secret" (p. 939), even though his own narrator appears less whimsical about his role.[2] He does at least recognize explicitly that, even historically speaking, all facts are not significant, and derides the putative research which might reveal "combien de petits pois ou de fraises on a consommés" (p. 940). He is, nonetheless, maliciously inconsistent.

The narrator denounces and foreswears contrived effects of surprise (p. 923), but later produces several. The "Avertissement" insists the names in the work are not ciphers for specific individuals, but such disclaimers, standard in the *roman à clef*, really invited the reader to guess, and *Charroselles* in particular transparently represents the writer Charles Sorel. In the name of truth he mocks the "confidant" device for discovering the hero's feelings, affirming his fidelity to public and varied sources of information, yet he admits at the same time that he has not been totally constrained by such limitations: "à n'en point mentir, j'y ai mis aussi un peu du mien" (p. 936).

If, in other words, one expects a particular kind of novel--any particular kind--he will not find it here.[3] But such an expectation would in any event have been unfounded, created by factors (that is, reading habits) mostly extraneous to Furetière's own text. It admits no presuppositions, will not allow itself to be classified. The only assumption is the reader's familiarity with fictional devices; but the manipulation of them, though not exactly subtle, is nonetheless far from straightforward. The mock-epic opening, for example, jests about the overworked pattern of beginning *in medias res:* "Je ne veux point faire aussi de fictions poétiques, ni écorcher l'anguille par la queue, c'est-à-dire commencer mon histoire par la fin, comme font tous ces messieurs . . ." (p. 903): but this disingenuous narrator then does exactly what he has denounced, telling first the Nicodème-Javotte story before suspending it to fill in the "Histoire de Lucrèce" (p. 917). Lucrèce and Javotte later meet in the same convent and become friends, in function of the very "maudite coutume qui règne il y a longtemps dans les romans" according to which "tous les personnages sont sujets à se rencontrer inopinément dans les lieux plus éloignés, quelque route qu'ils puissent prendre"; moreover, in the same passage, the narrator depreciates "ces rencontres [qui] donnent quelque liaison et connexité à l'ouvrage qui sans cela serait souvent fort disloqué" (p. 1020). On the other hand, he still gets his revenge on the convention by ironically declaring it, in this instance, absolutely inconsequential in the plot: "Je ne crois pas néanmoins que ce hasard serve de rien à l'histoire." A disappointed "reader" is made to intervene and reproach him with concluding the Nicodème marriage too early in the story (p. 917), which he counters by saying that he has on the contrary done the reader a favor by laying to rest any anxiety about the outcome; but again there is a reverse irony, evident only much later, for the marriage so soon concluded ultimately is never realized. When the passage on Angélique's salon commences, he promises to omit some material so as not overly to defer "le mariage qui est sur le tapis"--this time a different marriage, one between Javotte and Bedout (p. 970)--and yet he *does* defer it, first with a long conversation at Angélique's, then with the interpolation of the allegorical "Historiette de l'Amour égaré" (pp. 983-1002); for forty pages the marriage waits in abeyance (to p. 1011), and then--it does not take place.

The referent informing all this discourse is the novel, whether its conventions are truly defied, or whether, as is also frequently the case, they are in fact followed. Javotte's elopement with Pancrace is a deliberate banality, one needing for that reason little elaboration: "Ils sont si communs que j'ai vu des gens qui, pour marquer l'endroit où ils en étaient d'une histoire, disaient: J'en suis au huitème enlèvement, au lieu de dire: J'en suis au huitième tome" (p. 1017); the narrator even adds a pleasantry about leaving the reader a blank page to fill in as he will. The beginning of Book Two makes a point of not guaranteeing it will end in marriage (p. 1025)--after Book One has just concluded with one elopement and one marriage--but despite all there is a marriage (pp. 1103-4). At other times, nevertheless, the narrator is loyal to what he says, abandoning Javotte and Pancrace for good, for example, after declaring he knows no more about them (p. 1019). The many seductions of Pancrace might, if related, serve somewhat to justify Javotte's capitulation, but the narrator will have none of this: "Je n'écris point ici une morale, mais seulement une histoire. Je ne suis pas obligé de la justifier" (p. 1018). And in this regard he keeps his objectivity. (The motives of Lucrèce after her conversion late in Book One also remain quite uncertain.)

Rather than a tissue of irrelevancies, Book One turns out in reality to be a web of interconnecting actions not at all gratuitously compiled. It is, in traditional mould, a series of love plots which in their social context much resemble moves in a chess game. The first axis is Nicodème's attack on Javotte, which can be symbolized as N ——➤ J (pp. 904-17); it is then interrupted by the story of Lucrèce and the marquis, M ——➤ L (pp. 917-42). This second vector could be made reciprocal (M◀——➤L) because Lucrèce is hoping for her part to trick the marquis, through his insincere marriage promise, into making of her a marquise. When that falls through, she tries the same strategy on Nicodème. Now this relation between the two plots was in fact already revealed in advance of her *histoire*;[4] the second thus joins the first in this manner (pp. 942-52):

$$N \longrightarrow J$$
$$M \longleftrightarrow L$$

Her pretentions to Nicodème, though are settled for a sum; and Bedout instead appears (pp. 953-1015), then Pancrace (pp.1003-19), to vie for her:

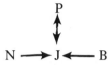

Javotte's infatuation with Pancrace eventually removes her from the center of this schema, and Nicodème disappears (p. 1009), leaving only Bedout. At this point Lucrèce re-enters (pp. 1019-24), although still in a convent ( a point of contact with the Javotte axis [p. 1020], as previously mentioned), and a new link (B ——►L) is established. In fact this attack too is reciprocal, for Lucrèce is laying a trap for Bedout--hence the marriage ending Book One. All of Book One (with exception of the "Historiette") is thus, when reassembled, a coherent nexus:

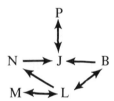

These lines are further reinforced by the acquaintanceship of Nicodème and Bedout and the friendship in the convent of Javotte and Lucrèce.

It is therefore the more unexpected that in Book Two no such design is to be found, despite a rugged semblance of order and plot. Two sordid, caricatural suitors, Charroselles and Belastre, pay court to Collantine whose powerful sexual drive is sublimated into legal wrangling: they are expected to "attack" her in a court of justice and defeat her there in order to win her hand. And it comes to a conclusion with her marriage to Charroselles, after which, in the closing paragraphs, *chicane* suddenly becomes the metaphor for domestic disharmony.

To say that much alone is to exaggerate its unity, however, for Furetière has undercut normal fictional assumptions much more aggressively than in Book One. The attack is immediate: " Si vous vous attendez, lecteur, que ce livre soit la suite du premier, et qu'il y ait une connexité nécessaire entre eux, vous êtes pris pour dupe. Détrompez-vous de bonne heure" (p. 1025). Only Charroselles, among the characters, carries over from Book One, and the story indeed is wholly unrelated to the preceding one. The narrator's utter sincerity is invoked with comic insincerity in an explanation where ligature is used as metaphor for liaison:

> Il est aisé de [farcir les poèmes héroïques] d'épisodes, et de les coudre ensemble avec du fil de roman, suivant le caprice ou le génie de celui qui les invente. Mais il n'en est pas de même de ce très véritable et très sincère récit, auquel je ne donne que la forme, sans altérer aucunement la matière. . . . Pour le soin de la liaison, je le laisse à celui qui reliera le livre. [p. 1025]

Next he further demotes the word *roman* itself, disassociating his own book from it: "Ce sont de petites histoires et aventures arrivées en divers quartiers de la ville, qui n'ont rien de commun ensemble . . .: ne l'appelez plus roman, et il ne vous choquera point" (pp.1025-26). Already in Book One the long conversational satire at Angélique's was evidence of topical interest tending to negate clear thematic coherence, but the plot was all the same too well structured to prepare the reader for what he encounters in Book Two, where it is a mere thread for satire and eventually is almost totally submerged by heterogeneous insertions.

This is not an uncompleted novel, since it possesses an unambiguous conclusion , but one manifesting willful disorder (which has its polemical uses but on esthetic grounds cannot escape being a failure). No work of art can have disorder as its sustaining principle, not even one which, like *Jacques le fataliste*, pretends to represent the randomness of objective experience, and still less novels like Zola's which have done much to forge our notions of "realism." The novels of Balzac and Thomas Hardy may often be subjectively depressing by virtue of their inexorable downhill course, without their artistic integrity being called into question; but there is something nihilistic about setting up a model only to tear it down, the way Alain-Fournier dismantles the dream world of *Le Grand Meaulnes*. It is because the progression is such as it is from Book One to Book Two that this cynicism becomes evident in not just its antinovelistic, but its anti-artistic, dimension.[5]

Furetière presents us not simply with an "endless" picaresque-type plot structure but rather with an amorphous whole, one which could be not indefinitely *ex*tended but indefinitely *dis*tended by throwing in any kind of stuffing anywhere. That is why the narrator can jest about writing arbitrarily at so much per page: "Si j'étais de ces gens qui se nourrissent de romans, c'est-à-dire qui vivent des livres qu'ils vendent, j'aurais ici une belle occasion de grossir ce volume et de tromper un marchand qui l'achèterait à la feuille"[6] (p. 1032). Almost hidden in the "Catalogue des livres de Mythophilacte" near the end there is a novel humorously entitled *La Vis sans fin*, or "le projet et dessein d'un roman universel, divisé en autant de volumes que le libraire en voudra payer" (p. 1083). These passages reiterate the dominant satire in that what is mocked is another bourgeois type, the professional writer. It was nearly impossible in Furetière's time to be supported on the *sale* of one's writings; the writer was generally under the tutelage of noble interests, or better still he was a person of leisure to whom esthetics was a pure luxury. However greatly personal factors may figure in Furetière's contempt for Charles Sorel, his sarcasm is particularly unrelenting where it concerns Charrosselles' preoccupation with literature as merchandise. This is what makes the character, in this perspective, an essential bourgeois, despite his claims to nobility; and at the same time it necessarily debases his writings, which emanating from such motives are made to appear a trivial kind of commodity.

There are nonetheless two attenuating considerations. First, the "form" is not as utterly lacking as the narrator himself pretends, since the plot is resolved; in this respect Book Two repeats the tendency in Book One to give the lie to its own pompous pronouncements. And secondly, none of the assorted pieces more or less piled into Book Two, especially toward the end, is absolutely irrelevant, at least to the bourgeoisie and novel motifs. Even the Mythophilacte inventory concerns an author, books, and bourgeois mentality, and the "Somme dédicatoire" is an elaborate burlesque of literary custom. But these set pieces assume too much autonomy with relation to plot: the last mentioned occupies eight whole pages of what are imaginary chapter summaries for four volumes. Art demands more than just conceivable or arguable relevance, however, and exacts a sense of ensemble that even pervasive wit (not to say malice) cannot alone supply. There is some real talent in Furetière, but it is fundamentally he who has least respect for its literary potential. His attack on the *roman* is related to Scarron's, but it is much more negative, because Furetière wants to reduce esthethic criteria to a minimum.

As suggested earlier, the satire in this novel is two-pronged, because the work is directed not just against the novel but equally against the bourgeoisie. Consider the double cutting edge of a comparison like the following, explaining Bedout's prompt forgetting of Javotte: "l'amour n'est pas opiniâtre dans une tête bourgeoise comme il l'est dans un coeur héroïque; . . .l'intérêt et le dessein de se marier est ce qui règle leur passion Il n'appartient qu'à ces gens fainéants et fabuleux d'avoir une fidélité à l'épreuve des rigueurs, des absences et des années" (p. 1009). There is a characteristic logic to the bourgeois mind that is implicitly disparaged; for instance, the pairing between a *fille de procureur* (Javotte) and an *avocat* (Nicodème), is somehow as much in the nature of things ("une grande affinité et sympathie") as that of a maid to a valet (p. 909). Furetière's terms never leave any doubt about his contempt for the bourgeois mentality, poles away from the elevation of a *roman*, as illustrated by the bourgeois obsession with marriage: "Ils ne font jamais l'amour qu'en passant et dans une posture forcée, n'ayant autre but que de se mettre vitement en ménage. Il ne faut pas s'étonner après cela si le reste de leur vie ils ont une humeur rustique et bourrue qui est à charge à leur famille et odieuse à tous ceux qui les fréquentent" (p. 911). The opposing view, understood here, is aristocratic: marriage is a formal structure, having little claim on one's emotional or sexual behavior.

From the outset the word *bourgeois* itself generates pejorative connotations within the text, completely undisguised in the adverbial form *bourgeoisement.* Everything the bourgeois does reeks of bourgeoisism: his domesticity, his petty practicality (going to get his own laundry: "Comme Nicodème était bon bourgeois et bon ménager, il alla le chercher lui-même" [p. 948], his niggardliness (locking up the bread cupboard [p. 955]),[7] his inability to break out of his small ways (his sense of debauchery is going to the theater and then the cabaret [p. 963]). The bourgeoise for her part tends house (p. 929), folds her napkin and carries out her own plate when getting up from table (p. 913), can converse with other women only about prices and practical affairs; Javotte and her mother are forever reeling balls of wool or "bourgeoisement occupées à ourler quelque linge pour achever le trousseau de l'accordée" (p. 946). It is representative of Javotte's bourgeois mentality that she thinks letters serve only business purposes (p. 961): an example of the fact that she has no (romantic) imagination. A man's personality functions exclusively in terms of his profession; the only part of *Cinna* that esthetically interests Vollichon is the rhetoric of the cases argued before Auguste (p. 964). Even the *chicaneur* whose satire forms the substance of Book Two is a bourgeois type (the robe too in Furetière has almost exclusively bourgeois connotations, *noblesse de robe* notwithstanding),[8] and the "Jugement des bûchettes" (pp. 1056-57) in "langage chicanourois" is an example of trivial mentality disguised in pedantic technicality.

The bourgeois trait par excellence is pervasive money-consciousness; and if there is a connection, as some have asserted, between lucre and filth, then it is difficult not to conclude that the bourgeois's suspicion of conspicuous cleanliness is an aspect of it ("la propreté qui plaît à tous les honnêtes gens est ce qui choque le plus ces barbons" [p. 916]). Furetière's "Tarif ou évaluation des parties sortables pour faire facilement les mariages" (pp. 919-20) satirically lists nine levels of husbands a girl can anticipate, according to where her dowry falls in the range from 2,000 to 600,000 pounds,[9] "la corruption du siècle ayant introduit de marier un sac d'argent avec un autre sac d'argent." It symbolizes the mercenary conviction that everything has its clear silver value, based as it is on specific ratios to the price of the groom's office (*charge*).[10] When Villeflatin thinks of Nicodème as a potential husband of Lucrèce, he can comment only at this level: "il lui dit ... qu'il avait du bien; il n'en fit point d'autre éloge, car il croyait bien par ce mot avoir dit tout ce qui s'en pouvait dire" (pp. 941-42). Another interpolation, the "Etat et rôle des sommes" in Book Two (pp. 1095-96), while entirely different in nature, also confirms the attitude that everything must be paid for at a contract price. And the *historiette* about Amour, mostly satirical gossip and useless to the main plots, has at least one possible link with them in Amour's final determination to have no more doings with mercenary love-making (p. 1002).

Like Scarron, Furetière plays for humorous effect on the names of his characters, several of which are précieux: Nicomède, Angélique, Phylalète, Phylippote, Polyphile (=‘amours multiples’), Belastre (= *belâtre* or *bel* + *astre*). Some have a Dickens-like quality emphasizing their bourgeoisism (Vollichon) or simply their baseness (Villeflatin = *vil* + *flatter*). No young woman of quality would be named Javotte (usually a maid's name, as in Marivaux); *Bedout* irresistably suggests a small mind, in part via *bedeau* ‘beadle’, or else a bourgeois ‘paunch’ arising from sedentariness (*bedaine*, *bedon* = ‘stomach’); and *Pancrace* (*pan* + *crasse* ‘dirt’) indubitably evokes an eminently untidy or unsanitary person. Even more damning is the affectionate bourgeois habit of nicknaming a spouse: Vollichon and his wife are "Mouton" and "Moutonne" (p. 1012).

In social behavior, its attitude towards the family is what most sets the bourgeoisie apart from the nobility. Its daughters would rather marry anyone than no one, and look uninspirationally to the practical: "Je veux un homme qui soit un bon mari et qui gagne bien sa vie" (p. 947: the voice is that of Mme Vollichon, but she is speaking about a husband for her daughter). The male for his part speaks just like Arnolphe in *L'Ecole des femmes*: "je voudrais qu'une femme vécût à ma mode, et qu'elle ne prît plaisir qu'à voir son mari" (p. 959); he locks his women up as in a harem, his own private property, and receives callers in his home only for himself, and only for business at that (p. 912). His concept of marriage, as expressed in Bedout's letter to Javotte, is neither romantic nor noble; its pompous rhetoric can evoke no more exciting image than a consummately domestic life together "dans une étude où nous apprendrions à jouir des bonheurs d'une vie privée et tranquille" (p. 962). And as if that were not bad enough, the bourgeois must have his children under foot; "car c'est la coutume de ces bons bourgeois d'avoir toujours leurs enfants devant leurs yeux, d'en faire le principal sujet de leurs entretiens, d'en admirer les sottises et d'en boire toutes les ordures" (p. 967). First Vollichon's son asks in front of everyone to be taken to the toilet, then he is thrust into the conversation: "Mme Vollichon ne parla plus . . . que des belles qualités de son fils, de ses mièvretés et postiqueries. Ce sont les termes consacrés chez les bourgeois et les mots de l'art pour expliquer les gentillesses de leurs enfants." Next little Toinon appears with his hobby-horse, and this brings on a grotesque romp:

> Toinon rentra peu de temps après dans la salle en équipage de cavalier, c'est-à-dire avec un bâton entre les jambes, qu'il appelait son dada. Vollichon prit aussitôt une manche de balai qu'il mit entre les siennes, et, courant après son fils, ils firent ensemble trois tours autour de la table, ce qui donna occasion à Nicodème d'appeler cette course un tournoi. [p. 967]

Laurence, watching, and being herself a finer spirit, can only laugh and muse about "la sottise des bourgeois qui quittent l'entretien de la meilleure compagnie du monde pour jouer et badiner avec leurs enfants, et qui croient être bien excusés en alléguant l'affection paternelle" (pp. 967-68).

The bourgeois lacks refinement, not only in taste but in language; when Villeflatin wants to ask Lucrèce how far her relationship with Nicodème has gone, the only word he can think of is *copule*--which "grosse parole" fills her with confusion (p. 946). On the other hand, nothing shows up the bourgeois worse than his awkward and unnatural attempts to be polite, which only spawn "de longs compliments bourgeois" (p. 1015), or to rise otherwise above his nature: Charroselles wants to play noble, and thinks he can go about it with a mangey team and buggy. The bourgeoise who turns from her household to delicacies is scored for pretending too much (p. 929); her real lack of familiarity with things of quality will incline her to make foolish judgments (witness Collantine's admiration for Belastre's poetry [p. 1064]). The secret aspiration of the bourgeois to nobility gives rise to an elegant pun during the marquis's pursuit of Lucrèce: "les promenades à Saint-Cloud à Meudon et à Vaugirard étaient fort fréquentes, qui sont les grands chemins par où l'honneur bourgeois va droit à Versailles."[11]

It follows that nothing could be worse than the bourgeois's sense of gallantry, the essense of which he does not understand; and in being chivalrous, he manifests only a ridiculous attempt to be what by nature he is not:

La seule galanterie qu'il fit ce jour-là, fut qu'il voulut peler une poire pour sa maîtresse; mais comme c'était presque fait, elle lui échappa des doigts, et se sucra d'elle-même sur le plancher de la chambre. Il la ramassa avec une fourchette, souffla dessus, la ratissa un peu, puis la lui offrit et lui dit encore, comme font plusieurs personnes maintenant, qu'il lui demandait un million d'excuses. [p. 959]

Bedout's efforts at elegance in his letter can draw on only artisanal metaphors which are quintessentially bourgeois, and even lead him into a most impolite équivoque: "je voudrais que nos deux coeurs, passant sous la presse du mariage, reçussent de si belles impressions, qu'ils pussent être après reliés ensemble avec des nerfs indissolubles" (p. 962). Similarly, Collantine sees her chicane battles with Belastre as a parallel of the amorous rituals of knighthood, and he replies with an awkward legal metaphor:

puisque, sans vous fâcher, it faut plaider contre vous, je veux intenter un procès criminel contre vos yeux, qui m'ont assassiné, et qui ont fait un rapt cruel de mon coeur; je prétends les faire condamner, et par corps, en tous mes dommages et intérêts.
[p. 1060]

His love letter, in the same vein (p. 1062), is, like Bedout's, a portrait of his bourgeois mind out of its element.

Of course Bedout and Belastre are hardly dandies; but a bourgeois who is, such as Nicodème, just goes to the opposite excess by taking his instructions from *Le Grand Cyrus* and *Clélie* (p. 911). He wastes his "style poli" on Javotte though, who, having neither curiosity nor ear for metaphor and therefore no idea what *servir* and *donner un coeur* can stand for, lowers it all to bourgeois banality with her singlemindedness for marriage and her childish, domestic *papa* and *maman*. All her replies, in which the verbs are characteristically qualified by "ingénument" or "naïvement," bear the mark of bourgeois dullness; in addition, her passivity renders doubly absurd Bedout's gallant declarations about his destiny being in her hands (p. 966).

The more affluent and more polished of them still betray that ineffaceable bourgois spirit. The narrator's long examination of attitudes toward mud touches on this (p. 927 ff.); for to appear in polite company one is required to appear unspotted even in the rain (a sign of an aristocratic esthetic implying being above concrete materiality), yet the bourgeois either cannot afford--or is too parsimonious to afford--a carriage: hence the tergiversations which Hyppolite, who wants to be elegant, cannot countenance and cuts off: "tout cela n'importe; que ne venait-il en chaise?" (p 928). She gives further proof of her *arrivisme* and its dependence upon identifiable, objective criteria for social acceptability, when she justifies this stance with: "Car comment jugerez-vous d'un homme qui entre en une compagnie si ce n'est par l'extérieur?" (p. 930).

Although Furetière has been credited with creating a feeling for the dramatic possibilities to be found in bourgeois existence, I do not think this can seriously be argued in the light of his unremitting mockery. Lucrèce's pregnancy is dramatic to her, even potentially a moving and desperate dilemma, but this is not what Furetière calls attention to; it is not a grand theme, and Lucrèce is incapable of heroism. So is all the bourgeoisie. At his most romantic, the bourgeois elopes with the girl; but it is in truth a small gesture, deflated by its facility: "Elle fut facilement enlevée par le moyen d'une échelle qu'on appliqua aux murs du jardin, qui . . . n'avaient été faits que pour conserver ses choux, qui sont bien plus aisés à garder que des filles" (p. 1019).

All this sarcasm is not accompanied by unequivocal admiration for the nobility. But the nobility have style if nothing more, and a complete lack of the bourgeois's petty vices; in this comparison even their flaws have redeeming aspects. They are teased, for instance, about not paying their debts: the marquis "payait si bien que cela faisait tort à la noblesse" (p. 940);[12] but if that is so, still it is a sign that they are not *bourgeoisement* obsessed with money. The nobility too, it is recognized, have their silly trademarks: they typically wear feathers, for example (p. 923), and Vollichon even calls them "plumets" (p. 1011) as a synonym for gentlemen. But the weight of the evidence is on the reverse satire. The nobility has an ingrained, if not inbred, elegance, "certaine habitude de civilité et de politesse qui dure toute la vie" (p. 911), and the potential even of a bourgeoise like Lucrèce can only be realized in a noble environment:

C'est dommage qu'elle n'avait pas été nourrie à la cour ou chez des gens de qualité, car elle eût été guérie de plusieurs grimaces et affectations bourgeoises qui faisaient tort à son bel esprit, et qui faisaient bien deviner le lieu où elle avait été élevée. [p. 918]

Still, any refinement is better than none. Laurence, "femme d'esprit," has been improved by familiarity with *le beau monde* (p. 963), noble or not, and suffers in the presence of a Mme Vollichon; she vainly tries to translate Vollichon's rocky humor into precious witticisms (p. 965). And Javotte turns out to have possibilities too, only dimly suggested by her coquettishness in dress and delicate feminine pride at the beginning (pp. 907-9). Being bourgeoise, she thinks refinement should be purchasable in a book (p. 1003); but once her eyes are opened to her initial stultification, she can, by studying finer models, lift herself into a higher frame of mind and quite astound her father and everyone else when the time comes obediently to sign the marriage articles.

Another continual subject of the novel, that of modernity, cuts across class lines to a degree, though we see its manifestations particularly among the bourgeoisie: the changing styles (p. 905), the fashionable hairdresser (p. 907), "le luxe et la délicatesse du siècle" (p. 928). The marquis and Lucrèce relate how any costume can be meticulously criticized item by item (pp. 931-32), and the marquis proposes a "grand conseil des modes" with a judiciary structure and authority to issue certificates of compliance (pp. 933-34). The satirical portrait of Nicodème and his cousin, "gens du bel air" changing from daytime robe to "grands canons et les galands d'or" (pp. 907-8), is also that of the young modern, aspiring to the stylishness of his betters; and in such ways the modern and bourgeois themes join. There is every reason to believe that here Furetière is capturing an authentic discovery of his time. Fads can develop coherence and evolve rapidly only when there is a stable social group with good and rapid communications; these conditions obtained in the court of Louis XIV (by this time the Versailles court), and secondarily among the Paris nobility and especially bourgeoisie. (The time lag in the provincial imitations of Paris vogues itself gave rise to a comic disparity.) There were at once noble fashions imitated by the bourgeoisie, and others that changed just as rapidly but were identifiably bourgeois. But the well-established bourgeois views these developments negatively, from a fundamentally conservative position, as a sign of corruption and the depravity of youth (p. 942); of this the best proof is the gradual loss of respect for the father (p. 1011).

The *précieuses* are a good example of this dependent phenomenon: for in this book preciosity is bourgeois, although it is clearly derivative, not elaborating its own code but imitating a model: "on tâchait d'imiter tout ce qui se pratique dans les belles ruelles par les précieuses du premier ordre" (p. 970). The *académie bourgeoise* which Angélique's salon represents must seem to the author like a contradiction in terms, again for the reason that it is inauthentic. The bourgeoisie can achieve style in its own eyes only by aping the nobility; it learns to play at gallantry too. For instance, delicacy prescribes that gifts be not offered directly to a lady, but it permits losing a sum to her at the gaming table. Nonetheless, the bourgeois who spends money expects *quid pro quo*, and beneath his tactful gift lies this mercenary assumption which the narrator underscores as follows:

> Je crois même, pour peu que nous allions en avant, comme on se raffine tous les jours, qu'on pratiquera la coutume . . . de bien faire son marché, et de dire: Je vous envoie tel présent pour telle faveur, et d'en prendre des assurances: car, en effet, les femmes sont fort trompeuses. [p. 922]

Love does not come naturally to the bourgeois, so what he cannot learn of it from observing gentlemen he derives from books. In this regard, *Astrée*, the instrument of Javotte's enamoration, is a more deadly "venom" than others for the bourgeois, because its pastoral characters do not seem to represent an experience socially unattainable to him (p. 1006). Javotte literally learns to live a certain experience through the novel, picturing Céladon in the form of Pancrace, and then, as Astrée, herself falling in love with him--but it is a *vie de roman*, something vicarious. Pancrace even realizes that to succeed with her he needs to go back to reading *Astrée*, and tries to complete the identification through adoption of the heroes' names as their own *noms de roman* (p. 1007). This precious conceit is itself of course a mark of escape into fantasy, but it is also a recognition of the fact that novels not only copy life but shape it as well.

Of course Furetière like Scarron was writing a *comic* novel and, although his characters are none of them actors, the conception of comedy is still intrinsically linked with theatrical comedy. The "Avertissement" appropriates to the work the familiar Molière theory of comic catharsis: that the depiction and ridiculing of vices leads to their correction. Comedy--and by extension comic fiction--is good medicine:"Voilà comment, lecteur. je te donne des drogues éprouvées" (p. 901). Thus it is natural for the narrator to define his discourse not only in reference to novelistic but also to theatrical categories: "l'on ne joue pas ici la grande pièce des machines" (p. 917). And that this aspect of the work is related fundamentally to the bourgeois theme is evident in the opening pages, where the narrator dispenses with grand decor in these terms: "quoique toutes ces belles choses se fassent pour la décoration du théâtre à fort peu de frais, j'aime mieux faire jouer cette pièce sans pompe et sans appareil, comme ces comédies qui se jouent chez le bourgeois avec un simple paravent" (p. 905). It is therefore inappropriate to think of it as a *representation* of bourgeois life; it is instead, quite specifically, "une comédie qui se joue chez le bourgeois." It is not for nothing that Furetière subtitled his work *ouvrage comique*. For while *roman* as conceived in 1666 is not normally "bourgeois," comedy on the contray is. The comparison of *chicane* procedures to particular antics of Scaramouche (p. 1073) is apt more than just as literary metaphor, and it is perfectly natural for the same reason that Racine should have transferred as he did some ideas from this novel into his comedy *Les Plaideurs*.

There are other analogies as well, first in occasional farcical scenes (much rarer, though, than in Scarron) such as the cascading retreat of Nicodème (p. 948) which earns him, for Mme Vollichon, the epithet "Brise-tout," and also in the conventional comic ending of marriage in both Books One and Two. Furetière has tried to derail the ordinary spectator's assumption that the final marriage will come about, but that does not change the outcome which, as in a play, owes something to the strategy of *péripéties*. Comedies shared with novels the trait of ending but never beginning with marriage, as is recognized in the final lines of Book One: "S'ils vécurent bien ou mal ensemble, vous le pourrez voir quelque jour, si la mode vient d'écrire la vie des femmes mariées" (p. 1024). Of course it was not much later that Mme de Lafayette had something more to say about that notion.

# Notes

Antoine Furetière (1619-1688), *Le Roman bourgeois, ouvrage comique*, 1666. Edition: Since there is no modernized edition in print, I have had to use for reference the text edited by Antoine Adam in *Romanciers du XVII<sup>e</sup> siècle* (Paris: Gallimard [Pléiade], 1958), pp. 900-1104. In my quotations the spelling will, however, be modernized.

[1] *Le Roman jusqu'à la Révolution,* p. 277.

[2] Coulet finds his procedure the exact reverse of Scarron's: "Scarron pour faire apparaître la gratuité de l'invention romanesque, affectait d'élaborer son oeuvre sous les yeux du lecteur sans savior où il allait; Furetière, qui prétend ne rien inventer, montre qu'il sait d'avance tout ce qu'il a à dire" (ibid., p. 274). In fact, though, this posture is not perfectly consistent: "Mais je ne suis pas assuré qu'il [Nicodème] vienne encore paraître sur la scène" (p. 1009).

[3] Cf. Coulet: "Le lecteur qui espérait trouver un roman réaliste à la place du roman romanesque est déçu et irrité" (op. cit., p. 277).

[4] This word often meant a specific type of narration (first person) as in the *Roman comique* or *Manon Lescaut*, but could also apply to other intercalated stories, which is the case here and in *La Princesse de Clèves*.

[5] Cf. Henri Coulet: "La vision que Furetière a du monde est aux antipodes de la vision romanesque qui arrange le réel et l'organise: sa vision à lui désorganise, déconsidère le réel; il ne veut pas intéresser ni plaire" (op. cit., p. 277).

[6] "Tromper le marchand" is an allusion not only to fattening the volume but also to the frequent phenomenon where an author wrote one or more volumes of a serial novel but left the publisher (and public) up in the air by never completing it.

[7] Balzac's Grandet will provide evidence of the permanence of this trait, with his careful and stingy metering of flour, butter and sugar.

[8] The same is true in Racine's *Les Plaideurs* of 1668.

[9] Only the highest category (100,000 to 200,000 *écus*) leads to the promised land, accession to nobility by marriage to "un président au mortier, vrai marquis, surintendant, duc et pair."

[10] The *charge*, a measure of bourgeois pretentiousness here, was purchased and could be resold, therefore had a market value as well as prestige. There are additional rules appended which can modify the chart ratios: great beauty might promote a girl by one step; servile or base origins caused her to be sold at great discount.

[11] See p. 937, n. 2: *aller à Versailles* is apparently a euphemism for "être renversé," i.e. 'tumble' in the English sense--which is precisely what Lucrèce will do during one of these walks.

[12] The heavily indebted noble is already a comic theme in *Dom Juan* (1665) and reappears regularly thereafter, for example in Regnard's *Le Joueur* (1698).

# Chapter 3

## La Princesse de Clèves

The title of Segrais's *Nouvelles françaises* (1656) had announced the substitution of familiar settings for the conventional antiquity of the heroic novels, and his friend Mme de Lafayette in 1662 similarly began her *Princesse de Montpensier* on a decidedly French note that might be described by the musical term firm attack: "Pendant que la guerre civile déchirait la France sous le règne de Charles IX, l'Amour ne laissait pas de trouver sa place parmi tant de désordres et d'en causer beaucoup dans son Empire." Except for the precious personification of Amour, the opening of *La Princesse de Clèves* is in this respect entirely comparable to it: "La magnificence et la galanterie n'ont jamais paru en France avec autant d'éclat que dans les dernières années du règne de Henri second" (p. 241). For her readers, this was in both instances a throwback of only a century or a little more; most of the names and the main historical events would have been still quite familiar. Within this context the novelist develops what was called *la petite histoire*, not the conquests of kingdoms but the loves and intrigues of the court. This novel is representative of the *nouvelle historique* at a stage where it took on greater length and complexity and, having supplanted the *roman* in the early 1660s, itself became "petit roman." [1]

In *La Princesse de Clèves*, as in all of Mme de Lafayette's works, the heroine's name stands affirmatively and unselfconsciously for the whole. Mme de Lafayette confidently assumes the responsibilities of a narrator, leaving aside the scruples of the supposedly objective observer-historian seen in our previous chapters, and renouncing too the kind of compilation where the characters do all the talking. The four interpolated stories are short (from two to seven pages only) and neither suspend the interest of the main plot nor cause one to forget which characters are responsible for relating them. She abandons too, as was customary in *nouvelles*, the classical beginning *in medias res* where necessary antecedents to the action are accounted for in subsidiary narrations by the characters themselves; none of the stories here provides essential background information on the main characters. And she attempts a technical feat probably unmatched by any of her predecessors in fitting a private fiction containing only two wholly imaginary characters (Mme and Mlle de Chartres) into a complicated network of historical facts and dates; this achievement testifies to great ingenuity on her part even if she had to alter some biographical data to do it.[2] In the main the story is clearly inscribed within the chronological boundaries of the return of the court to Paris in November 1558 and its return in the fall of the following year, although in the last few pages time is distended in the functional equivalent of what in the cinema would be a fade-out. Rare were the novels in the century following which even approached its temporal control and coherence.[3]

*Magnificence* and *galanterie*, the consummate qualities which distinguish the social world of this novel, are symbolized in the chief model for both pomp and love, "galant, bien fait et amoureux" (p. 241), Henri II. There is a mytho-feudal assumption here that rank and prowess coincide; the king "réussissait admirablement dans tous les exercices du corps" (p. 241) and is himself the best horseman in the kingdom (p. 355); after him come some of the novel's leading heroes, Guise and Nemours, who with Ferrare are best at jousting (p. 304). On the feminine side of the court the real monarch is an abstraction, refinement: "*Le goût* que le roi François premier avait eu pour la poésie et pour les lettres, *régnait* encore en France" (p. 242);[4] the queen, the Dauphine, and especially *Madame, soeur du roi* are associated with "les belles choses," poetry, comedy, music.

Such propositions, disarming in their uncanny transparency, are simply the postulates of this vision and cannot be contested. They will not be nuanced by Mme de Lafayette's spare vocabulary nor her restrained and self-sufficient style. Her range of diction is astonishingly slim, and she never colors her presentation with similes. The same adjectival and metonymic repertory returns endlessly with a stubborn confidence in its own adequacy that to us must seem almost disingenuous. Mme de Chartres is characterized by her *bien*, *vertu*, and *mérite* (p. 248), Saint-André by *mérite, agrément, magnificence* (p. 245); Nevers's three sons are *parfaitement bien faits* (p. 243). These qualities are all social in that they bespeak the values of the society that rocognizes them; the considerable adjectival use of nouns lends them an air of tangibility, as in the rapid characterization of the Chevalier de Guise as "un prince aimé de tout le monde, bien fait, plein d'*esprit*, plein d'*adresse*, et d'une *valeur* célèbre par toute l'Europe" (p. 243), and again in the more developed portrait of Nemours:

> Ce qui le mettait au-dessus des autres était une *valeur* incomparable, et un *agrément* dans son esprit, dans son visage et dans ses actions que l'on n'a jamais vu qu'à lui seul; il avait un *enjouement* . . . , une *adresse* extraordinaire . . . , une *manière* de s'habiller . . . , et enfin un *air* dans toute sa personne . . .
>
> [pp. 243-44]

This court of "belles personnes" and "hommes admirablement bien faits" does not seem to demand further definition; the abstract and essentialist vocabulary stands for (but to today's reader does not describe) the ethos of a class.[5] Jonathan Culler rightly notes that when Mme de Lafayette writes such sentences, "she displays the immense confidence in her readers that this mode of writing implies. Language need only gesture towards the world. . . . One [today] can no longer say 'he thought what was natural on such an occasion' without writing an obscure and problematic sentence."[6] Yet there is an inevitable sense too in which this sentence was always ambiguous.

All the characters' qualities point to each other and thus seem almost interchangeable, a tautological dynamic epitomized in a few phrases about Navarre: "sa valeur était soutenue de *toutes les autres grandes qualités*: il avait un esprit vaste et profond, une âme noble et élevée, et une égale capacité pour la guerre et pour les affaires" (p. 243). The complementarity is so harmonious here because he is--as could be inferred once we understand this logic--a king. Redundancy is unavoidable: he is what he is, and this will show in all his particular facets.

The novel's leading couple, by rank but also by virtue of their function as heroes, share in the unexceptionable superlatives. Mlle de Chartres, "une beauté parfaite," is queen among the novel's several queens, inspiring admiration even in a context where the admirable is commonplace (p. 247); she shines like a diamond, her white skin and golden hair radiating "un éclat que l'on n'a jamais vu qu'à elle" (p. 248). Likewise, Nemours is described as virtually beyond comparison, "un chef-d'oeuvre de la nature" (p. 243). All of the greats fall in love with her; and he for his part is irresistible, apparently even to Queen Elisabeth. It is a function of the superlatives to impel these two characters towards each other, this fate being implicit in their heady aristocratic perfection which they instinctively if unconsciously recognize: "se voyant souvent, et se voyant l'un et l'autre ce qu'il y avait de plus parfait à la cour, il était difficile qu'ils ne se plussent infiniment" (p. 263). The narrator takes even this in stride, and can soon dispense with epithets; it is indicative of their stature and dignity that they are evoked simply as *ce prince* and *cette princesse*. But their story like themselves is unexampled, as the text often reminds us. Their singularity is an essential part of their nature as characters; and that most extraordinary of decisions, to confess her love to her husband, is entered into by the Princess, in large part, precisely because it is so exceptional.[7] Thus everything about this novel is highly stylized. Whatever is distasteful is avoided, even in its historical data; all that is retained must contribute to the sense of elevation of the drama being enacted.

What does it take to constitute a story? None can be told except in function of certain implicit assumptions about the answer to this. It is taken for granted by Mme de Lafayette, for example, that the story can be confined in its chronological span within the limits of a certain movement or "adventure" in the life of the hero (true also in epic tradition), despite the work's apparent assimilation, by virtue of its title, to the biographical genre: this is the story not of a lifetime, but of a marriage and a love. Similarly, it is clear that, for this author, there is nothing to be told which emanates from the experiences of the common man. Picture Mme de Clèves and Nemours as ordinary beings, and the story evaporates. As in classical French tragedy, the superlatives have a purifying and valorizing function. The grand hero, freed from contingency, becomes representative of everything; the archetypal, not the typical, can alone pretend to universal significance.

This is the relation of the passions and inner struggles of a great lady (and two great men), in whom uniquely the narrator is interested. The world of objects is invisible except when they can be charged with intense symbolic value (the stolen portrait, Nemours's cane). Visual notation is starkly absent; nothing has color, for example, except in the context of the heraldic amorous gesture: the colors worn (as a private message to the Princess) by Nemours at the tourney, and their reappearance in the ribbons she ties. The seasons are simply a gauge of social rhythms; November brings not cold, rain or wind, but the return of the court to Paris. Details are unimportant to Mme de Lafayette. If one thinks of Stendhal's criterion--"Il n'y a de vérité que dans les détails"--then certain of her passages can be made to seem like abdications of a novelist's responsibilities: "il était difficile d'avoir une conversation particulière. Il en trouva pourtant les moyens" (p. 257); "il demanda congé au roi pour aller à Paris, sur quelque prétexte qu'il inventa" (p. 365). Material necessities, looked after by valets and maids in the novel's social climate, can be taken for granted and merit no attention. Noticeably lacking too is any allusion to society at large; one has no sense of Paris as a crowded city. There is only capital-letter Society, le monde; no bourgeoisie, no peasantry, not even servants are spied by the reader (even Clèves's emissary dispatched to follow Nemours is styled a gentilhomme).

Yet all this abstraction is made to contribute to the intensity of what the story *is* about. For the noble society has a hermetic closeness about it despite its occasional geographic dispersal, that has been not unfairly compared to that of a hothouse. The Princess cannot escape it by going to Coulommiers: Mme de Mercoeur lives close by to provide access to her, despite the surrounding walls. There is nowhere to hide in a circle so small that, when Clèves tells of his chance encounter with Mlle de Chartres just after her arrival, Madame can confidently assert that the person described does not exist (p. 250).

The celebration of this society's virtues in the opening pages is, however, subtly infused with suggestions of a less laudable countercurrent, partly through muted ironies which only slowly are brought to fruition. The second paragraph hints at a certain grotesque inelegance in the person of Diane de Poitiers, in an insidious but unremarkable juxtaposition of her image with her granddaughter's: "elle paraissait elle-même avec tous les ajustements que pouvait avoir Mlle de la Marck, sa petite-fille, qui était alors à marier" (p. 241). Only a few pages later is it explicitly stated that she is no longer either young or beautiful (p. 244). Imperceptibly, the narrator damns with faint praise. Diane, for example, never draws pejorative adjectives, yet nothing good is ever said of her and the impression is nonetheless conveyed of a cranky, proud, imperious woman. Her failure to appreciate the Princesse de Clèves of course cements this negativity. Mme de Chartres underlines her lack of merit and fidelity, and indeed can give no reason for the king's loving her (Madame de Lafayette, it would seem, cannot get over Henri's attachment for this woman twenty years his elder). In this way, the reader is given the deceptive impression that the narration is neutral, and that his reaction to the characters is personal. But this is never true in any novel; it just means that the steering of the reader's attitudes by the narrator's "rhetoric" operates largely in subliminal ways.

The social glitter, although it is integral to the scene and by no means denounced as fundamentally inauthentic, is soon revealed for what it is: the surface structure only of a deeper structure too intricate to be perceived by the unapprenticed. As early as the fourth paragraph, remarks concerning Diane's rival, the queen, translate the pomp into the façade of a "profonde dissimulation" which veils a lust for power ("une grande douceur à régner" [pp. 241-42]). While still under the influence of the *magnificence et galanterie* which distinguish the court from the very first sentence, the reader learns that its soul is *"ambition* et galanterie" (p. 252): the dazzling appearance is, in other words, the ornamental expression of ambition. A frenzy of activity is divided into *plaisirs* and *intrigues*, which would seem at first glance to correspond respectively to the initially posited domains of *galanterie* and *ambition,* but are, upon closer inspection, equally applicable to both and bespeak the complex interweavings at multiple levels of all the goings-on. Love and power are not discrete categories at all, but isomers of the same matrix:

> Il y avait tant d'intérêts et tant de cabales différentes, et les dames y avaient tant de part que l'amour était toujours mêlé aux affaires et les affaires à l'amour. Personne n'était tranquille, ni indifférent; on songeait à s'élever, à plaire, à servir ou à nuire; on ne connaissait ni l'ennui, ni l'oisiveté, et on était toujours occupé des plaisirs ou des intrigues. [p. 252]

Even though this agitation is in fact highly organized, it is this aspect of the novel which is hardest to grasp for today's reader, to whom the unfamiliar names, titles, and relations seem a maze. This element of confusion does entail one empathic advantage, however, which is that it puts him in a perceptual situation analogous to that of Mlle de Chartres, who is likewise a stranger to the court, and thus naïve and vulnerable. "Ainsi il y avait une sorte d'*agitation sans désordre* dans cette cour, qui la rendait très agréable, mais aussi très dangereuse pour une jeune personne" (p. 253). She is drawn without realizing it into the orbit of the Dauphine, one of five heads with whom the women of the court are bound to affiliate (p. 252), and thus becomes identified with the Guise faction throughout.

That is why the opening pages of the novel are of such real fundamental importance: their ordering of the social world implicitly constitutes an anthropology--that is, the structure underlying the manifestations of activity. The immanent lines of power which are essential to the text's dynamics will totally escape the reader who cannot perceive it, and for this reason the accompanying chart attempts to summarize them graphically, first in schematic fashion, then with details added.

Key to table:

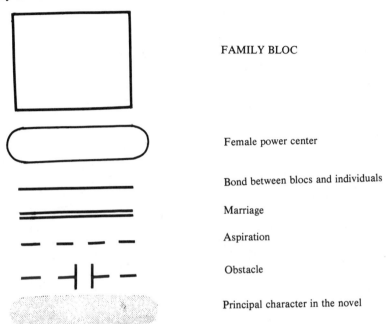

FAMILY BLOC

Female power center

Bond between blocs and individuals

Marriage

Aspiration

Obstacle

Principal character in the novel

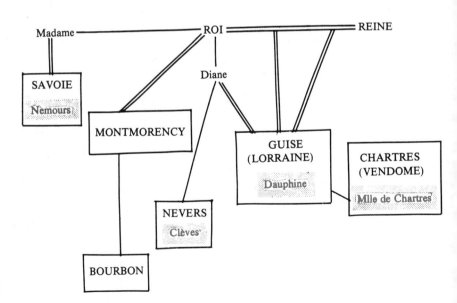

TABLE 1

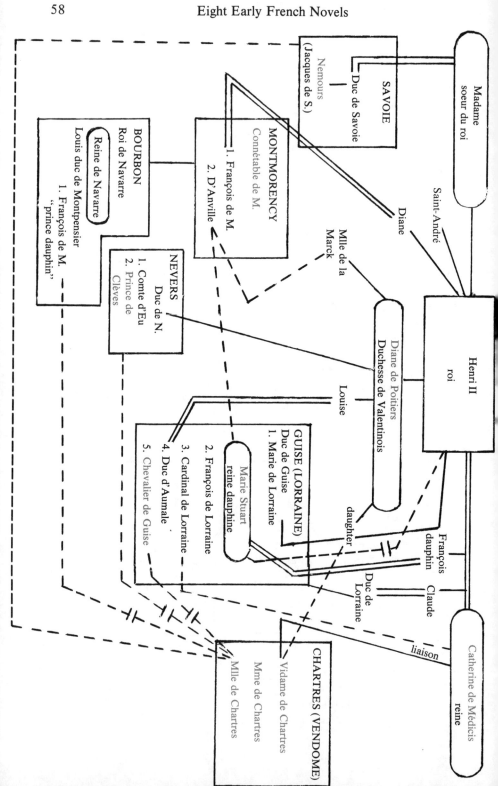

Note that this is not a genealogical table, although community of interest goes in hand with family ties.[8] Oppositions along two major axes explain most of what occurs within the novel's plot and sub-plots. The primary opposition is between the Montmorency and Guise parties (p. 244), in which Diane, through her control of access to Henri II, wishes to play broker. Only Saint-André has a sufficiently strong personal position with the king to be independent of involvement in this struggle (p. 245). Although Diane has a tie with the Guises through her daughter's marriage (she would have one as well with Montmorency but for d'Anville's refusal to marry her granddaughter, Mlle de la Marck), she still must side essentially with the Montmorency clan to counterbalance the strength of the royal marriage with Marie Stuart (a Guise), which has bypassed her--and which of course she opposed. Montmorency's one direct link with the king is illegitimate, and is thus much weaker. A further but indirect bond between the Guises and the throne lies in the marriage of Claude de France with the Duc de Lorraine, the Guises being the lesser branch of the house of Lorraine; and the Duc de Guise is, along with Saint-André, a personal favorite of the king. Most lines of aspiration are blocked by specific obstacles which are functions of this overall power balance. Marie Stuart tells how Diane and Montmorency prevented, during the previous reign, a marriage between her mother and Henri that would have further cemented the Guise fortunes (pp. 255-56). We know in addition that Diane has a particular antipathy for the Cardinal de Lorraine and the Chevalier de Guise. The Bourbons must, in the interests of their own political strength, side with Montmorency against the Guise ascendancy.

But there is also a second axis, less directly concerned with access to Henri (in which Catherine was rather powerless): it is the opposition of Diane and Catherine: many of the strategic problems of the Chartres bloc result from this. Diane, having hoped to marry her daughter to the Vidame (p. 249), cannot forgive him for preferring a liaison with the queen. She attacks his lineage by preventing the marriage of Mlle de Chartres with a Montpensier, after the Duc de Nevers has himself, because of his vaguely defined relationship with Diane, blocked his own son's design to marry the girl. (It is worth noting that Mme de Chartres's perceptions of these real and operative lines of force are, despite her disabused and knowing posture, most imperfect: she does not understand, for instance, why neither Clèves nor Guise will marry her daughter [p. 254]). But since the Prince de Clèves does not share his father's reasons for solidarity with Diane, Nevers's death will finally make that marriage possible. At the same time, the Cardinal de

Lorraine's jealousy of the Vidame for Catherine's favor (or favors) creates a strain between the Guise and Chartres blocs and specifically interdicts a marriage between Mlle de Chartres and the Chevalier de Guise (to whom Catherine, moreover, is personally hostile).

It can be seen too that the five chief women of the court all represent different blocs. There are the three queens, Catherine (linked with Chartres), the Dauphine (Guise), and the Reine de Navarre (Montmorency-Bourbon: she exerts influence on Navarre and, through him, on Montmorency [p. 252]); Diane, linked more directly with the king and having ties also with the Guises; and Madame, soeur du roi, who marries the Duc de Savoie, cousin of Nemours. *Nothing in the structure would prevent the marriage of Nemours with Mlle de Chartres.* That such a marriage does not take place is an accident of the novel's chronology, since she has already married Clèves by the time Nemours arrives on the scene.

After several dense pages devoted to external description of the court, the main story suddenly begins--"Il parut alors une beauté à la cour" (p. 247)--with no change of tone. But within the same paragraph we quickly find ourselves carried inside the maternal mind of Mme de Chartres. With utter lack of ostensible self-consciousness or apologies, the narrator assumes all knowledge needed for the story, and simply narrates without even calling attention to point of view or sources of information. In the quintessence of classical style, the limpid and pure appears artless. The narrator passes with complete fluidity in and out of individual consciousnesses, in one passage slipping from Mlle de Chartres to Clèves to Guise, back to Mlle de Chartres, and finally to Mme de Chartres (p.259). In this way, as complete a view as desired can be given of any particular nexus, ever in Mme de Lafayette's impeccably unobtrusive manner.

While exercising this kind of Protean omniscience, the narrator at times momentarily welds our viewpoint to a particular character, as when the Princess's fascination with the sight of Nemours leads us insistently from eye to heart:

Les jours suivants, *elle le vit* chez la reine dauphine, *elle le vit* jouer à la paume avec le roi, *elle le vit* courre la bague, *elle l'entendit* parler, mais *elle le vit* toujours *surpasser* de si loin tous les autres et se rendre tellement *maître* de la conversation dans tous les lieux où il était, par *l'air* de sa personne et par l'agrément de son esprit, qu'il fit, en peu de temps, *une grande impression dans son coeur.*[p. 262]

In the two pavillion scenes spied upon by Nemours, his voyeurist perspective is similarly emphasized by a narration of exactly what he himself could see, with no intrusion of thoughts or supplementary information about those being observed. Without a knowledge superior to that of the characters, of course, the narrator could not give relief to their own lag in comprehending the significance of events; but sometimes this function can be served too by the characters who themselves interpret what they observe, as when Mme de Chartres or Guise takes note of the symptoms which prove that the Princess, unknown to herself, is falling in love. At other times, though, the narrator is superior to all present observers, and thus records what no one of them in fact saw or even thought. This is translated as the expression in the conditional of what someone could have seen but did not: "Si Mme la Dauphine l'eût regardée avec attention, elle eût aisément remarqué que les choses qu'elle venait de dire ne lui étaient pas indifférentes; mais, comme elle n'avait aucun soupçon de la vérité, elle continua de parler, sans y faire de réflexion" (p. 291).

Frequently, of course, the narrator's viewpoint virtually merges with the Princess's or with Nemours's: "il était difficile de n'être pas supri*se* de le voir quand *on* ne l'avait jamais vu" (pp. 261-62); "l'*on* ne peut exprimer la douleur qu'*elle* sentit" (p. 275; cf. p. 367). But just as easily the narrator draws back to give voice to an irony which, purely between narrator and reader, calls attention to the Princess's private reactions, as when she finds the portrait of Elisabeth "plus beau qu'elle n'avait envie de le trouver" (p. 299), or reacts to Nemours's injury: "Mme de Clèves le crut encore plus blessé que les autres" (p. 306). An all but unnoticeable adverbial touch can suggest the semi-awareness of the character, for example: "M. de Nemours envie à Mme de Clèves d'avoir ces tableaux" (p. 364). Empathy with the état de ce nombre [de portraits] et c'était *peut-être* ce qui avait donné primary couple is of course induced principally by the statistical preponderance of their viewpoints, but it can also be forced in subtle ways that harness the play of the reader's imagination: "Mme de Clèves sortit de la chambre de sa mère en l'état que l'*on* peut *s'imaginer*" (p. 279; cf. pp. 345-46). Once, but once only, is there recourse to an exclamation point to assure that the reader will not miss the point: "Quel poison, pour Mme de Clèves, que le discours de Mme la Dauphine!" (p. 291).

A few points might briefly be made about such variations as they relate to dialogue and (interior) monologue. In a detailed study of a passage such as the description of Mme de Chartres's attitudes and instruction to her daughter (p. 248), it could be shown that the terms of the text approach those of indirect discourse--that is, the sentences without direct quotations sound much like the very things she herself might have said--and that at the same time, the propositions therein being recorded in a manner which makes them grammatically indistinguishable from facts ("elle lui contait *le peu de sincérité* des hommes . . . ; elle lui faisait *voir*, d'un autre côté, *quelle tranquillité suivait* la vie d'une honnête femme"), there is a suggestion of sympathy with these opinions. We slip from imperfects to preterites[9] in such a way as to combine summaries of trains of thought within characters with illustrative bits of specific conversations. On the other hand, there are sourceless direct quotations where presumably not a word is omitted.[10]

There are similar variations in the representation of thought. Often, thought is directly interpreted by the narrator in a clear statement that distills what is presumably in effect a more complex frame of mind, for example: "*Ce qui troublait sa joie, était* la crainte de ne lui être pas agréable, et *il eût préféré* le bonheur de lui plaire à la certitude de l'épouser sans en être aimé" (p. 257). At other times it is reported indirectly in an approximation of what would later be called *style indirect libre* (the phrasing closely paralleling what the character's own might be), and this procedure can indeed turn into direct "quotation," as if the character were *talking* to himself: "*Elle* trouva qu'il était presque impossible qu'elle pût être contente de sa passion. Mais quand *je* le pourrais être, *disait-elle*, qu'en veux-*je* faire?" (p. 330).[11] In any case, a state of confusion within a mind is never expressed in ways that are themselves confused, and the logical coherence of Mme de Lafayette's "monologues" distinguish them radically from what we since Joyce call the interior monologue.[12] But it also occurs that the narrator refuses to arbitrate the pure truth of mind in order to show the uncertainties of biased perceptions: "*Soit qu'*en effet il eût paru quelque trouble sur son visage, *ou que* la jalousie fît voir au chevalier de Guise au delà de la vérité, *il crut qu'*elle avait été touchée" (pp. 262-63).

One of the most original aspects of the treatment is that thinking in the novel occupies time; the person lost in thought stares blankly, or sits silently absorbed, or even travels a certain distance which is noted when he comes to himself.[13] Some of the long monologues should perhaps be called soliloquies, because they are recorded exactly as if spoken: *disait-elle, disait-il, s'ecriait-il, s'ecria-t-il.*[14] They are never overheard, however; indeed Nemours' dramatic monologue towards the end (pp. 369-70) is the more striking because, exceptionally for him, there are no witnesses. If this is melodrama on his part, it is staged only for himself, since the Princess will never know about it. Thus it seems to vouch for his otherwise suspect sincerity--as if the narrator were telling of it only because it is true.

Throughout, Mme de Lafayette displays her confidence in her reader's ability to assimilate the narration on its own terms. For example, the ultimate fate of numerous characters is foreshadowed, which is to be expected in this kind of fiction which supposedly exposes the secret causes of great happenings. Even today most readers probably know enough of Mary Stuart to be struck by her evocation of dire forebodings in the company of a Mlle de Chartres who does not believe in auguries (p. 256). Technically this is, in truth, a bit facile, as is the invention of an astrologer's devious prediction of the strange mode of Henri II's death (pp. 296-97). But quite aside from the historical fact that these prophecies after the fact were "fulfilled," there is another kind of fictional convention at work here. One of the notable differences between the laws of fiction and those of nature is that prophecy in fiction (this is especially noticeable in theatre), unlike that in real life, *always* comes true. Nemours, as if he knew he is operating in such a privileged literary ambiance, becomes a novelist himself and invents his own prophecy, which he then thrusts upon Mme de Clèves as a kind of ineluctible necessity: "On m'a prédit, lui dit-il tout bas, que je serais heureux par les bontés de la personne du monde pour qui j'aurais la plus violente passion. Vous pouvez juger, madame, si je dois croire aux prédictions" (p. 297). Hence the contemporary reader would doubtless have perceived an ironic justice in his later being granted precisely what he has just cried out for in anguish: a single, unequivocal declaration of the Princess's love--and nothing more (p. 369).

Such more or less theatrical norms also inform other aspects of the plot,[15] and testify to an assumption of close analogy between theatre and narrative fiction which is characteristic in this period and has been remarked in the foregoing chapters. Familiarity with the conventions of theatre, in other words, was part of the conditioning through which the reader could perform as an educated reader of fiction, however apparently divergent the media.

As in a play, Mlle de Chartres's arrival at court immediately sets events in motion: within two days Clèves and Guise are hopelessly in love with her. Gallantry is hardly Clèves's element, exceptional prudence being his most noticeable character trait (p. 243); still he is thunderstruck (literal sense of *étonnement*) when he sets eyes on her, and she is just as abruptly conscious of being gawked at, embarrassed somehow by the electricity in the air (pp. 248-49). Mme de Chartres, proud if not vain as well ("extrêmement glorieuse" [p. 248]), is out to sell her daughter, socially speaking, at the highest possible price. It is Clèves's good fortune that Guise, who has the rank, quite explicitly cannot afford her (p. 253). The book's bitterest irony is that the austerely tutored girl will be smitten however by the court's most notorious lover, feeling nothing more than esteem for her worthy husband. In order to communicate forcefully to the reader, before the marriage takes place, that she has no love for Clèves, the narrator takes us on a tour of the concurring opinions of Clèves, Mlle de Chartres, and finally her mother (pp. 257-59). All her signals seem ambiguous to Clèves--who is obviously prepared to place upon them the most favorable construction--and he must recognize his inability to force a reaction, much less an inclination, in this passive creature. By his long series of negatives ("vous n'avez *ni* impatience, *ni...*, *ni...*," etc. [p. 258]), he testifies to the obviousness of her immoveable indifference. The starkly impersonal clause "Ce mariage s'acheva" (p. 259) stands in grim comparison with the spectacular theatricality of her subsequent meeting with Nemours, which, significantly, follows almost immediately thereupon in the text (pp. 261-62).

By that time the Princess is curious and even eager to see Nemours (p. 261)--in effect predisposed to love him. At the ball where she is already the center of attention, a hum of anticipation marks his arrival as everyone watches him make his way (over some seats) to where she awaits him, the king like the voice of destiny having decreed that they should dance together.[16] This time, in contrast to Clèves's unilateral *étonnement*, the surprise and admiration are reciprocal as the two, bedazzled, recognize each other instinctively, spontaneously. It is a magic moment, a scene out of a fairy tale, and Guise for one immediately reads it as a presage of their future love (p. 262).

But despite analogies with stage drama, this novel is very unlike any play in the relative importance it accords to unuttered thought and nervous silence. The discretion of the narrator's expression, parallel to that of court manners, causes their love to develop in the tension of near-silence and understatement. Months elapse before *inclination* evolves in the text into *passion violente* (p. 310), and there is a further significant lag before the Princess can face words like "folle et violente passion" herself (p. 352). Not until very late in the work is the simple verb *aimer* finally applied to her and Nemours, and then it is only in attenuated form ("Mme de Martigues ne savait pas que Mme de Clèves *aimât* M. de Nemours, ni qu'elle en *fût aimée*" [p. 364]). And only in the last dozen pages does the Princess actually allow herself to yield to emotion, a milestone to which the narrator draws particular attention: "Mme de Clèves céda *pour la première fois* au penchant qu'elle avait pour M. de Nemours" (p. 383). They communicate, above all, tacitly, with blushes and pregnant silences (p. 293); and when they speak, their discourse is filled with non-specific grammatical markers: "Il y a *des personnes* à qui *on* n'ose donner d'autres marques de la passion qu'*on* a pour *elles* que par les choses qui ne *les* regardent point," Nemours says to her (p. 293). That does not really make the message less comprehensible--"Mme de Clèves entendait aisément la part qu'elle avait à ces paroles" (p. 294)--but it permits her to declare to Clèves with a degree of honesty that nothing explicit has been said ("des choses que l'on ne m'a pas encore osé dire" [p. 336]).

No one would argue now, as some of the early readers did, that the interpolated stories are irrelevant to this deliberate evolution. The stories in *La Princesse de Clèves* are usually counted as four; but we are justified, I think, in including as well Marie Stuart's short relation about her mother. Parentheses in the following summary indicate intermediate stages in the transmission, not those represented in the primary narration.

| *Histoire* | *Subject* | *Narrator* | *To whom told* |
|---|---|---|---|
| H 1 (pp. 255-56) | Marie de Lorraine | Marie Stuart → Mlle de Chartres | |
| H 2 (pp. 264-69) | Diane de Poitiers | Mme de Chartres → Mme de Clèves | |
| H 3 (pp. 281-88) | Mme de Tournon | (Sancerre)→(Clèves) Clèves──→Mme de Clèves | |

| H 4 (pp. 299-301) | Ann Boleyn | Marie Stuart | → Mme de Clèves |
|---|---|---|---|
| H 5 (pp. 314-21) | Vidame de Chartres | Chartres→Nemours (Nemours) → | (Mme de Clèves) |

Whether or not she overtly subscribed to it, Mme de Lafayette obeys the unofficial time rule of framing the main action within a twelvemonth, leaving to the subsidiary narrations the function of expanding the chronological dimensions. Histoires 1, 2, 4 all go back forty-five or fifty years; 3 and 5, two and about ten years respectively.

The single most obviously significant fact which such a listing makes clear is that the stories are all told for the benefit of the same person; they are the major vicarious input into her education concerning life at the court. They are all pertinent to her as well, but obliquely; the thematic ties, although unstated, are genuine. In fact Mme de Lafayette takes some care to justify the function of the stories in general and of H 2 in particular. The first passage about Mme de Chartres in the work informs us, "elle faisait souvent à sa fille des peintures de l'amour; . . . elle lui *contait* . . . les malheurs domestiques où plongent les engagements" (p. 248): H 2 is thus a logical component of her overall mode of instruction by precedent. The particular relevance of stories about the court comes from her seeing in it "un lieu où . . . il y avait *tant d'exemples* si dangereux" (p. 252). From this point in the text there is more than a page of transition before H 2 commences, and Mme de Chartres herself, in framing the earlier context for her narrative, specifically asserts the direct pertinence of the previous reign to the present:

> Si je ne craignais, continua Mme de Chartres, que vous dissiez de moi ce que l'on dit de toutes les femmes de mon âge, qu'elles aiment à *conter les histoires* de leur temps, je vous apprendrais le commencement de la passion du roi pour cette duchesse, et plusieurs choses de la cour du feu roi qui ont même *beaucoup de rapport avec celles qui se passent encore* présentement. [p. 264]

The Princess too confesses her crying need for enlightenment, evoking as an example of her ignorance her erroneous impression that "M. le connétable était fort bien avec la reine." The story of Diane then is instructive to her both because many of its personalities are still central at court and because the same structures of intrigue still persist ("deux cabales dans la cour, telles que vous pouvez vous les imaginer" [p. 267]); but the basic polarity underlying its necessity is that of appearance versus fact. It serves as an introduction to vicious court politics and, in addition, as a lesson in the instability of power, evidenced in the reversal of fortunes which brought Diane to power at the death of François I (she is destined, of course, to be abruptly overthrown in like fashion).

The other stories are, similarly, relevant in multiple indirect ways rather than as any conspicuous parallel to Mme de Clèves's personal experiences. H 3, however, does have a significant impact on the subsequent action. Again, through it, appearances prove deceiving, but this time the woman the Princess has misjudged is a personal friend, and she has been dead wrong in assessing her character ("je croyais Mme de Tournon incapable d'amour et de tromperie" [p. 288]). It is a story of the duplicity and infidelity she will come to fear above all else; and Mme de Tournon was a widow as she will be, who thought of marrying Sancerre, but was inconstant. In Sancerre we observe reactions that will later characterize Clèves himself.[17] Even more to the point is Clèves's role as confidant, one who cannot understand having things held back from him and who, by insisting on the importance of complete trust, plants in his wife's mind the seed of her future confession; indeed the narrator--exceptionally--interrupts the story at this juncture to call particular attention to its perceived pertinence for the Princess herself:

> Je vous donne, lui dis-je, le conseil que je prendrais pour moi-même; car la *sincérité* me touche d'une telle sorte que je crois que si ma maîtresse, et même *ma femme, m'avouait* que quelqu'un lui plût, j'en serais affligé sans en être aigri. Je quitterais le personnage d'amant ou de mari, pour la conseiller et pour la plaindre.
>
> Ces paroles firent *rougir* Mme de Clèves, et elle y trouva *un certain rapport avec l'état où elle était*, qui la *surprit* et qui lui donna un *trouble* dont elle fut longtemps à se remettre. [p. 284]

This message is further reinforced by Sancerre's conclusion that his whole tragedy resulted from a lack of confidence between himself and Estouteville.

In H 4 we again see the risks of love, the fickleness of passions, but above all the danger of jealousies. Ann Boleyn was vulnerable not because she was in fact guilty of anything but simply because the incriminating appearances were plausible. Only uncompromising virtue, virtue beyond suspicion, could be secure. Infidelity is once more a major factor in H 5, but in this case the personal involvement of Mme de Clèves in reading the letter that occasions it is probably even more consequential than the content of the story itself: suddenly it is clear that she is no longer a bystander. The Vidame de Chartres being at its center, we have moved now into her own family, and for several excruciating hours she has believed herself the personal victim of what has transpired. She registers in succession the pain of her own sense of betrayal, and the horror of the dreadful letter written by another deceived woman.

The last of the five interpolated stories ends when the novel is scarcely half over, as if by this time the Princess could be presumed to know enough to find her own way. But having come to realize that social appearances are unreliable, she shies away and turns steadily in upon herself. Society is manoeuvre and feint, authentic causes usually being hidden. One can never tell if even such a thing as an illness is genuine--nor does she herself abjure use of such conventional pretexts. The main movement of the novel is away from the outside, objective world and towards moral analysis--we would say moral and/or psychological, a distinction that in the seventeenth century had no currency. Still that larger world continues its course, marking time by means of events of public history while the heroes concentrate more and more on their personal dilemma; and finally the court recedes almost entirely from sight. Time too, like other aspects of objective existence, is seen through the Princess's experience and counts less specifically toward the end, the seasons passing unnoticed. The feelings and conduct of three people alone usurp the foreground. From the day when she first hid something from her mother (p. 270), she had in fact been closing herself in. Just at the point when the court is most in turmoil--at the death of Henri II--she most obviously begins taking her distance from it, failing even to make an appearance during the long vigil. And as the court fades from her eyes, she fades from its eyes too, being apparently forgotten thereafter except by Nemours, his intercessor Chartres, and Mme de Martigues (p. 378).

Yet she never wished to be the judge of her own conduct. The mother who promised to help guide her instilled in her a notion of love which placed it under the sign of danger, the opposite of *vertu*--source of *éclat* and *élévation* (p. 248), at least when it is combined with beauty and noble birth. The sole happiness (that is, the only safety) comes from loving one's husband and being loved by him, a doctrine to which her daughter subscribed but could not implement. *Péril* rears its head at the mention of love almost as allegorically as danger in the *Roman de la Rose*: "Mme de Chartres voyait ce *péril* et ne songeait qu'à *en garantir* sa fille" (p. 253). When she saw that marriage's love was not forthcoming, she insisted only on its obligations, her final strategy being to create such an air of inviolability about her daughter that it can itself become a form of protection against advances, a weapon of dissuasion: "Mme de Chartres joignait à la sagesse de sa fille *une conduite si exacte* pour toutes les bienséances qu'elle achevait de la faire paraître une personne *où l'on ne pouvait atteindre*" (p. 260). Having decided that she must be prevented from frequenting Marie Stuart, in whose house Nemours can find her, she willfully deceives her into believing Nemours's love is for Marie; the Princess's ensuing jealousy has the effect, however, of bringing her to a new awareness of her own state (p. 275). In their final talk before her death, Mme de Chartres feels she must finally be explicit and speaks to her daughter of her *inclination* for Nemours, carefully selecting such a euphemism so as not to suggest too much--not to push her understanding too far--and even then burying it beneath an avalanche of words like *violence, devoir, réputation, malheurs*, finally evoking the ultimate levelling horror: *tomber comme les autres femmes* (pp. 277-78). She has spoken; the door is closed. The Princess, who has been all along rather reassured than oppressed by so much protection, feels abandoned, in need of some outside force: "Elle se trouvait malheureuse d'être *abandonnée* à elle-même, dans un temps où elle était *si peu maîtresse* de ses sentiments et où elle eût tant *souhaité d'avoir quelqu'un* qui pût la plaindre et *lui donner de la force*" (pp. 278-79). This need--and this lack-- will help her excuse her own sense of weakness: "si j'avais encore Mme de Chartres pour aider à me conduire" (p. 333). It explains her recourse to Clèves himself, whom she entreats with words: "conduisez-moi" (p. 334), "réglez ma conduite" (p. 339). She wants out of the freedom which, to her mind, has been thrust unwanted upon her.

We are led up to this confession scene not only by the logic just described, but also by a series of hints of her craving for such a salutory unburdening. Indeed she was prepared to lay all at her mother's feet when fate sent the fever which prevented execution of this resolution. Clèves in the second histoire has stung her with his deprecation of "l'artifice de soutenir, aux yeux du public, un personnage si éloigné de la vérité" (p. 283) and, as we have seen, stressed his own propensity for confidence. Those specific passages return to her mind (p. 303), and in the anguish following her reading of the letter to Chartres, her distressed and desperate soul recalls first the image of her mother before shifting that maternal role to Clèves (p. 310). And, of course, just as this confessional temptation beckons her, the Dauphine exclaims in innocent but bitter irony, "il n'y a que vous de femme au monde qui fasse confidence à son mari de toutes les choses qu'elle sait" (p.327). What all this amounts to is a discourse of constraint; although she believes her confession to result from individual decision, she is pressured into it in many subtle ways.[18]

Much emphasis has traditionally been placed on sincerity in *La Princess de Clèves*, but it is not an unproblematic notion with respect either to its motivations or to its effects. It is true the word appears often in the text, marked as one of the heroine's admirable qualities. But while her sincerity shines in contrast to the falsity around it, it represents an illusory ideal, and in the relationship between the two Clèves its results are disastrous. Are we to take the clause "la vérité persuade si aisément lors même qu'elle n'est pas vraisemblable" (p. 376) to mean that Mme de Lafayette really believes, in Rousseau's manner, that truth is always inherently persuasive? Probably such a conviction is compromised by a latent, but more disabused, experiential doubt.

There is, for one thing, no such thing as innocent language. Despite Mme de Lafayette's reputation for limpidity, this fact, far from being an interpretive paradox, is essential to a reading of the text. Especially does it govern signification in the province of love, where the erotic is overlaid with the remnants of a chivalric code and stylized by its assimilation to the art of war (Chartres is "également distingué dans la guerre et dans la galanterie" [p. 243]). The unsuspecting, like Mlle de Chartres, might take certain expressions of love as pertaining to *sentiments* whereas they in fact designate *forms of conduct*. The characterization of Henri II as "galant, bien fait et *amoureux*" in the opening paragraph is part of an exterior description: he is publicly *amoureux*, and such an affirmation is based on the *témoignages éclatants* to which the same sentence refers. *Aimer* is a kind of recognizable behavior, and when the Dauphine says "il est certain que M. de Nemours est passionnément amoureux" (p. 289), she reveals that Nemours, despite his apparent and promised discretion--which is always in doubt--is publicly bearing the signs conventionally associated in his circle with the state of being in love. This is evident for example in what he says to Mme de Clèves: "Les grandes afflictions et les passions violentes... font de grands changements dans l'esprit; et, pour moi, je ne me reconnais pas depuis que je suis revenu de Flandre. *Beaucoup de gens ont remarqué* ce changement" (p. 293). And if he is irresistable, this is in large part a function of his reputation for being so, as the Princess later acknowledges: "M. de Nemours était de tous les hommes celui que je craignais le plus" (p. 342).[19]

Indeed nothing proves early on that Nemours is not primarily motivated by his gamesterism, his awareness that his sexual prestige requires that he claim this particular trophy. He has all the aplomb that she lacks, thinks fast like a shrewd courtier, and always has the self-possession and wit to escape dangerous verbal traps with consummate grace (pp. 297, 346). All this skill he brings to bear against her innocence, taking a certain pleasure in deflowering it[20] and forcing both her sentiments and her vanity by reminding her that he has sacrificed a queen in her favor. There is a suggestion of the rake about him that from afar prophesies Laclos's Valmont; his insidiousness is reflected in the frequency of his speaking, like the Temptor, *tout bas*. Nemours's mouth is sealed only as long as there is a chance of his being defeated (in this game the attacker does not advertise his own defeats); once assured that he has essentially triumphed, he must call in a witness (Chartres): "Il n'a pu s'imaginer qu'il était aimé sans *vouloir qu'on le sût*" (p. 351). When Clèves lies dying, Nemours's thoughts are purely egoistic; he jealously fears the competition of the sick man for the Princess's attention, but takes hope in his death (p. 373).

Since courting in our day no longer follows the same meticulous models, some aspects of the joust may escape the reader; but even in Mme de Lafayette's time the vocabulary of love was fundamentally ambiguous because, reinforced by preciosity, it often gave a narrow ritual significance to a term otherwise having altogether different usages. Are we to infer from a sentence like "Ce prince vit bien qu'*elle le fuyait*, et en fut sensiblement *touché*" (pp. 295-96) that Nemours's heart is melting? It would be to overlook the fact that *fuir* and *être touché* can indicate specific steps in the stylized courtly mating dance. Doubtless the Princess does not flee for the purpose of communicating her participation in it to him; the point is that he interprets the flight as if she did. She believes there is some measure of safety in the inexplicitness of love's discourse, but this impression is owing only to its specialized indirection. Thus their love is far from being as mute as it appears. The reason Nemours can affirm "je n'ose vous parler" (p.

341) at the very moment when he has seized upon a pretext to clarify his pretentions is precisely that an expression like *n'oser parler* is one of the elegant manners of saying *je vous aime*. That he can in some bad faith think of her as "une personne à qui il n'avait encore jamais parlé de son amour" (p. 367) is evidence of the code's discretion; it does not, of course, mean that there is any secret between them about their love (he will say later, "Quoique je ne vous aie jamais parlé, je ne saurais croire, madame, que vous ignoriez ma passion" [p. 383]), though it may well show that even one's own inner thoughts may tend to confuse the literal and ritualized meanings of words.

Throughout, Nemours acts in function of that courtly code, looking devoutly to it for guidance at moments of great strain. Guilty of a damaging indiscretion, he judges himself unworthy ("je suis indigne") and concludes with chivalric rigidity that this imposes a penance of utter silence--which really means that he is outwardly to display *tristesse* and *crainte respectueuse* (pp. 352-54). His next non-verbal sign is even more medieval and even more explicit (to her exclusively, which is the height of knightly fealty): he wears "her" color at the tourney.[21] But the code cannot account for behavior which does not obey its own schematic logic; thus Nemours is confused in a situation where its prescriptions fail him: "Si je n'étais pas aimé, je songerais à *plaire*; mais je plais, on m'aime, et on me le cache. Que puis-je donc espérer . . .?" (p. 369). In other words, *aimer* implies an engagement in further consequences which Mme de Clèves is suppressing, thereby defying the implicit syllogism:

> Qui aime se donne.
> Elle m'aime.
> Donc elle se donnera à moi.

The rules of a game never tell how to behave with someone who has not acknowledged their authority. But Nemours can construe love in no other framework, and his falling to his knees when she finally avers her love is an instinctive ritual gesture intended to capitalize on the avowal and precipitate its ramifications. To him a "je vous aime" is devoid of sense if it does not also signify "je me donne."

On the other hand, of course, Nemours is not totally "insincere" either; his qualification of his passion as "la plus véritable et la plus violente qui sera jamais" (p. 383) is confirmed by the narrator at the end ("une passion la plus violente . . . qui ait jamais été" [p. 394]), even as it flickers out.

But that just shows again how moot the question of sincerity finally is. The reality of his passion does not rule out the possibility that it was acquired through the enactment of a certain role and *induced by the very language utilized*, since there is no evidence that he or anyone else in his society can sort out such distinctions through the veil of ambiguous terminology. Not until *Les Liaisons dangereuses* will we encounter characters who can radically and lucidly divorce their thinking processes from their interpersonal manipulation of words.

Despite her nongallant posture, the Princess nonetheless becomes engaged on this ritualistic level in a game of tokens. The precious question of whether a swain should want his mistress to attend a ball (pp. 271-72) becomes the means whereby she can do him a covert favor by missing one. Now there is a certain apparent innocence about this on both sides, because he did not know his discussion would be repeated to her, and since, by his absence, he does not know she stayed at home in deference to the opinion he voiced; she has moreover an honorable pretext in her wish to avoid unseemly associations with Saint-André, who is giving the ball in question. But really everything in their highly conversant society is told, as they well know, and when the message--hers, in its turn--gets through to Nemours in her presence, she blushes as if to tell him the abstention was in his honor. The blush was not consciously controlled, to be sure--but she later wishes her mother had let its obvious meaning stand uncontroverted (p. 274). This gallant non-verbal signing continues in the second token, the symbolic rape of the Princess in the form of her portrait which is specifically a theft from Clèves her husband: "elle fut bien aise de lui accorder une faveur qu'elle lui pouvait faire sans qu'il sût même qu'elle la lui faisait" (p. 302). Rationalization again, because he does know--and so acknowledges--that she witnessed the act. While it could be argued that he stole the painting simply for his private pleasure, that cannot be proven, for there is no way that the knowledge of its being missing could fail to reach her--an event which she no doubt, like everyone else, would interpret as the act of a secret lover in their midst.

There are accidents which inform her of things Nemours did not specifically design for her perception, such as the rented room (toward the end of the novel) whence he can watch her garden. However, these invariably serve an ironic purpose: she is deeply moved by his disinterestedness ("*respectant* jusqu'à sa douleur, songeant à la voir sans songer à en *être vu*" [p. 380]); but this is quickly contradicted in the reader's mind by his determination to be recognized; "Pourquoi me réduire à la voir *sans en être vu* et sans lui parler? . . . Je la *respecte trop* longtemps" (p. 381). This is later excused by a deterministic-sounding phrase: "une passion dont je ne suis plus le maître" (p. 383), which is also rhetorical pretext. And the Princess shows that she too thinks partly at least in terms of ceremonial procedures, labelling their long discussion one which exceeds the norms for a *première conversation* (sometimes called *conversation réglée*)--a term which would not be out of place on the *Carte de Tendre*. Naturally this game is played by twos; and while the script calls for the male to "attack," in reality it is more like fencing. Women want Nemours as much as he wants them; and there is no way the Princess can herself be thought exempt from her own admission, "Par vanité ou par goût, toutes les femmes souhaitent de vous attacher" (p. 388)--*attacher* being the feminine euphemistic counterpart of *plaire*. Underneath, however, there is a finally insuperable gap between them, and it is her idealism: "les sentiments que j'ai pour vous seront éternels" (p. 389). Whether she believes that that is true because she is a woman or because she is of different kind than he, she is persuaded that such sentiments could not be the same to a man with Nemours's background; territory once "conquered," in war as in the *guerre en dentelles*, necessarily loses its interest.

For all the passion contained in these pages, there is an unromantic paucity of lyricism which can be attributed to a perspective which looks on love with a holy fear. The virtue preached by Mme de Chartres is less a positive ideal than a defense mechanism against the vulnerability of love, and must be practiced with "une extrême défiance de soi-même" (p. 248). The spontaneity of response motivated by passion escapes rational control and even awareness ("elle s'y était engagée sans en avoir presque eu le dessein" [p. 337]). It comes as a stranger to one's own self-image; the person in love fails, as Georges Poulet has said, to recognize himself.[22] One cannot even say, at least in his first such experience, "I am in love," as any teenager is preconditioned to do today; Mme de Clèves cannot detect at all the meaning of the new sensation. The long monologue following her reading of the letter to Chartres emphasizes this failure of self-knowledge ("mais elle se trompait elle-même" [p. 310]) and the terrible suffering this entails (*horreurs, affliction, désespoir*). Unable to trust herself, she thinks again, instinctively, of her mother.

Spontaneous gestures which are palpable signs to other observers reveal their meaning to her only after the fact; then she realizes her lack of control. Frequently such perception is accompanied by a sense of terror: "Lorsque ce prince fut parti, que Mme de Clèves demeura seule, qu'elle regarda ce qu'elle *venait de faire*, elle en fut si *épouvantée* qu'à peine put-elle s'imaginer que ce fût une vérité" (p. 336). What provokes it is her loss of sense of self, often recalled to the reader's mind: "elle ne *se reconnaissait plus* elle-même" (p. 329); "elle ne *se connaissait plus*" (p. 390). One is given the impression (explicitly rationalized by Jean Rousset)[23] that the false appearances characterizing the objective world yield progressively, in the course of the story, to a more convincing truth directed inward. But in reality the inner being itself contains only appearances, incomplete, and ultimately, for the Princess, unreliable. While one character may provisionally hold secrets kept from others, he does not know himself better than the others do, indeed often less well; the other's penetrating glance is more perceptive than is one's introspection. Mme de Clèves, too easily deciphered, is the polar opposite of a Mme de Merteuil; she is too obsessed with herself to be a successful social animal. Her *faux pas* when she catches her foot in her gown symbolizes her ineptness in concealing her passion--in trying to keep an unpenetrable partition between her private and public selves.

It has been quite plausibly argued, in an existential perspective, that the revealing blush or gesture is nothing other than an expression of one's freedom declaring itself despite the repressive force of controlling will.[24] Yet it is precisely this sense of loss of conscious control that frightens. The Corneillian *je suis maître de moi* has devolved into lack of mastery; Mme *de Clè*ves discovers first that she is "si peu *maîtresse* de ses *sentiments*" (p. 279), and then no longer even "*maîtresse* de ses *paroles* et de son visage*" (p. 303) or "maîtresse de *cacher* ses sentiments" (p. 307). The transition point is when she discovers the hiatus between her duty and her conduct (pp. 294-95): knowing that she cannot dominate her thoughts, she transfers her power of will to the project of suppressing all exterior signs of what is going on inside: "Elle ne se flatta plus de l'espérance de ne le pas aimer; elle songea seulement à ne lui en donner jamais *aucune marque.*" Such a realization is accompanied by great remorse and suffering: with *douceur* there comes *douleur* (p. 307); with pleasure, pain; with desire, fear. Guise's comments following Nemours's accident reveal to her that this inner force betrays even her public mask: "Mme de Clèves, *après* être remise de la frayeur qu'elle avait eue, fit bientôt *réflexion* aux *marques* qu'elle en avait données" [p. 306]). In consequence, she feels the weight of public suspicion, more even than is objectively justified. After the Chartres letter, she thinks she is healed ("elle n'avait plus rien à craindre d'elle-même" [p. 311]), but this rebounds in the almost giddy gaiety of the letter scene with Nemours. The mixups involved, nearly so exaggerated as to compromise the serious tone of the episode, highlight the exhilarating release of the only pure and unmixed joy (p. 328) the Princess will ever know.[25] This pleasure is possible, though, only because of her secure sense that here she is operating within controlled circumstances and authorized by her husband: this outside pretext and apparently riskless situation make possible her only happy scene with Nemours in the whole novel. What she does not know--but the reader is given to believe--is that her love has made her a faithless friend: because of her frivolity, and scarcely thinking of them, she serves ill both the Dauphine and Chartres, causing them adverse prejudice and perhaps ultimately death.

Fear is reinforced by a second and more concrete experience: pain. The awful, sleepless night with the Chartres letter has taught her "les inquiétudes mortelles de la défiance et de la jalousie" (p. 330). It is the suffering which re-ignites and justifies fear, the fear of suffering, which will prove decisive. The idea of peril returns ("le hasard [=risk] d'être trompée") with a new immediacy; for the suffering has been as authentic as if it were warranted, and it matters little from the standpoint of her experience that Nemours was innocent. *Cruels repentirs* and *mortelles douleurs* in her ensuing reflexions re-emphasize her loss of control: "Je suis *vaincue* et *surmontée* par une inclination qui *m'entraîne malgré moi*" (p. 330). This translates, in terms more familiar to her, into shame: a feeling of being soiled by love and guilty—though innocent—of adultery. Her characterization of herself just before her confession as "maîtresse de [ma] conduite" (p. 333) takes on a supremely ironic connotation. And the confession itself is treated by her and Clèves as a shameful secret, as if she had a venereal disease: "je meurs de honte en vous en parlant"; "une chose qui me fait paraître si peu digne de vous et que je trouve si indigne de moi" (p. 339).

These words are echoed by Clèves in his jealous decline: "je n'ai que des sentiments violents et incertains dont je ne suis pas le maître. Je ne me trouve plus digne de vous; vous ne me paraissez plus digne de moi" (p. 362-63). In him the Princess witnesses another instance of inability to control the self. No one is worthy any more. Such terminological alterations testify of course to profound ambivalence between tenderness and ferocity; Mme de Clèves during this period oscillates unstably too, between her husband and Nemours. Her superego inspires faithful resolutions which promptly vanish when Nemours is seen (p. 356) or even imagined (p. 363). Clèves's dying words, though temperate, function as a sort of malediction and have the effect he desired, inspiring in her a self-horror (p. 377) and the feeling that both her lack of love for him and her desire to marry Nemours are crimes (pp. 377, 381).

Nemours's presence at the confession, besides reinforcing his characteristic posture as a spy, indiscreet and unseen,[26] is a functional necessity: it tells Nemours unambiguously that he is loved, so that he continues his pursuit; and its subsequent use in the plot produces the impasse which destroys the marital trust between the two Clèves. But his behavior only repeats other indications of a cruel and even sadistic repercussion of his love. Not only did he cynically use Clèves to insinuate himself into the Princess's presence at her moment of greatest suffering, he also derives "le plus sensible plaisir qu'il eût jamais eu" (p. 324) from her state, which he rightly judges favorable to himself. A little later we find another occasion (after the confession) where Mme de Clèves's "extrême tristesse" augments Nemours's love (p. 340). His pride demands (as will Valmont's) this reduction of the other: after the confession, we read, "il sentit pourtant un plaisir sensible de l'avoir *réduite* à cette *extrémité*. Il trouva de la *gloire* à s'être fait aimer d'une femme si différente de toutes celles de son sexe" (p. 337). Love has become a corrosive force; desire makes Nemours as mean as jealousy does Clèves.[27] The latter resorts to a Racinian subterfuge to force his wife's secret (p. 340), then tortures her with the knowledge gained, trying to augment her feeling of indignity. The loss of confidence resulting from Nemours's indiscretion regarding her confession, fortuitous but definitive, is another example. It is exacerbated by Nemours's lie as to its source (p. 347). (Whether or not it originated with Clèves, the anecdote clearly has made the rounds, since it has been related by Nemours to Chartres to Mme de Martigues to the Dauphine, and then to Mme de Clèves.) Her quandary over Clèves's role is a new source of suffering, since the logical alternatives—that he has, or has not, betrayed her confidence—seem equally inadmissable (p. 350). Hence the dramatic value of the way the confession scene was staged: since the Clèves cannot know that it was witnessed by an outsider, their problem is now insoluble, and all they can do henceforth is tacitly avoid it. But Clèves becomes an obsessed man, one whose contorted reason will come to see in the avowal a proof of dissimulation ("Vous n'avez pu me dire la vérité tout entière, vous m'en avez caché la plus grande partie" [p. 362]), and turns it against her, calling her the cruel woman who has made him the unhappiest of men (p. 363). And he dies a romantic death of love, the direct result of his despondency, heaping imprecation and guilt upon his tortured wife: "Je meurs du cruel déplaisir que vous m'avez donné. . . . Adieu, madame, vous regretterez quelque jour un homme qui vous aimait d'une passion véritable et légitime" (p. 375). His death in fact leaves her rudderless, as did her mother's, and even more overwhelmed with her own inadequacy and transgression.

Mme de Clèves's suffering while reading the Chartres letter is expressed in strong terms: "si *étonnée* et dans un si grand *saisissement* qu'elle fut quelque temps sans pouvoir sortir de sa place. . . . Elle se trouvait dans une sorte de *douleur insupportable*, qu'elle ne connaissait point et qu'elle n'avait *jamais sentie*" (p. 308). She knows the experiential equivalence of Nemours's infidelity: that is, she has suffered as much as if he had indeed been guilty. An implicit consequence of this incident is her shaken faith in the possibility of gauging his sincerity (that is, his dependability): "Elle fut étonnée de n'avoir point encore pensé combien il était peu vraisemblable qu'un homme comme M. de Nemours . . . fût capable d'un attachement sincère et durable" (p. 330). His imprudence in recounting the confession again raises the peril, her fear of the public and of insecurity, the very motives in the name of which she had made her singular confession:

> Il n'a pu s'imaginer qu'il était aimé sans vouloir qu'on le sût. . . . J'ai eu tort de croire qu'il y eût un homme capable de cacher ce qui flatte sa gloire. C'est pourtant pour cet homme, *que j'ai cru si différent* du reste des hommes, que *je me trouve, comme les autres femmes*, étant si *éloignée de leur ressembler*. . . . Je serai bientôt regardée de tout le monde comme une personne qui a une folle et violente passion . . .; et c'est pour éviter ces malheurs que j'ai hasardé tout mon repos et même ma vie. [pp. 351-52]

In perceiving that like others Nemours has trumpeted his triumph, she must deny his exceptional nature; he is no longer like her, his "difference" is annulled. (Yet he has the astonishing, cynical temerity later to assert that he has in no way abused his knowledge of the confession [p. 384]!) From this she deduces the necessary consequence that Nemours's love, like all others, is finite and transitory; he rejoins the general category ("*les hommes conservent-ils de la passion dans ces engagements éternels?*" [p. 387]) and his fickleness becomes not just a risk but a certainty ("la *certitude* de n'être plus aimée de vous" [id.]). Therefore his constancy can last only as long as do the obstacles to love's fulfillment. You are changeable, she tells Nemours; I am not. The result of union would inevitably be suffering: "J'en aurais une douleur mortelle et je ne serais pas même assurée de n'avoir point le malheur de la jalousie . . . le plus grand de tous les maux" (pp. 387-88). The total possession which is her idea of love turns out to be unrealizable because, she believes, of the other's inability to meet its conditions.

Thus the *repos* in the name of which she eventually refuses him is a protection from suffering more than a self-affirmation. Mme de Clèves has always been passive, and her instinctive solution is that of *Le Cid*: wait and see[28]--in both instances a symbol of the possibility of reaching a satisfactory resolution of conflicting imperatives. It is a paradox that critics have paid so little attention to Mme de Clèves's own explicit reasoning behind her ultimate withdrawal, but the explanation doubtless lies in its failure to appear definitive. By itself it would command attention, but it is complicated by her equivocal return in later passages to evocations of *devoir, repos,* and *bienséance.* Duty she invokes as a fateful, invincible obstacle, even though she admits without difficulty that it subsists only in her imagination (p. 389). The narrator suggests her own uncertainty about her motives in alluding to "toutes les raisons qu'elle *croyait* avoir pour ne l'épouser jamais (p. 393). Yet they are placed in a clear ratio which is important for their interpretation: "Les raisons qu'elle avait de ne point épouser M. de Nemours lui paraissaient *fortes* du côté de son *devoir* et *insurmontables* du côté de son *repos*" (p. 392). The end of love now appears infallible, unhappiness certain, not worth the wager--yet the prize perhaps impossible to resist. In all this neither *bienséance* nor virtue is involved. "Car le fond du problème," writes Doubrovsky, "c'est un choix de valeurs, un choix déchirant entre les valeurs délibérément choisies d'un code aristocratique et les valeurs spontanément élues de la passion."[29]

These two sets of values translate into security versus risk. Viewed in these terms, the austerity of her final choice appears less heroic than it has often been represented. Passion, as Georges Poulet has noted, cannot be conceived here in terms of duration, which comes only with *repos*, a negative state. Flight in the face of danger, her mother's counsel ("retirez-vous de la cour" [p. 278]), becomes her own instinctive mechanism: "il n'y avait de sûreté pour elle qu'en s'éloignant" (p. 303). *Repos* is always associated with physical separation from Nemours.[30] This is the opposite of facing up to one's challenge in the Corneille manner and overcoming it: it is a retreat from threat into the bosom of stability. Ultimately, as has often been pointed out, she desires the peace of death, and indeed her denial of self is a form of suicide. In fact this meaning has been latent in all of her conduct, as in the confession: the sentence "elle s'était creusé un abîme dont elle ne sortirait jamais" (pp. 336-37) prefigures her descent into the tomb, and soon thereafter we encounter this more pointed reference: "si la mort se fût présentée pour la tirer de cet état, elle l'aurait trouvée agréable" (p. 346). Only later does she realize that death is a real alternative. Her mind is finally set too, let us remember, by a close brush with it. There is of course a religious meaning to this--"des vues plus grandes et plus éloignées" (p. 393) point her towards the next life as she renounces this one--but it is also because she has had the opportunity to feel the presence of death as friendly, providing a detachment from earth which comfortably fulfills her own notion of *repos*.

The fact that divergent readings of this novel--and especially its conclusion--have been possible suggests some general considerations concerning its pervasive ambiguities. It contains, for example, numerous sentences which can be taken as ironic and/or ambiguous or simply unclear. Does the affirmation that Mme de Chartres "ne craignait point de donner a sa fille un mari qu'elle ne pût aimer en lui donnant le prince de Clèves" (p. 258) mean that she failed to exercise proper caution, or that she was confident her daughter would come to love Clèves, or that she thought it didn't matter? Does "M. de Clèves se trouvait heureux" (p. 258) mean he was happy, or just that he got what he asked for? Mme de Chartres's parenthesis about Diane's ability to influence the king ("je ne sais par quels moyens" [p. 265]) could be read either as a stylistic discretion on her part or a sign of trenchant irony; "les accidents qui peuvent arriver par les lettres" (p. 392) could refer either to *accidents de coeur* or the chance the letters may fall into the wrong hands.

These uncertainties are often ascribed to Mme de Lafayette's compressed and convoluted syntax, which does present problems. In fact, though, we might as well consider them just highly visible instances of fundamental polyvalences which everywhere abound; ultimately every sentence is ambiguous, or rather polysemic, just as is the work as a whole. As in Racine, classical discretion and restrained diction (often called paucity of vocabulary) leave room for the deepest semantic ambiguities. Serge Doubrovsky has every right to speak of the "juxtaposition d'un monde cornélien et d'un monde racinien, le paradoxe d'une tragédie racinienne avec des personnages cornéliens" (p. 38) because the novel has lent itself to just such a range of readings. Doubrovsky himself brings to light a remarkable new paradox, namely that Poulet's rendering of *passion* in *La Princesse de Clèves* sounds exactly like a definition of freedom: whereas the Cartesian lucidity of Mme de Chartres fails, the individual reveals himself most fully through the total response of his passions.

The value structure of the novel has also been cast in antipodal modes. The exterior values evident in the early parts pose an ambiguity concerning its overall progression: whether Mme de Clèves's own elevated moral standards are essentially social in nature, a standard imposed from without; or are simultaneously social and personal, being interiorized in Corneillian fashion; or on the contrary are purely individual, announcing the supremacy of private absolutes. In other words, they can be seen as wholly exterior in orientation, the duty to family and vows being a social standard ("cette réputation que vous vous êtes acquise" [p. 278])--even duty to oneself being interpreted as an interiorized form of convention. On the other hand, expressions such as *se manquer* or *se connaître* can be adduced to show the Princess's firm imposition of her own standards on her conduct, in the face of unavailing though forceful outside pressures.

Any reading of the text that constructs its sense in linear projection seems to run into difficulties. For instance, Doubrovsky's own argument that blushes are a significant expression of the spontaneous elections of passion cannot explain Mme de Clèves's twice blushing in the presence of her husband (pp. 249, 259), and his assertion that the work lacks any transcendant dimension[31] cannot be proven. The observation that a given element is nowhere overtly signified in the text does not clearly justify the inference that the text actually operates a meaningful exclusion of that element. That "virtue" and "duty" are not evoked in *La Princesse de Clèves* in a specifically religious context does not prevent a religious connotation attaching to them: it was after all an aspect of the classical esthetic to touch only obliquely on Christianity in works not of directly Biblical inspiration. And if Mme de Chartres and M. de Clèves in dying are hardly set forth as models of pious resignation, much less repentence and conversion, again their religious sentiments cannot on that basis be absolutely denied. There is a passing allusion to Mme de Chartres's piety (p. 279) in the face of death; her mention of "le bonheur que j'espère en sortant de ce monde" and her intention to prepare for the moment (p. 278) would be read by any contemporary of Mme de Lafayette as appropriate Christian decorum in a novel, which was not to him a religious or philosophical medium; and the stoic connotations of admirable constancy in Clèves's death (p. 376) likewise admit of a Christian interpretation.

No text indeed can ever be purely unequivocal; all words and all assemblages of words are necessarily polysemic. No sign is imposed by immanent nature, thus there is never a single true meaning of anything. A critic, whatever his tack--and without one there is no critical function--is always contributing to the valorization of multiplicity. Yet these truths seem somehow more salient in the presence of some texts (and their interpretations) than of others, and they are particularly pertinent in the rarefied atmosphere of classical restraint encountered here. *La Princesse de Clèves* has given rise to the most varied and antithetical interpretations, and however much one reader may incline to prefer the gist of certain ones, the others can seldom be excluded with any finality. Ultimately only ideological bias (this expression being broadly construed) permits one to confer satisfactory codifiable meaning on the text. Doubrovsky suggests, and with some justice I expect, that this work can be better appreciated (that is, the multiplicity of its significance recognized) more readily now than in the preceding two centuries of faith in human perfectibility (p. 51). An "optimistic" reading which would reflect confidence in the human will would represent an era of progress, but do little justice to the text's darker implications. The story in some sense changes over time, emerging with new complexities.

To us, Mme de Clèves is likely to appear incapable of working out a functioning and satisfactory relationship between her own sense of self and her sense of society. There lurk menaces and fears that the author undoubtedly could not have expressed more explicitly had she wished to. But one is scarcely impelled to think of *La Princesse de Clèves* as a novel of anxiety; it seems to convey no marked intuition that anything is manifestly amiss in the structure of the world as it is. Socially and politically, the framework is in many ways the same one we find in *Les Liaisons dangereuses*, except that in the latter work the confidence in social equilibrium has been lost, and the nobility is destructively at odds with itself.

In the end, years trail away, passion fades, and death claims its own, leaving the reader to determine as he will whether the heroes have gone away in the proud silence of heroic (or Christian) stoicism, or whether they have been eclipsed like hollow men, "not with a bang but a whimper."

## NOTES

Marie-Madeleine de Lafayette (1634-1693), *La Princesse de Clèves*, 1678. Edition: *Romans et nouvelles*, eds. Emile Magne and Alain Niderst (Paris: Garnier, 1970), pp. 237-395. There have been numerous excellent essays on this novel; particularly recommended are those mentioned in the notes to this chapter and Jean Fabre, "L'Art de l'analyse dans *La Princesse de Clèves,*" *Publications de la Faculté des Lettres de l'Université de Strasbourg*, 105, *Mélanges II* (1945), pp. 261-306.

[1] Frédéric Deloffre, *La Nouvelle en France à l'âge classique* (Paris: Didier, 1968), p. 101. Moses Ratner asserts that "the 'nouvelle' was, in fact, to a considerable extent, the drama of the married woman" (op. cit., p. 61); cf. Dorothy Frances Dallas, *Le Roman français de 1660 à 1680* (Paris: J. Gamber, 1932), pp. 168-204.

[2] Charles Dédéyan furnishes a thorough account of these problems and Mme de Lafayette's solutions to them in ch. 9 of *Madame de Lafayette* (Paris: Société d'Edition d'Enseignement Supérieur, 2nd ed., 1965).

[3] Although she wilfully modifies her sources, Mme de Lafayette rarely stumbles into an illogicality, as in a "peu de jours après" [p. 271] where a close look reveals that *après* cannot refer to anything. But given the silken shifts from imperfect to preterite tenses and back, such a trifle is almost certain to pass unnoticed.

[4] Throughout this chapter, I will make use of italics for emphasis without special mention of that fact; Mme de Lafayette never uses italics.

[5] It is also taken, in classical esthetics, to be essential to the work's claim to broad significance. "Individualiser un personnage, ce serait, selon les classiques, lui enlever sa valeur de persuasion puisque son exemple ne saurait plus s'appliquer qu'à un nombre restreint de lecteurs. *La femme la plus belle du monde* suscite l'amour et la sympathie de tout le monde, précisément, mais *une femme brune*, par exemple, n'est plus du goût de tous les lecteurs. Aussi Du Plaisir conseille-t-il aux romanciers de ne pas donner de leurs personnages une description physique exacte" (A. Kibédi Varga, "La Désagrégation de l'idéal classique dans le roman français de la première moitié du XVIIIe siècle," in *Studies on Voltaire and the Eighteenth Century*, 26 [1963], 965-98, p. 975).

[6]*Structuralist Poetics* (Ithaca: Cornell Univ. Press, 1975), pp. 134-35. The actual example he uses is taken from *La Comtesse de Tende*: "il pensait d'abord tout ce qu'il était naturel de penser en cette occasion" (*Romans et nouvelles*, p. 410).

[7]"Un aveu que l'on n'a jamais fait à son mari" (p. 333); "la plus grande marque de fidélité que jamais une femme ait donnée à son mari" (p. 334); "il n'y a pas dans le monde une autre aventure pareille à la mienne; il n'y a point une autre femme capable de la même chose" (p. 349). To contemporary readers it appeared indeed extraordinary. Gérard Genette uses the example of the confession in discussing what he calls the "théorie classique du vraisemblable": "Rodrigue provoque le comte *parce que* 'rien ne peut empêcher un fils bien né de venger l'honneur de son père'; inversement, une conduite est incompréhensible, ou *extravagante*, lorsque aucune maxime reçue n'en peut rendre compte. Pour comprendre l'aveu de Mme de Clèves, il faudrait le rapporter à une maxime telle que: 'une honnête femme doit tout confier à son mari'; au XVIIe siècle, cette maxime n'est pas admise . . . la conduite de la Princesse est donc incompréhensible en ce sens précis qu'elle est une *action sans maxime*" (*Figures II* [Paris: Seuil, 1969], p. 75). Cf. also the introduction of Tzvetan Todorov to *Communications*, 11 (1968), pp. 1-4.

[8]On the basis of objective genealogy, the chart would have to be further complicated. The king of Navarre, for example, is brother-in-law of Nevers, which reinforces the Diane dependency; on the other hand, the Vendôme family is linked to the Bourbons. But such ramifications would be almost infinite; I have limited myself to relationships figuring in the text of the novel.

[9]"Elle en parlait *souvent* à Mme de Chartres: --Est-il possible, *disait-elle*. . . --Il est vrai, *répondit-elle* . . ." (pp. 263-64). Genette has called this procedure the *pseudo-itératif*: "scènes présentées, en particulier par leur rédaction à l'imparfait, comme itératives [i.e. repetitive, as by the imperfect tense], alors que la richesse et la précision des détails font qu'aucun lecteur ne peut croire sérieusement qu'elles se sont produites et reproduites ainsi, plusieurs fois" (*Figures III*, pp. 152-53).

[10] As in the dialogues pp. 323-25, 332-34, 339-40.

[11] Cf. Genette: "la convention romanesque . . . est que les pensées et les sentiments ne sont rien d'autre que discours, sauf lorsque le narrateur entreprend de les réduire en événements et de les raconter comme tels" (*Figures III*, p. 191).

[12] Cf. Jean Rousset, *Forme et signification* (Paris: José Corti, 1962), p. 42.

[13] There are several examples, the first being Clèves's first encounter with Mlle de Chartres (pp. 248-49); he later meditates his wife's confession en route to the Louvre (p. 338). Another passage between the two Clèves shows that a silence is not a void but is filled with reflections: "Ils étaient si occupés l'un et l'autre de leurs pensées qu'ils furent longtemps sans parler" (p. 350).

[14] Cf. n. 10 above and the two Nemours monologues, pp. 352-53 and 369-70.

[15] There are several stage-type conveniences whereby a scene is fortuitously interrupted just when it has perfectly played itself out: Clèves arrives to interrupt the Princess and Nemours (p. 294) and twice a call for Clèves from the king spares him and his wife the pain (and the narrator the dilemma) of continuing their conversation (pp. 323, 336).

[16] Cf. Stirling Haig, *Madame de Lafayette* (New York: Twayne, 1970), p. 115.

[17] His jealous desire for vengeance, for example: "Si elle vivait, j'aurais le plaisir de lui faire des reproches et de me venger d'elle en lui faisant connaître son injustice" (p. 287).

[18] Cf. Michel Foucault's discussion of confession as constraint in *La Volontè de savoir* (Paris: Gallimard, 1976), pp. 79 ff.; "L'obligation de l'aveu nous est maintenant . . . si profondément incorporée que nous ne la percevons plus comme l'effet d'un pouvoir qui nous contraint" (p. 80).

[19] As Roland Barthes has pointed out, "la passion n'est jamais que ce que l'on en dit: de l'intertextuel pur" ("L'Ancienne Rhétorique," in *Communications*, 16 [1970], p. 212). Being "irresistible" functions in the same purely discursive way.

[20] "Il s'en faisait aimer *malgré elle*, et il voyait dans toutes ses actions cette sorte de trouble et d'embarras que cause l'amour dans *l'innocence de la première jeunesse*" (p. 303).

[21] The beauty of this manoeuvre is that it at the same time pleads his love and his discretion, which has been so compromised, by the very fact that she alone can read this sign: "Ce prince crut pouvoir paraître avec cette couleur, *sans indiscrétion*, puisque, Mme de Clèves n'en mettant point, on ne pouvait soupçonner que ce fût la sienne" (p. 355).

[22] *Etudes sur le temps humain* (Paris: Plon, 1950), pp. 122-32.

[23] *Forme et signification*, pp. 17-44.

[24] "La passion est une expression *plus libre* de nous-mêmes que notre volonté. Elle manifeste nos valeurs spontanées, par opposition à celles que nous tenons des autres. . . . La vérité des corps s'insurge victorieusement contre la fausseté des esprits. . . . Une rougeur ou un geste, *c'est* l'amour, avant même que nous soyons conscients d'aimer. Quand nous nous mettons à réfléchir, nous avons déjà choisi, et c'est ce choix existentiel que nos corps expriment spontanément" (Serge Doubrovsky, "*La Princesse de Clèves*: une interprétation existentielle," *La Table Ronde*, 138 [June 1959], pp. 45-46).

[25] There is a similar sense of release in her avowal of love toward the novel's end, but it is tainted with the fear of uncontrol and indecision: "Elle fut *étonnée* de ce qu'elle *avait fait*; elle *s'en repentit*; elle en eut de la *joie*" (p. 390).

[26] Cf. Rousset, pp. 26-27.

[27] Mme de Lafayette maintains a balanced view of Nemours, all the same, by portraying him more sympathetically in the monologue scenes (pp. 352-53, 369) where he appears more disinterested, more genuinely concerned for the Princess.

28"Attendez ce que le temps pourra faire" (p. 389); "Laisse faire le temps, ta vaillance et ton roi" (*Le Cid*, V. 7).

29Doubrovsky, p. 46.

30"Laissez-moi en repos!" she exclaims to him (p. 341); when she sees less of him, "elle s'en trouvait dans quelque sorte de repos" (p. 343); the memory of Nemours draws her out of "un certain triste repos qu'elle commençait à goûter" (p. 379); cf. also p. 332.

31"S'il n'y a aucune transcendance vers un avenir humain, il n'y a pas davantage de transcendance vers le Divin. La complète absence de Dieu est frappante. . . Il est difficile d'imaginer livre plus dénué de tout sentiment cosmique" (Doubrovsky, p. 50).

# Chapter 4

## Gil Blas

In this century it has become customary to detail Lesage's weaknesses rather more than his strengths, and some have found his once-acclaimed classic irretrievably dated. A recital of the author's "inabilities"[1] doubtless has its interest in a discussion of the general history of the novel, but it would be foreign to our concerns here inasmuch as it is an activity which consists not in reading the text but in naming its absences. Most of the arguments have centered on whether this large and drawn-out work can be said to possess a satisfactory structure, an important criterion, in our time, where judgments of merit are at stake; or whether on the contrary, even though it undeniably has a beginning and an end and contains a life story within its perimeters, it must be considered an essentially amorphous stringing together of tales and satirical pieces. The themes that on the positive side can be invoked as structuring devices are mostly dismissed by Vivienne Mylne on the grounds that the ordinary reader is unlikely to perceive them. But this contention will not satisfy our purposes, because it allows no room for the fact that elements not consciously perceived may still function subliminally, or even rest entirely latent at a first reading only to emerge to full awareness at some later one. Besides, it fails to recognize that, as Roger Laufer stresses, the author wrote every word of his text.[2] We might recast this for reasons of critical perspective to say that no word is incidental to the being of the text. But I will leave this debate in the background for a while and come around gradually to what I see as the dominant themes. Even if they do not invest *Gil Blas* with what one is prepared to call structure, they do give it texture, provided of course that their playing a significant role at all can be firmly established.

How greatly a work is "dated" is all the same not an entirely subjective judgment, although the effect of obsolescence will vary from reader to reader in function of his own literary culture. Although it is a commonplace that works age badly when they contain too many topical references, especially where satire is involved, the allusions are not really what have particularly faded in *Gil Blas*. Even for a reader of 1715, a caricature such as Sangrado would in all likelihood have satirical validity with or without precise awareness of a living model in the person of

Hecquet. What has been lost is rather, as Mylne observes, the style of reading appropriate to a novel such as this. Neither the tone, the subject matter, nor the characters are as strange to the modern reader as the mode and pace of the narration; and although similar remarks are pertinent to *Le Roman comique* and *Le Roman bourgeois* as well, in the case of *Gil Blas* it is apparently only in the last fifty years that this reaction has been widely felt. No doubt it will also some day apply to Stendhal, Balzac, Dickens. Our purpose here is neither to rehabilitate (that is, evaluate), nor to reconstitute as such (because it cannot be done) the perceptions of an eighteenth-century reader, but to read the text, and give an accounting thereof--not, for reasons of economy, in extensive detail, but with whatever clarity the critical optics of our own era permit.

     *Gil Blas* situates itself from the start unambiguously in the tradition of comic novels. Although the story is entirely related as if by the hero himself, the *je* of the "Déclaration de l'auteur" is not Gil Blas; nor is the source of the chapter titles, in which the character Gil Blas is transposed to *il*. The conventional division into short chapters is itself a fiction marker; the individual titles draw attention to the action and on occasion serve as a humorous device in their own right, for example chapter III.10: "Qui n'est pas plus long que le précédent." And even the earliest editions bear the real author's name. Thus, although Lesage toys with the narrative convention less than previous comic authors--this change coinciding with the choice of a first-person narrator--scrupulousness of the narrator as faithful historian ("pour dire la chose en fidèle historien" [VII.1]) is here invoked only for ironic purposes, and the status of the fiction is deliberately transparent. Such had not always been the case in previous pseudo-memoirs, for example those of Gatien de Courtilz.

     As in the earlier comic novels we have looked at, there is much in the text that refers to literature; but in *Gil Blas* the object of satire is to a far lesser degree the mode of being of romance itself. "Si j'imitais les faiseurs de roman, je ferais une pompeuse description . . ." (VII.2): such explicit parody is not lacking, but it extends to other literary referents too. Scipion takes on the mock-Homeric epithet "le fils de la Coscolina," and there are pastoral elements (such as the pastoral motif of the festivities at Olmeda in II.9), as well as more general literary metaphors (a petition to the king is "revu, augmenté et corrigé" like a second edition [VII.12]). Lesage could not be unaware that his novel would call forth comparisons with Spanish picaresque fiction, and indeed he authorizes the analogy, inasmuch as both Gil Blas and Scipion are at some point in the work referred to as *pícaros*.[3]

The referent here, even though this label takes on a certain social sense, is specifically literary, since for the French reader *pícaros* existed only in literature. Equally obvious are certain parallels with *Don Quijote*, particularly after Gil is joined by Scipion; and while the *Quijote* is not mention in *Gil Blas*, Cervantes is.[4] There are, however, certain allusions which point toward it: "un imprimeur de livres de chevalerie, qui s'était enrichi en dépit du bon sens" (VIII.9), not to mention Gil's own confession of a fondness for chivalric tales (X.7). And like Cervantes and others, Lesage also inserts references to his own book: not just "ainsi qu'on peut lire dans le chapitre suivant" (VII.10) but throwbacks to previous volumes: "comme je l'ai dit dans le premier volume de mon histoire" (VII.8). Indeed, inasmuch as Gil Blas is an "author" and literature "exists" in his world, certain of the more playful conventions of earlier comic narration can be incorporated with less obtrusive effect into his. He can in his own right allude to his reader, even lend him discourse ("Oh! tout beau! Monsieur Gil Blas, me dira-t-on . . ." [VIII.5]) or dialogue with him (VIII.9), just as he can address himself.

In *Gil Blas* the literary satire centers less on generic conventions than on literature as a social institution, and more exactly on authors on the one hand and critics/public on the other, with more attention given to the former. Fabrice is naturally the prime example, he for whom writing is a kind of addiction, making and breaking his fortune by turns; when he swears off (XI.7), it is only to come obsessively back (XII.7). Although Fabrice is hard put to gain a living by what he himself calls "ma marchandise" (VII.13), less emphasis falls on this practical struggle of the artist than on caricature of certain authorial manias: "author" connotes ambition, and even more so vanity (even the archbishop "n'était pas auteur impunément" [VII.3]) and disputatiousness ("Ils étaient sur la fin du repas, et par conséquent en train de disputer" [XI.14]). In most of this the target is fairly general, although there is specific reference to Fabrice's preciosity (VII.13) and Triaquero's "ton de la bonne compagnie" (X.5). And if the critics who comment upon their works are equally pretentious and narrow, the authors' own indulgence never extends to other works than their own. Gil Blas keeps an ironic distance from them all, sampling Fabrice's sonnets "entre la poire et le fromage" (VII.13), despairing both of Fabrice's mentality and of the futility of a vocation without honor (or honors), and even offering to reward him for a genuine effort to reform.

Of course there is plenty of sarcasm left for other purposes, and it goes in hand with the simple lines along which characters are drawn. From early on, the social world encountered by Gil denotes a typology. The cave episode for instance precipitates a medley of underworld associations: Léonarde, with the physiognomy of a witch, is identified with Hebe as Gil is with Ganymede, while the thieves are "dieux infernaux"; the cave itself is implicitly hell, and explicitly both labyrinth and tomb (I.4-5). (So strict are the associations formed that Gil, when he later meets Rolando in Madrid, supposes by metonymy that there must be a cave about [III.2]). Medicine and its practitioners are of all characters the most rigorously classified, and for them Lesage's barbs are relentless. Virtually no one ever recovers from an illness with their help. The only effective remedy is that given to the archbishop of Grenada (VII.4), but no doctors are mentioned; the aunt of Don Manrique (X.12) is cured, but perhaps mostly through her nephew's presence. As for Gil Blas himself, he nearly dies, then recovers only after being abandoned by his physicians (IX.8). Their dupes are not viewed with much compassion either; Sédillo's logic, in succombing to Sangrado's unvarying treatment of hot water and abundant bloodlettings, is worthy of a Dr. Pangloss: "Je vois bien qu'il faut mourir, malgré la vertu de l'eau, et quoiqu'il me reste à peine une goutte de sang, je ne m'en porte pas mieux pour cela. Ce qui prouve bien que le plus habile médecin du monde ne saurait prolonger nos jours, quand leur terme fatal est arrivé" (II.2). Sangrado is without doubt a caricature of the Hecquet whose methods he embodies,[5] but numerous other doctors also traverse the scene, with absolutely unexceptional results. As doctors are pompous and ignorant, ecclesiastics are ambitious and hypocritical. Hypocrisy seems indeed to be an essentially religious attribute, adhering in particular to the archbishopric.[6] And on those occasions where one encounters what appears to be a rhetoric of reversed values, it is well to be suspicious of parody: Léonarde's celebration of the virtues of underground cloistering (I.6), as Vivienne Mylne has remarked, is a parody of arguments in favor of monastic life.[7] Other professions have their own, equally set traits. The thief's duty is to steal as the judge's is to hang (III.2); the police have their own seamy secrets, making them vulnerable like their prey, but in comparison thieves are, on balance, more honorable.[8] Raphaël's story in V.1 shows him to be perfectly consistent, every episode revealing treason, infidelity, self-interest; he too is a stereotype, incapable of love as of any other virtue, and presides in Valladolid over a sort of academy of thieves. Thieves are, indeed, a sort of paradigm of social man ("Eh! voit-on d'autres gens dans le monde?" [I.5]): fair booty includes the affairs of the poor (I.17).

The story of Gil Blas is carved into many slices by the interpolations of numerous *histoires* related by other characters he meets: Rolando and three others of the thieves (I), Doña Mencia (I), the barber Diego (II), Don Pompeyo de Castro (III), Raphaël (IV), Don Alphonse (V), Laure (VII and XII), Don Roger de Rada (VIII), Don Gaston de Cogollos (IX), Scipion (X). Of these thirteen stories, two--those of Raphaël and Scipion--cover over fifty pages apiece. In addition, there is the *nouvelle* in IV.4, unambiguously announced as such and bearing its own separate title: "Le Mariage de vengeance." Besides being told in a particular style, with a tone and diction reminiscent of *La Princesse de Clèves*, it differs from all the *histoires* in its non-Iberian setting and the fact that the narrator (Elvira) does not figure in the story (though she is granddaughter of one of the principal characters).[9] Such massive invasion of the primary narrative cannot be fortuitous and has often been scored as a flaw, particularly in the case of this *nouvelle* and the "Histoire de Don Pompeyo de Castro" whose narrator has no direct dealings at all with Gil Blas, who in fact only by eavesdropping hears it told. But all these stories are plainly the stuff of the book, even if modern readings have been inclined to treat them rather as stuffing.

In some cases one can point without undue straining to a reasonable significance to be inferred from them through parallels with Gil Blas's own experiences. For instance, Laufer describes the thieves' stories as representations of the options open to an available young man,[10] and they do expose the high road, the low road, plus some other roads to where their narrators are now. Likewise, he justifies Elvira's nouvelle--as I have done for the nouvelles in *La Princesse de Clèves*--as pertinent in the light of Aurore's project for seducing Don Luis Pacheco, in the main narrative. It is even possible to find tortuous arguments rationalizing the thematic relevance of every last *tiroir*, and no one has tried more valiantly than Laufer. But I think it is all to no avail, and that a much more satisfactory way out lies in admitting the place of narrativity itself as a motif of narration in *Gil Blas*. For in terms of the text's own discourse, all these interpolations are only, so to speak, the tip of the iceberg. There are at least eighteen other occasions where we are told that someone told his or her story, without its being textually encoded, in addition to at least seventeen where Gil attests he related his own. Moreover, this question of pertinency is of explicit interest to Gil Blas as narrator, although the gist of its implementation is not to make the interpolations pertinent if the criterion is direct reinforcement of the primary narrative. One is entitled to see both humor and a paradoxical literalness in Diego's apology for relating his unremarkable story "puisque nous n'avons rien de meilleur à faire" (II.6); Gil Blas himself adds afterward that there was really much more to it, but which does not bear repeating (II.8). Similar remarks designate the unnecessary details filling three-quarters of his mother's story, which he omits from his own (X.2). But words are the stuff of life here, and just as the novel embraces the gamut of narrative substance, from frivolous escapade to austere drama of passion, so does it recognize that narrating can be indifferent, advantageous, or dangerous. Gil's mortifying "aventure de l'hôtel garni" (I.16) is brought upon himself by too much telling (Scipion, similarly, is nearly retaken captive for telling his story unguardedly to the curé de Galves in X.10), and one of his masters dies for inventing a fiction to enhance his fatuous image (III.8).

The narrative also entails metacommentary on writings—for which Gil Blas is, as a matter of fact, qualified in terms of the fiction, being himself a writer if not an author. Since he is the conduit through whom all the subsidiary stories are relayed, they are plausibly laminated with his style which renders the whole relatively homogeneous, with little difference even between his own discursive passages and those which supposedly render oral speech. This lack of differentiation between spoken and written style is characteristic of the whole French classical period. It is originally to Gil's talents not as manipulator but as stylist that he owes his ascendency first with the archbishop, later with de Lerme and Olivarès: "j'avais appris à tourner une phrase. J'étais devenu une espèce d'auteur" (VII.12). De Lerme's praise gives him a vehicle for relaying to the reader an appreciation of his own merits, which indeed apply to the novel as a whole: "Tu n'écris pas seulement avec toute la netteté et la précision que je désirais, je trouve encore ton style léger et enjoué" (VII.3). Polish and urbanity associate *Gil Blas* with other fictional memoirs which were traditionally narrated by aristocrats, whence Mylne suggests, rightly I think, that it represents the fusion of three kinds of work: the satiric or comic novel, by virtue of its essential subject matter; the Spanish picaresque, in the plot line of its first half; and fictional memoirs for its "tone."[11] But Gil learns from his political experience that the consequences of writing too are highly serious. Critics have disagreed antipodally over the years as to whether Gil Blas has any psychological density as a character, but I think Laufer is justified in any event in saying that the *fil* or thread is not the footloose Gil Blas of the story but Gil Blas the narrator, who is, in the terms of fictive conventions, a constant.[12]

When a hero goes on the road, his travels inevitably take on a value symbolic of life itself. Phases on one level will suggest completion of cycles in the other: for instance, Gil returns home at the very moment his father expires (X.2). Life line and narrative line become inextricable; "les sautes entre les chapitres, les parties ou les livres, traduisent immédiatement le sentiment du hasard et de l'aventure."[13] Gil's destiny, as marked in his face and hand (VII.9), is to alternate between joy and pain; he learns to read this pattern like his reader, and thus comes to interpret downfall as the happy omen of imminent prosperity (VII.16). Raphaël proposes to transform his narrative into a book, and quickly adds: "je suis jeune encore, et je veux grossir le volume" (IV.11). "Life" in other words is the book to come: in fiction, writing and living are metaphors of each other, and the expression "la vie des hommes telle qu'elle est" (in the "Déclaration de l'auteur") must be understood as a *literary* reference, not the assurance of a nonliterary signified.[14]

For the grist of the narrative is extracted principally from books. Not that *Gil Blas* is in the aggregate very romantic: its irony excludes the proper tone, and the plot lacks a heroine. But it is full to overflowing with the commonplaces of heroic romance of several varieties: foundlings, hermits, caves, pirates; disguises, mysterious rendez-vous, secret doors and staircases; duels, kidnappings, rescues; malediction, nearly miraculous encounters, and even a hint of the supernatural: Siffredi considers the *connètable*'s experience unnatural (IV.4); Don Alphonse enters a sort of enchanted castle inhabited by an angel: *Sèraphine* (IV.10); Gil himself tells of a miraculous elixir which makes bad wine exquisite (VII.9). In Captain Chinchilla, Gil encounters the very caricature of the swashbuckling adventurer: "Il me conta dans quelles occasions il avait laissé un oeil à Naples, un bras en Lombardie et une jambe dans les Pays-Bas" (VII.12). For good reason one event is characterized as "dénué de vraisemblance" (IV.4); Lesage could have had no misgivings about what such words meant. One can exclaim with Etiemble: "Que dire des invraisemblances...!"[15] only if one begins with the gratuitous assumption that the work should correspond to some extraneous norm for what is "realistic." Such a criterion could never be derived from *Gil Blas* itself, which embraces not *reality* but all the traditional materials of *narrative*.

In the beginning was the University of Salamanca. This is the fiction's pretext—and Gil's own—for removing him from Oviedo in the first place, and also has a certain symbolic value, first of all because as a destination it bespeaks his unusual intellectual gifts, and in so doing immediately sets him apart from the conventional pícaro. For all practical purposes Gil Blas has no family; it only serves to posit him, then dispatch him in a certain direction on a few ducats and a mule, of which he is promptly dispossessed because they are accompanied by his parents' worse-then-useless admonition not to take other people's belongings. However learned, he lacks basic techniques of self-defense, acquisition of which must therefore be the first order of business: "Loin de m'exhorter à ne tromper personne, ils devaient me recommander de ne pas me laisser duper" (I.2). This initial cycle is neatly closed with his capture by thieves and Gil's sarcasm about the value of his education: "voilà le digne neveu de mon oncle Perez pris comme un rat dans une ratière" (I.3). Gil the scholar is finished, although he is briefly revived further on when, for want of a better heading, he proposes to go from Astorga to Salamanca "où je tâcherai de mettre mon latin à profit" (I.13). But when it comes to actually donning a student's gown, his values are crucially tested: "Pourquoi m'habiller en licencié? Ai-je envie de me consacrer à l'état ecclésiastique? Y suis-je entraîné par mon penchant? Non, je me sens même des inclinations très opposées à ce parti-là" (I.15). Once more, in a moment of indecision, the university surfaces as potential destination (I.17) just before Fabrice sets his friend on the new domestic track which will dominate from book II on. Several passing references to the university, when Gil finally does go to Salamanca with Aurore in IV.5, recall discreetly the Gil Blas that might have been, and which Scipion, in symbolic fashion, more or less was: for the latter did serve a "pédant de Salamanque" and in fact thereby acquired his education in that city (X.12); thus it is not unfitting that he should say "je... parlai comme un docteur de Salamanque" (X.11), a metaphor Gil nowhere applies to himself.

The early devaluation of expectations–the dupery, then the cave, then prison–set up Fabrice's cynical tutorial which closes the first book and launches a very long but remarkably steady rise powered by self-interest and ambition. "Je veux porter l'épée"(I.15) is overly heady, since properly speaking the sword was the prerogative of the constabulary and aristocracy; nonetheless a sword is purchased,[16] and the fancy outfit that goes with it ("habit de cavalier" also hedges on the distinction between horseman and *chevalier*), naïvely outlandish though it is, is shelved each time Gil enters domestic service, to be retained and resurrected later as his symbol of distant hope. As in his first adventure, where he was beguiled by the first person to accolade him with hyperbole and deference worthy a lord, Gil falls again, in the "hôtel garni" episode, for the seductions of hearing himself styled "le seigneur Gil Blas de Santillane" (I.16). He becomes valet of, successively, the *licencié* Sedillo, Sangrado, an unnamed "cavalier," and Don Mathias de Silva (the *petit-maître*), the last of whom, just before his death, promotes him to *secrétaire* (III.8). Gil has thus moved already from the state of the lowliest petty bourgeois into noble service, and at this point takes, along with a group of his peers, the burlesque oath never again to fall into a *condition bourgeoise*. And indeed, he never does: despite the humour, an important threshold has been crossed, for in this company Gil is transformed into a "joli garçon" and adopts his master's social values just as he playfully adopts his name (III.4).

Henceforth Gil is more choosy: "Je ne voulais servir que des personnes hors du commun" (III.9). If he then enters the service of the comedienne Arsénie, it is first because in a sense she qualifies as "hors du commun" (an actress is off the ordinary social scale, and there is a disingenuous play on words rationalizing her "nobility"), and second because he is no longer qualified as a valet but as "une espèce d'homme d'affaires" with some financial responsibility. When he reverts to the station of valet, it is for Don Vincent de Guzman, "vieux seigneur fort riche" (IV.1); then for Don Gonzale Pacheco, "vieux seigneur" (IV.7), and finally for the Marquise de Chaves (IV.8): by now Gil Blas is serving the highest society (with her prized salon, the Marquise almost certainly represents the widely-famed Marquise de Lambert). Thereafter, he allows himself to pass for *cavalier*, benefitting again from the ambiguity of this designation, and then, pushing perhaps a play on words even further, briefly plays *chevalier d'industrie* in the company of Raphaël, Ambroise Lamela, and Don Alphonse.[17] All this is accomplished with a minimum of heroism; when faced with a sword, Gil renounces love and flees without regret (IV.9). Only later, to signal his own transformation in stature, does he on the contrary try to provoke a duel for the love of Séphora (VII.1).

In the second half of the novel, Gil is never less than secretary or *intendant*, first for Don Alphonse and then for the archbishop of Grenada. His being submitted to a literary interrogation to qualify for the latter post is a sign that his culture and intelligence are hereafter to be factors in his itinerary. He makes special note of the down bed in his private room (VII.3), which is itself a sensuous contrast with any picaro's litter. Although Gil's confidence in his future gain is now entire, he must also realize that a "fortune faite" is entirely and irrevocably lost when favor is lost. But another milestone too is marked during this episode: the ability to discern among men--"connaître le terrain," says his tutor Melchior de la Ronda--is introduced as an important asset at this level.

While he is next, thanks to Laure, right-hand-man to the Marquis de Marialva, another event confirms for Gil the ascendency of his destiny. He hears the prediction: "Il ne vous reste plus guère de malheurs à essuyer, et un seigneur vous fera une agréable destinée qui ne sera point sujette au changement" (VII.9). Now any reader senses that, however suspicious the character who delivered it, prophecy in fiction, unlike prophecy in real life, is always fulfilled; and Gil's mental calculator immediately goes to work compounding his interest. And though he loses faith in it for having imagined too promptly that it referred to Marialva, the prediction is not lost sight of, for Fabrice has it in mind when placing him as secretary--soon superintendant--to Count Galiano (VII.14). After all this his life style is definitively reoriented: "J'étais . . . trop affectionné aux commodités de la vie; je ne pouvais plus, comme autrefois, envisager l'indigence en philosophe cynique" (VII.16).

By this time the phrase "Seigneur Gil Blas de Santillane" can be pronounced without irony. After a few months as *intendant* to Don Diègue de Monteser, he is rapidly promoted to secretary and favorite of the Duc de Lerme and protégé of the king (VIII.2-5), and even the proud Don Rodrigue now calls him "seigneur de Santillane." To mark his succession to the master class, Gil must now have a valet of his own (VIII.7), excel in vanity and "forget" himself with the other *parvenus* (VIII.13), playing the flawless courtier: "Je leur dis des *riens* en fort beaux termes, des phrases de courtisan" (IX.1). His eventual downfall cannot infirm this social metamorphosis. When he praises Scipion in these words: "Si nous disons ordinairement que nous n'avons pas de plus grands ennemis que nos domestiques, nous devons dire aussi que ce sont nos meilleurs amis, quand ils sont fidèles et bien affectionnés" (IX.8), his *nous* situates the perspective decisively on the side of those who rule. He becomes lord of his own manor; then even closer to power, and for much longer, with Olivarès. And although Gil never explicitly dared hope for actual ennoblement, and reacts with amazement when it comes--"sans que j'en aie l'obligation à mes parents" (XII.6)--it is the logical capstone of his climb. "La race des Santillane," evoked by Scipion with unsarcastic good humor (XII.13), will soon have lost sight of its mean origins.

Nor is Gil Blas alone in his rise, for the general movement of the work is upward. At first, Fabrice moves in the same direction, with rather an advance on his friend, who as late as VII.13--hardly thinking this description will one day fit himself--is "fort étonné de l'avoir entendu traiter de don, et de le voir ainsi devenu noble, en dépit de maître Chrysostome le barbier, son père" (VII.13). Fabrice is of course useful as a witness too, since as Gil's compatriot he alone can truly measure the distance travelled, and he marks his awe by a sudden switch to *vous* when he realizes just how great it is (VIII.9). Even Laure, when she reappears, sets her sights no lower than dukes, counts and marquis (VII.7). And Gil learns upon entering the court that Don Rodrigue de Calderon was de Lerme's domestic before becoming his secretary (VIII.2). Of course Scipion, whom Gil has already described as a copy of himself (VIII.13), offers the most obvious parallel when he tells his own story in book X, for their climb has been similar up to the point where he attached his fate to that of Gil Blas.

An economic dimension complements the purely social, as what began with a necessary concern for livelihood turns finally to a preoccupation with status, and need changes to greed. We must not forget that the soul of Pedro Garcias, in the fable constituting the prefatory "Gil Blas au lecteur," was material. Proliferation of numismatic terminology in all but eleven of 133 chapters sustains the theme.[18] From Sangrado comes an early lesson not only in easy gains but in finagling on commissions (II.4), and what begins as just a penchant for venality changes at court, thanks to de Lerme's explicit offer of partnership, into a passion. But it is interesting that cupidity derives not from the poor man's awe, but the rich man's craving, for lucre: "je me sentais plus avide à mesure que je devenais plus riche" (VIII.9). Gil's first marriage, arranged for him by Scipion like an avaricious father for the love of one hundred thousand ducats (IX.1), was to have been the culmination of this drive. Gil's renunciation of all this is not initially a willing one, but fortune has arranged for him even greater wealth in the service of virtue.

The meals in the novel frequently symbolize changing fortunes, as in the case where bread and water is all Gil gets for what was to have been an order of partridge and rabbit (I.9-12). It is this occasion (in prison) that causes Gil to reflect ironically on how good the food was in the robbers' cave. In poor times onions, bread, and cheese might have to suffice, or at inns cabbage soup and rabbit (II.6-8)--behind which always lurks the suspected substitution of tomcat. Not inappropriately did Sedillo will to Gil Blas, along with four volumes of a breviary, Le Cuisinier parfait and a treatise on indigestion (II.2). Improvements in worldly knowledge and accoutrements are regularly accompanied by commensurate change of fare, for which Gil also acquires an irreversible fine taste, contributing as much as the other things to the distance between him and pícaro.[19] Following his first stay at court, Lirias offers him and Scipion "des repas de bernardins" (X.7)--the last of the temptations of the flesh still to hold its spell over them.

Parallel to these plots runs a moral tale which, however, is less rectilinear. It is not strongly underscored, and bad conscience, although it can be felt, rarely has an upper hand over Gil's other motivations; but the stress given to this theme toward the end asserts its right to our attention, as did the somewhat ambiguous little allegory in "Gil Blas au lecteur." Moral commentary is hardly absent from the first half of the novel, though it is frequently disguised as other forms of discourse. Gil's role for instance in the bloody attack on Doña Mencia's party is related as if to reflect only on his cowardice:

> Je ne laissai pas pourtant, bien que tremblant de tous mes membres, de me tenir prêt à tirer mon coup; mais, pour dire les choses comme elles sont, je fermai les yeux et tournai la tête en déchargeant ma carabine; et, de la manière que je tirai, je ne dois point avoir ce coup-là sur la conscience. [I.9]

The concluding words reveal a concern to undercut his own share in the responsibility: present only by constraint, he was too frightened to shoot straight. The reader is never encouraged to weigh heavily the degree to which Gil has been an outlaw. His association with Raphaël and Ambroise in books IV-VI is not excused by the same duress, but their first act together, a virtuous one, is to save Polan and Séraphine (V.2); the only other is the hoodwinking of Samuel Simon (VI.1), and one cannot help but surmise that the victim's being a Jew (and a usurer) implicitly attenuates the guilt. Gil's good side is suggested on the other hand by the fact that, albeit without design, he is responsible for unearthing the den of thieves (III.2). To be sure, his basic rectitude is always a bit too wavering for moral lessons to emerge with much clarity. His virtue does not quite deserve reward: although he declines an invitation to make league with Raphaël, for example, he is dismissed for having kept his company (III.2-3). The notable exception to his general lack of moral resolve is his decision to flee the debauchery of Arsénie's house in the name of "un reste d'honneur et de religion" (IV.1).

This apparently firm reaction on his part does not, however, betoken a conversion. Soon thereafter, this Gil who later calls himself "un homme naturel" (VII.1)--that is, disinclined to artifice--discovers with some fascination, in Aurore's interest, his own abilities for play-acting and prevarication. In the process he identifies himself with the dubious role of go-between, which he is subsequently asked to play by Aurore's uncle Don Gonzale (IV.7). Two missions of the same sort on behalf of Philip IV confirm Gil as a kind of specialist in what he euphemistically calls his "rôle de Mercure"; but, as English Showalter has remarked, "Gil Blas's virtue goes no farther than to find that particular work distasteful and unrewarding."[20] He chooses virtue over vice if it also coincides with his self-interest, narrowly construed. Troubled by his imposture as Laure's brother he goes through a whole inner debate only to arrive at a conclusion which is as morally clear as it is pragmatically undecisive: "Enfin, après un sévère examen, je tombai d'accord avec moi-même que, si je n'étais pas un fripon, il ne s'en fallait guère. . . . C'est dommage qu'il n'y ait pas autant d'honneur à cela que de profit et d'agrément" (VII.10). Nonetheless, one is encouraged to suppose that Gil has some moral fiber for not having sunk even lower than he has. De Lerme, after hearing a somewhat edulcorated relation of his past, commends him in these terms (which, in retrospect, one might have to take with a grain of salt): "Combien y a-t-il d'honnêtes gens qui deviendraient de grands fripons, si la fortune les mettait aux mêmes épreuves!" (VII.2).

From this point on, rather more attention is drawn to Gil Blas's moral and even human qualities, which decline in tandem. A chapter title declares: "Les moeurs de Gil Blas se corrompent entièrement à la cour," and Gil himself adds: "j'y devins plus dur qu'un caillou" (VIII.10). His mind and character have that elastic property which Fabrice's jargon calls "l'outil universel" (VIII.9), and Scipion--"un chien de chasse pour découvrir le gibier" (VIII.7)--is chosen for the same qualities. Sins of sex are viewed with no special horror in *Gil Blas*, but soliciting for the prince is nonetheless Gil's least honorable role, for the codes of honor and gallantry held the corruption of an innocent maid to be particularly blameable; but as it happens, the girl involved is not the virgin she was thought to be. The consequences in the case of Lucrèce, in book XII, are much graver.

This process of moral decline is analyzed as a loss of self, as Fabrice confirms: "Gil Blas n'est plus ce Gil Blas que j'ai connu" (VIII.13). In attempting to be a *seigneur*, which he is not, "je n'étais plus le fils de mon père et de ma mère" (id.); and the conversion that results from his illness and near-death in the tower of Segovia (IX.8) is translated as a restitution of that identity: he remembers his parents, is "rendu à moi-même" (and notably not "à Dieu"). His own authentic nature is thus restored, as he himself puts it to his mother: "c'est cette malheureuse maladie qui vous a rendu votre fils. Oui, c'est ma maladie et ma prison qui ont fait reprendre à la nature tous ses droits" (X.2). The sense of guilt over his previous self-estrangement now accuses him of murdering a father who however had no love for him ("Je me regardais . . . comme un parricide"); and by reaction against that alienated state, he reorients himself toward the antithesis of the court, namely the country, frugality, and humility. On this moral level also, Scipion's story mirrors Gil's. With a more distinctly criminal inclination owing to the Bohemian blood in his veins, Scipion pilfers without scruple, yet eventually proves that "un fripon peut fort bien devenir un honnête homme" (X.10).

The death of Antonia paves the way for a more honorable repetition of the first rise to power, Olivarès providing the opportunity for service in good conscience for a man who has by now learned to enjoy wealth without being possessed by it (XI.7). He nonetheless promises to obey Olivarès without scruple, and pays for it when entreated once more to procure for his prince. This assignment he duly carries out, even though the sight en route of Raphaël and Ambroise being led to the stake confronts him with a grim vision of what might have been, and even though the honored victim this time is Laure's daughter.[21] But the terror passes quickly--there is no melancholy in this hero--and Gil's reaction when Olivarès congratulates him on his success suffices to show that his newfound virtue is as moderate as was formerly his vice:

> C'est ainsi que Son Excellence me dora la pilule, que j'avalai tout doucement, non sans en sentir l'amertume; car depuis ma prison je m'étais accoutumé à regarder les choses dans un point de vue moral, et je ne trouvais pas l'emploi de Mercure en chef aussi honorable qu'on me le disait. Cependant, si je n'étais point assez vicieux pour m'en acquitter sans remords, je n'avais pas non plus assez de vertu pour refuser de le remplir. [XII.3]

The eventual fate of Lucrèce and of Laure brings on no painful qualms, only the resolution never to do that again. The lack of emotion in such passages, or the brevity of its expression, has often been cited, indeed, as a grievous failing in Lesage. Never is there a serious moral test which is encountered and accepted as an occasion for affirming the meaning Gil Blas has chosen to instill in his life, and nothing in the novel itself gives rise to any such expectation. After all, fortune and morality cease after book IX being at odds, with the sole exception of the Lucrèce episode, since the successive interventions of Don Alphonse and Olivarès make it possible for Gil to grow ever richer by being relatively virtuous. All extreme forms of signification are avoided. The work ends, too, with a very temperate kind of contentment for Gil, in the company of a new wife whose beauty is deliberately described as less than perfect (XII.13).

Much of the preceding pages has consisted in various forms of paraphrase, which I hope serve to bring out the main conclusions which my reading of *Gil Blas* imposes: that there is a pattern to its plot, although it is diffuse and cumulative; and that there is also a symbolic meaning which emerges, although it is not univocal. There is no reason to believe that depiction of growth of character was one of Lesage's goals, or even that he would have seen much meaning in such a concept. It is time to add that no aspect of the work is allowed to override humor, and this is perhaps best illustrated by a few examples of that form of humor which most ostensibly flies in the face of Christian morality, namely the sexual innuendo referred to in Lesage's time as *équivoque*. It is interesting here partly for its delicacy, in contrast to the vulgarity of chamber pots (which are *almost* absent from *Gil Blas*) and the ribaldry common to stage farces. Frequently the *équivoque* is a manner of euphemism--a sophisticated rhetorical device, particularly in combination with wit. When Don Vincent's agony is accompanied by a doctors' quarrel over what Hippocrates meant by *orgasme*,[22] nothing but the word itself explicitly indicates that the joke involves more than the perpetual medical satire (IV.3). On the other hand, the physiological sense of Raphaël's impatience in love implies a satire of all such gallant euphemisms: " ... mais je voulais aimer physiquement, et je me rendis un soir sous les fenêtres de la dame, dans le dessein de lui dire que je ne pouvais plus vivre si je n'avais un tête-à-tête avec elle dans un lieu plus convenable à l'excès de mon amour" (V.1). Now in principle, the *équivoque* is equivocal, and can thus be read two ways. For example, Gil learns that Jacinte and "un bon ami," both serving ailing masters, "comptaient d'assembler les dépouilles de leurs maîtres par un hyménée dont ils goûtaient les douceurs par avance" (II.1). Which "douceurs"? The phrase can of course be taken as a pure metaphor for wealth, but the following sentence draws the connotation in the direction of the sensual: "J'ai déjà dit que la dame Jacinte, bien qu'un peu surannée, avait encore de la fraîcheur." Some time later, the woman arranging Gil's own clandestine courtship of his pretended widow says of her: "Entre nous, la dame est un morceau appétissant. Son mari n'a pas vécu longtemps avec elle. Il n'a fait que passer comme une ombre" (III.5). This asserts that she is still fresh and comely, but also suggests that by such a wispy marriage she was just barely (if at all) deflowered; it even allows the reading that since the husband was nearly dead, she (virtually) had intercourse only with a ghost. Hints of impotence lend themselves easily to equivocation: when Mergeline tries to take up where she left off with the mortally frightened Diego after they are nearly caught in the act, her governess intervenes: "que feriez-vous de ce pauvre garçon? Il n'est pas en état de soutenir la conversation" (II.7).

By referring to the "équivoques claires" prevalent in the banter heard at Arsénie's (III.5), however, Gil Blas reveals interestingly that an *équivoque* is not necessarily equivocal, and thus characterizes a particular kind of society which like Laure displays "beaucoup plus d'esprit que de vertu." Indeed she punningly excuses her own promiscuity as a sort of consequence of theatricality by saying: "le public en rit, et nous sommes faites, comme tu sais, pour le divertir" (id.). She has a knack for splicing an ordinary metaphor onto a specifically sexual connotation: "Je m'attirai les regards de plusieurs cavaliers. Il y en eut qui voulurent sonder le gué" (VII.7). It is easy to see why in time *équivoque* came to stand simply for an indecent joke.

There is, however, a particular series of equivocations that seem to culminate piquantly in the novel's closing sentence. They all involve an uncertain irony concerning paternity. The first has to do with Lucrèce, Laure's fourteen-year-old daughter:

> Si quelque lecteur malin, rappelant ici les entretiens particuliers que j'eus à Grenade avec Laure, lorsque j'étais secrétaire du marquis de Marialva, me soupçonne de pouvoir disputer à ce seigneur l'honneur d'être père de Lucrèce, c'est un soupçon dont je veux bien, à ma honte, lui avouer l'injustice. [XII.1]

In fact, Gil Blas spent only about a day in Marialva's service in book VII, although it was at that time that he was apprised of Laure's intention to marry him. But does "ma honte" suggest impotence? The next instance relates to Olivarès' growing affection for Don Henri, which he takes as evidence of a blood bond, even though he knows that is objectively contestable:[23]

> Tu vois par là, mon ami, que la nature se déclare. Je n'eus garde de dire à monseigneur ce que je pensais là-dessus; et, respectant sa faiblesse, je le laissai jouir du plaisir faux ou véritable de se croire père de don Henri. [XII.6]

Such irony prepares the way for the paragraph which effectively ends the book with a pirouette:

Il y a déjà trois ans, ami lecteur, que je mène une vie délicieuse avec des personnes si chères. Pour comble de satisfaction, le ciel a daigné m'accorder deux enfants, dont l'éducation va devenir l'amusement de mes vieux jours, et dont je crois pieusement être le père. [XII.14]

Is this meant to shed any doubt on the matter, because of Gil Blas's age? What are Heaven and piety doing here in the company of such innuendo? The important thing to recognize is the maintaining to the very last word of a calculated effect of humor, which prevents any heavy sententiousness being ascribed to the final phases of Gil Blas's philosophizing.

A few remarks now, before proceeding further, on the chronology of the novel. The first six books of *Gil Blas*, which contain not a single datable event, provide no basis for an articulated chronology of the whole; the last six, with numerous historical allusions, do. It would probably not be worth going into this in detail were it not for the fact that Etiemble has repeatedly stated, and others have repeated after him, that Lesage's chronology is so bad that he marries off an octogenarian at the end of the story.[24] But to my knowledge Etiemble has nowhere documented this assertion, and I can see no reason why we should accept it.[25] I hope it will be clear that it does not require an excessively microscopic reading of the novel to reach the conclusions expressed here, but it does necessitate some internal accounting in terms of the text itself and whatever exterior anchors that it supplies.

Almost all the early engagements of Gil Blas are short, whence the impression of discontinuity; and time is dealt with somewhat vaguely, more or less as in a picaresque novel. The typical pattern is that events of just a few days given in some detail are followed by a quick leap over a quantity, specified or not, of days, weeks, or months, after which another slower sequence begins.[26] For example, here is a résumé of time sequences in the first three books, where 1-$n$ indicates countable sequences; $x$ an unknown number of time units' jump, and $x$ alone an unspecified interval:

Book I: 1-4 days + 6 months + 1-2 days + 15 days + 3 weeks + 4 days + $x$ days + 1-6 days.

Book II: 3 months + 8 days + 1-3 days + 3 days + $x$ days + 6 weeks + 5 days + 1-3 days.

Book III: $x$ days + 2 days + 8 days + $x$ + 2 days + 1 day + $x$ days + 1-3 days + $x$ + 1-5 days + $x$ days + 1-4 days + $x$ + 3 weeks.

There is never an occasion in the novel where more than eight or nine consecutive days' action can be kept track of, and the frequency of lacunae which could be matters of either days or years makes the establishment of a chronology by summation quite impracticable.

With the introduction of the Duc de Lermes in VII.12, on the other hand, a clear historical context is established: the dates are not in the text, but de Lerme was prime minister from 1598 to 1618. There is a thematic logic to this, in that after a certain point Gil Blas's progression carries him from the private into the public domain.[27] Thereafter the indicators become more precise, and several mentions of intervals in Gil's life as well as historical events permit some reconstruction even with respect to the first six books. While I agree with Vivienne Mylne that the names of writers thrown in for local color do not constitute grounds for dating the story, in fact they mostly fit without difficulty. Zabaleta (1610-1670) would apparently be too young for his mention in II.7, but not Vélez de Guevara (1579-1644); Moreto (1618-1669) could not have been born by the time he is named by Fabrice (VII.13), but Lope de Vega, Cervantes, and Gondora present no problem.

The procedure followed in the following table of time allocation by books is simple. Although specific durations cannot be calculated for most of the books in the novel, *minimal* times are easy to figure--that is, the length of time which, at a minimum, would be required for the events narrated as specified. Those dates which are in brackets are retrospective and will be rationalized by the subsequent discussion.

| I | 8 months | [1605-1606] |
|---|---|---|
| II | 6 months | [1606] |
| III | several months | [1606-1607] |
| IV | 10+ months | [1607-1608] |
| V | 1 day | [1608] |
| VI | 2 weeks | [1608] |
| VII | 5+ months | [1609] |
| VIII | 10+ months | |
| IX | 4-6 months | [1617] |
| X | 3 months | 1618 |
| XI | several years | 1618- |
| XII | several years | -1648 |

Book X begins precisely when de Lerme is named cardinal (1618) and lasts only about three months; book XI begins fourteen months before the death of Antonia and soon thereafter of Philip III (1621). Gil Blas's government service for Olivarès ends with the Portuguese wars in 1640; but we follow Olivarès to his death in 1645, at which time Gil returns to Lirias and remarries, completing his story three years thereafter (therefore in 1648). Now in X.6 we are told he has not seen Raphaël and Ambroise for ten years; and the last occasion was in book V, which sets the date for book V rather firmly in 1608. In XII.3 we learn in addition that he has not seen Laure for fourteen years, which was in VII.10, but these two dates cannot thereby be so well fixed because of the large interval loosely covered in the last two books. Book VIII is also very vague, as the events described in the service of de Lerme could cover as little as one year or, in relation to this calendar, as much as eight or nine. Paradoxically, in terms of day and week counts the most "historical" sections of the novel are the least precise.

Working backward, one can reconstitute with the data in the second column an entirely plausible chronology whereby the novel begins in about 1605, Gil Blas being then exactly seventeen years old. There is therefore no reason why Gil could not have been born as late as 1588, in which event he would be, at the moment of his marriage to Dorothée in book XII, fifty-seven years of age, and could without the slightest tinge of ridiculousness refer to himself as "un homme qui commence à vieillir" and who doesn't look his age by ten years (XII.14). Similarly, he would have every reason to place himself at about mid-career at a point when he was about thirty (IX.9), and might still be called a young man by the king in 1621 (XI.2) at thirty-three (although the king himself, it is true, would have been at this juncture only sixteen, and Olivarès thirty-three or -four).

The egregious chronological errors of Lesage therefore come down to this: 1) Don Pompeyo de Castro refers in his story to the king of Portugal (III.7), whereas there was none from 1580 to 1640--years of Spanish domination. This Lesage acknowledged in a preface to books VII-IX in 1724, although he did not correct it until the edition of 1747, where he simply switched the reference to Poland. The effect on Gil Blas's story is negligible. 2) Gil tells Scipion when they return to Valladolid (in IX.1), "j'ai longtemps exercé ici la médecine," whereas all that is related of it in book II could fit into two months, or very amply into three months or so.

3) Gil says in XII.13 that Antonia has been dead for twenty-two years, whereas it has been twenty-four or twenty-five years. That is all. The twelve books are, on the whole, a remarkably good fit.

But that fact is of minor concern to most readers. More significant in the long run is what might be called the book's fetch. Jean Cassou classed *Gil Blas* among

> certains livres dont la lecture produit, avant toute chose, une impression de durée. Au-delà du temps que le lecteur a mis à les absorber, il a eu connaissance d'un déroulement, il s'est lui-même accru, non plus d'une "tranche de vie", mais d'une masse, d'une épaisseur de vie. [Op. cit., p. 195]

(It is extraneous to our subject whether, as Cassou further asserts, this is because the author has aged in the process.) No one will deny that Gil's twenty years spent in the service of Olivarès disappear rather quickly over the horizon, but I have no difficulty agreeing with Maurice Bardon when he says: "Le panorama successif d'une existence, voilà ce que Lesage a prétendu nous donner, et il serait puéril de contester qu'il y ait réussi."[28]

Remembering the ties we have earlier evoked between the idea of comic novel and the idea of comedy, and the fact that comedy is to this day a generic term standing for theater in general, we find with no surprise that comedy is everywhere in *Gil Blas*. Like stage comedy, and others of the novels discussed, it has an abundance of characters named for their attributes, usually via Spanish translation: Sangrado suggests *saignée*, for instance, and Descomulgado *excommunié* (III.3); other names are transparent even without translation: Séraphine, Astuto, the doctor Oloroso, the dance master Ligero. And still others are doubtless meant, through anagram or slight transposition, to suggest well known proper names, such as Oquetos for Hecquet and de la Fuente for Fontenelle. The numerous plots and subplots are loaded with elements drawn from the whole theatrical spectrum. Slaps and references to "coups de pied au cul" (X.11), accidents involving chamber pots and enemas (II.7, VII.16), fisticuffs (II.4, VIII.9), and such fleeting characters as the Matamore-type captain Torbellino, are all straight out of farce. The kind of *turqueries* which occupy a good portion of Raphaël's story, where for example he redeems his mother and sister from slavery in Algiers (V.1), are commonplaces of comic plots[29] (note too Raphaël's allusion to the immodest comedies performed in the "Turkish" style).

Dozens of novels also involve such episodes of slavery in Barbary, and many of the romantic motifs already listed are inextricably mixed up in the tradition of comedy as well. Satires of doctors and hypocrites are of course staples of Molièresque comedy, not to mention various other types such as the *petit-maître,* the bourgeois aping nobility, jealousy,[30] cowardice ("je frissonais de crainte" [VII.11]), and allusions to cuckoldry ("la sûreté de votre front" [II.7]). Numerous situations duplicate stage effects: two persons laughing at the same thing but for different reasons (IV.5), domestics trying to mimic the gallant and coquette roles of their masters (III.5). One of the thieves in book I presents the reversal of the typical *reconnaissance* by which comic dilemmas are resolved, in that he is the plebeian substituted for a noble child who therefore loses, rather than gains, his titles when his real patronymic is discovered. But there are several other *reconnaissances*, one kind being the discovery of Sirena's identity with Catalina--two characters turn out to be just two faces of one, the situation of Mme Turcaret in Lesage's own *Turcaret* (1709). Alphonse is an adopted son who turns out to be a unique inheritor when Leyva owns him. And as everyone knows, comedies usually end in marriages, as notably does Aurore's: "Il fut résolu que . . . nous dénouerions notre comédie par un mariage" (IV.6). Here event and metaphor fuse. Gil Blas's own marriage is of course accompanied by a burlesque *reconnaissance*, that of Scipion and his estranged wife Béatrix (X.9), whereby the episode terminates in a sort of double marriage.

Frequently, their resemblance with precedents makes these situations more like specific quotations from the comic repertoire. Both Sédillo, ridden with gout and urinary problems, seated in an armchair with all his limbs on pillows (II.1), and Gonzale Pacheco, asthmatic "momie vivante" (IV.7), vividly recall *Le Malade imaginaire.* Sangrado talks like the Sganarelle of *Le Médecin malgré lui,*[31] and Gil resembles him later in the same episode by the taste he acquires for the practice of medicine the moment he is first paid. The clothes merchant who values his outfit at sixty ducats "ou je ne suis pas honnête homme" (I.15) exploits a famous line from *Les Fourberies de Scapin:* "Parbleu, Monsieur, je suis un fourbe, ou je suis honnête homme: c'est l'un des deux" (II.6). Gil's argument with Ligero over the relative cost of philosophy and dancing lessons resembles the dispute between the different tutors in act II of *Le Bourgeois gentilhomme*, as the "béate" Jacinthe who has gotten Sedillo's nephew run out of the house (II.1) parallels the expulsion of Damis in *Tartuffe*. In addition, the last half of the novel draws widely on Leroux's *Dictionnaire comique* of 1718.[32] More tragic tones are to be found in some dramatic scenes, notably a repetition of Chimène's stance in *Le Cid*: Séraphine refuses to exact personally her vengeance on Don Alphonse--her brother's slayer--but vows instead to have him pursued, entreating him meanwhile to do his best to escape (IV.10). But tragic quotations also serve, as often they did in the comedy of the time, for comic effect by contrasting with the silliness of the situations where they are placed. Thinking at first that it is for himself that Aurore sighs and intrigues, Gil scans his memory for theatrical precedents by which to inspire his tongue; and the ensuing scene with Aurore (IV.1-2) shows traces of the result: "Ah! madame, serait-il bien possible que Gil Blas, jusqu'ici le jouet de la fortune et le rebut de la nature entière..." (cf. Phèdre: "Et moi, triste rebut de la nature entière . . ." [IV.6]). Another mock-Racinian accent: Gonzale, appreciative spectator of Euphrasie's feints, assures Gil: "J'ai vu couler des pleurs véritables" (Thésée: "J'ai vu, j'ai vu couler des larmes véritables" [*Phèdre* V.3]).

The institutional theater is equally manifest, beginning with the play offered by Diego's uncle at Olmedo, the occasion for numerous ironies about the excesses of tragicomedy (perhaps directed particularly at Crébillon *père*). Comedians figure among the most fatuous of critics, seldom gauge accurately how the public will react to a new play, and above all disdain the authors they live by: "Traitons-les toujours en esclaves" (III.11). Don Pompeyo's mere two-day passage in Madrid, besides providing an inlet for his story, serves only to let him express his highly negative opinion upon a performance by the "théâtre du prince" (III.6), which, one may be sure, means *la troupe du roi*--that is, the Comédie Française. Similarly, Gil's stay with the Marquise de Chaves furnishes a satire of a pretentious salon whose refined taste excludes any esteem being accorded to such low genres as novel and comedy (IV.8)--Lesage's two genres. This tendency turns starkly *ad hominem* in book X, where under the name Gabriel Triaquero ("triacleur" implies charlatan) Voltaire and his "ton de bonne compagnie" are derided, as this "poète à la mode" is shown after a performance of his play hopping from loge to loge to offer his head modestly for laurels.

And, to be sure, numerous comedians figure prominently in the story. Melchior Zapata, first encountered as a vagrant example of the miseries of the profession (II.8), later reappears with Laure in the troupe of Grenada, which receives Gil "comiquement" (VII.8). The theater exerts a sort of gravitational force; both Laure and Phénice, chambermaids of actrices, share in their life style and finally become *comédiennes* in their own right. Gil's portrait of the actor is complex, despite numerous articles of satire, but the novel brings out, more than any one professional tic, the ambiguities of this "vie comique" (VII.7) which at once degrades, offering up Laure at her début like merchandise to the highest bidder (VII.7), and genuinely lifts to a higher stratum of social associations, however unstable. Thus the earlier pleasantries about the "nobility" of actresses are invested subsequently with a degree of experienced validity; Phénice describes her station as one intermediary between bourgeoisie and nobility, a liberal profession in both a socioeconomic and a moral sense: "une condition libre et affranchie des bienséances les plus incommodes de la société."[33] The noble metaphor is not entirely facetious, although it is always tinged with irony. Laure relates: "Je regardai mon talent comme un titre de noblesse. Je pris les airs d'une femme de qualité" (id.); but Gil's styling her--not to her face--a "princesse de théâtre" (VII.6) is a corrective to such delusion. Raphaël's story has already served to make the point that actors cannot accede in real life to the attributes of the roles they play (V.1). This de- or re-classing function is only one aspect of the estrangement of self which seems endemic to the trade, as symbolized by the loss, by theatrical convention, of identity. Gil seems not to understand initially how "Estelle" can be Laure. On one level this is a mere reflection of the practice of taking stage names, yet it goes in hand with an inclination, as Laure herself acknowledges, to see herself transformed into someone else ("Je me parus tout à coup à moi-même une autre personne" [VII.7]), no longer mindful of her origins. The comedian is caught in a cross-current which ultimately is that of the stage itself, representing life, according to one of its pretentions, while being absolutely other than life. He too can lapse into confusing them. It is said of Lucinde, for instance, that "à force de jouer des rôles sanguinaires dans les tragédies, [elle] s'était familiarisée avec le crime" (V.1).

Comedy is also itself one of the most insistent of the novel's metaphors. Many situations are described as comedies, including those where Gil refers to himself playing the comic valet for Aurore--with a degree of success which is a subject of pride--and then for her uncle. He calls himself a "turlupin" (III.5), and Scipion a "personnage comique" (X.10). But the metaphorical and literal are close neighbors, Gil and others who have served comediennes providing a link between the two levels. Just as Eufrasie has shown that "les bonnes comédiennes n'étaient pas toutes à la comédie," Gil recognizes one in her chambermaid Béatrix, and counters with a comedy of his own: "par cette contreruse, je trompai les friponnes, qui levèrent enfin le masque" (IV.7). When she says to Gil, "vous jouez, à ce que je vois, un assez beau rôle sur le théâtre du monde" (X.1), Laure recuperates a lost metaphor--although she does not entirely avoid banality-- and restores to it some of its life. Moreover, it is pertinent to observe a similarity of function attributed to two related metaphors when Laure's "roman," on the plane of *narration*, becomes "une plaisante comédie" when *action* in the primary narrative supercedes that of the false *histoire* (VII.6).

The centrality of the stage motif in an overall reading of *Gil Blas* has been denied by Vivienne Mylne, for whom it does not "emerge as any more significant than, for instance, Gil Blas's remarks on doctors."[34] This is a failure, I think, to distinguish functions of different orders. However obstinately the author rips away at doctors, it cannot be argued that medicine is in any way a metaphor either of life or of narrativity; no one would propose seeing it as a structuring device. But to the contrary, the text is perfused with comedy, which clearly can and does take on these values. To Wagner's proposition that "la place de l'art dramatique est si grande que l'un des thèmes essentiels est celui-ci: *le monde est le vaste théâtre de la comédie humaine*,"[35] Mylne replies: "One could even put up an equally convincing case for the theme: 'Life is a school, and man discovers his true nature only by undergoing the lessons of experience.'" But where are the "school" metaphors in *Gil Blas*? What this is saying is that one may *propose one's own* metaphor, which may be defensible as paraphrase of the plot; but it is not an argument based upon the terminological structure of the text. If stage metaphors do not give shape and direction to the narrative, they do at least inhabit the text, and the same cannot be said for just any symbolic device. They inform the vision of the world, all the more when one takes into account the intrinsic associations already present between comic novel and comedy. Still, Wagner's formula should be more strongly worded. I would say: comedy, narrativity, and the narrative are mutually supportive lines of force, and not to perceive them is to have missed something essential about *Gil Blas*.

Doubtless one could go even further, especially with the benefit of a thorough repertory of reference codes such as Roland Barthes elaborates in *S/Z*. It would, of course, be a gigantic task with this particular novel, but by following Barthes's suggestions one can easily spot a few important categories. With or without that guide, one of the most striking for the modern reader, whose classical culture is unlikely to equal Lesage's, is the prevalence of Greek and Roman referents.[36] Both generally mythological and specifically literary by turns, they are not confined to the utterances of Gil himself--who at seventeen, in an era when to be educated meant to know Greek and Latin, can say, "j'entendis un peu les auteurs grecs et assez bien les poètes latins" (I.1)--but emanate from a whole range of characters. After some time we and Gil learn that Scipion like him has absorbed a classical education ("vous connaissez les poètes grecs!" [IX.9]) from his Salamanca pedant. This says a great deal about the assumed readership of the novel. The function of such codes, as Barthes has shown, determines the intelligibility of the text for the reader. The classical codes are a common language, a ready reservoir of references, only for a marked stratum of society. The same can probably be said for a half-dozen hagiographic references in *Gil Blas*, which being so few can be assumed to be relatively esoteric in nature, and allusions to more modern literature, such as *Obregon* and the plays of Lope de Vega.

Explicit references to social class structure, on the other hand, are probably less marked in this sense, inasmuch as the prevalent code, although it is determined by the ruling class, permeates the others as well. The upper class does not share its respect for class hierarchy. Assumptions of this order are nonetheless an instructive code for the modern reader to examine, since they no longer strike him as manifest. Chief among these is of course the self-evidence of innate merit embodied in the significance of blood, the original force which, preceding psychology, always seeks its own kind. A peasant raised as a nobleman still gravitates to underlings (as in the third thief's tale in Book I: "J'aimais beaucoup mieux jouer avec les valets, que j'allais chercher à tous moments dans les cuisines ou dans les écuries" [I.5]), just as Don Alphonse, although a foundling, bears an inner assurance of his noble birth (IV.10).

The cleavage between the nobility and everything beneath it is expressed to Lucinde with particular starkness by the Duc de Medina Celi, whose wife she has accidentally offended:

Quand de grands seigneurs s'attachent à de petites créatures comme vous, elles ne doivent point pour cela s'oublier. Si nous vous aimons plus que nos femmes, nous honorons nos femmes plus que vous; et toutes les fois que vous serez assez insolentes pour vouloir vous mettre en comparaison avec elles, vous aurez toujours la honte d'être traitées avec indignité. [V.1]

The situation, as can be seen by the generality of the terms employed, is well codified and clearly distinguishes sentiment or feeling from honor. But even as human beings, the nobility are simply more important; God really is, so to speak, a respecter of persons. Neither Aurore nor anyone else involved gives the slightest thought to the cruelty inflicted upon Isabelle, who has faithfully loved Don Luis; here is how, disguised as Don Félix, she encourages him to treat her: "D'ailleurs, l'objet, entre nous, ne mérite pas tant de ménagement; ce n'est qu'une petite bourgeoise. Un homme de qualité ne s'occupe pas sérieusement d'une grisette, et croit même lui faire honneur en la déshonorant" (IV.5). Gil does not apparently take exception to this, although it might be said that the insistency with which he treats this episode as a "comédie" may be a disculpatory rhetoric designed to obviate any serious reflections on the moral import of the act; it would not be the only such occasion. But the sense of a real distinction is in fact shared by the lower classes. Gil Blas feels as instinctively in the case of Doña Mencia (I.10) as Don Alphonse does in the forest episode that suffering inflicted upon a noble is a much greater shame than another; and it is thanks to such distinguished instincts that Séraphina and her father are rescued–beneficiaries, in effect, of *roture oblige*. And when Gil is shocked to hear nobles called by their first names (III.10), it is not just because he fears the comediennes in question are succombing to an illusion of equality.

To be sure, this attitude blends in the subordinate's mind with the wisdom of self-preservation, and here there is a progression as successive lessons are learned. They can be more or less codified as the maxims of the poor, as when Gil observes, after daring to compliment the old skeleton Don Gonzale on his sexual attractiveness: "il s'applaudit de mes paroles: tant il est vrai qu'un flatteur peut tout risquer avec les grands. Ils se prêtent jusqu'aux flatteries les plus outrées" (IV.7). He also comes to realize the part that *prévention*, or mental set, plays in the respect paid nobility; after describing the amusing physique of the archbishop, he adds: "Malgré tout cela, je lui trouvais l'air d'un homme de qualité, sans doute parce que je savais qu'il en était un. Nous autres personnes du commun, nous regardons les grands seigneurs avec une prévention qui leur prête souvent un air de grandeur que la nature leur a refusé" (VII.2). But between this lesson and the next, the intervention of Melchior is required to make Gil understand further that no matter how ignominiously offended by a nobleman, and no matter how unworthy he is, the commoner must never, for his own sake, lose his respect (VII.5). The numerous repetitions of sarcasm regarding not so much the recently as the fraudulently ennobled--those *dons* who have simply arrogated to themselves the title--while constituting obviously a satirical observation on new patterns of social mobility, could also be read as the reflection of a certain bad conscience over perhaps deserved but fundamentally (because innately) unrightful promotion of the lower classes. They are comforted, on the other hand, by the old saw that even the most powerful are governed by their favorites, who in turn are governed by their valets (VII.12).

Other codes refer to known or assumed facts about history, astrology, racial traits like the jealousy of Italians or the avarice of Jews; medicine, needless to repeat; tics related to status or profession--comedians and *petits-maîtres* arise late, police steal, every merchant claims to be the uniquely disinterested paragon of his kind. These codes tie in with and permit much of the social satire, for instance in this thumbnail sketch of a tax farmer: "Le partisan, quoique des plus roturiers de sa compagnie, tranchait du grand; et sa femme, bien qu'horriblement laide, faisait l'adorable et disait mille sottises assaisonnées d'un accent biscayen qui leur donnait du relief" (III.3). The humor does not derive from any refutation of received opinion, but rather from confirmation of clichés about the *roture*, pretentiousness, and provinciality of an economic group. Many of the novel's bons mots are based upon wry renderings of accredited differentials between principles and behavior: "Je ne me plains pas de la justice, lui répondis-je. Elle est très équitable. Je voudrais seulement que tous ses officiers fussent d'honnêtes gens" (I.13).

It would be a mistake to assume that a text is producing its own generalizations when in fact it is only referring to them as a standard by which facts and behavior become understandable--that is, readable. For example, when Gil says, "Je pleurai même aussi, tant il est naturel de s'intéresser pour les malheureux, et particulièrement pour une belle personne affligée" (I.12), he is appealing to human nature ("tant il est naturel"), a complete although unwritten text known to the reader, as the criterion by which the normalcy of his behavior is determined. Such codes as this one, which one might call the rule of sympathy, are at the most general level of abstraction and recur often: "Ces sortes d'objets font toujours quelque impression sur les plus grands libertins même" (V.1); "On s'intéresse pour un brave homme qu'on voit souffrir" (VII.12). Almost any fiction, perhaps any narrative, would furnish examples. Other "rules" might be, or at least appear to be, more culture-specific. A lady who putatively writes that "si elle était assurée qu'il fût discret, elle ferait avec lui le voyage de Cythère" (III.8) can be understood only if both the mythic referent and the code of gallantry, within which the terms have assumed particular connotations, register. On the other hand, limited frameworks of this sort can in fact be linked to much more pervasive value systems. "Pour du courage, il n'en saurait manquer, puisqu'il est gentilhomme et Castillan" (IV.2) appears to evoke only a code of regional associations, but depends also upon a far more generalized appreciation of the code of honor, which itself approaches the status of law of human nature. That will vary, of course, with the specific historical context by which the terms of the text were originally conditioned. But here they stand for more than mere opinions because they are attached to, indeed pulsate with, the blood: "Il plaignit le sort de son oncle, quoiqu'il n'eût pas sujet d'en être fort touché; et la force du sang lui fit regretter un prince dont la mort lui promettait une couronne" (IV.4). In truth the referent is even more complex than we can with justice indicate. When, for instance, Séraphine says to Don Alphonse, "Les droits de l'hospitalité doivent être inviolables," (IV.10), her discourse is to be sure informed by the code of honor, but there is also a distant Homeric ring--socio-historical, or literary?

Many precepts of conventional wisdom are of course already fixed in the form of proverbs ("Bon sang ne peut mentir" [X.1]), often explicitly invoked: "Demeurez d'accord de la vérité du proverbe qui dit qu'*à quelque chose le malheur est bon*" (V.1). Other generalizations, whether or not they actually have the social function of proverbs, tend to be formulated in a similar manner, evoking through such motifs as *intérêt* the maxim of the classical period, for instance: "C'est ainsi que les hommes le plus sévères rabattent de leur sévérité, quand leur plus cher intérêt s'y oppose" (VII.4). A reader without specific cultural information would be hard pressed to determine whether most of these are authentic proverbs or original formulations. Comparably turned are even statements representing a much more limited point of view, such as "Les mets délicieux sont des plaisirs empoisonnés" (II.2). Numerous passages apply aphorisms of this sort to the understanding of feminine behavior, as in the following examples:

Ce sont de vrais caméléons qui changent de couleur suivant
l'humeur et le génie des hommes qui les approchent.
[IV.7]

. . . une femme douce et polie pouvait se faire aimer sans le
secours de la beauté, au lieu qu'une belle personne,
sans la douceur et la politesse, devenait un objet de
mépris. [II.7]

Une femme excuse jusqu'aux mauvaises actions que sa beauté
fait commettre. [VII.7[

Le plaisir de parler est une des plus vives passions des femmes.
[VII.7]

[Voler l'amant d'une autre] est une chose si naturelle aux
femmes que les meilleures amies ne s'en font pas le
moindre scrupule. [VII.7]

Lest one suppose these are characteristically masculine remarks, we should
add that the last three examples all come from Laure's story. In other words,
proverbial forms serve not only to make the outside world comprehensible,
but to explain oneself also. In the context of Laure's speech they also have a
disculpatory effect, as if, not being free to do otherwise, woman cannot
really be held responsible for her actions.

Although the proverb is a highly explicit form—and it matters little
that different ones contradict each other--it is possible also to speak of
implicit proverbs. That is, many passages which contain no such formalized
pronouncement are nonetheless based upon an unenunciated supposition
which can easily be inferred from the text and could be proverbially
expressed--sentences such as: "Ils . . . ne pouvaient concevoir qu'il y eût au
monde une femme qui trouvât mauvais qu'on la louât" (II.7), or "Elle avait
de la sagesse, mais elle était femme . . ." (V.1)

Satire is never very far away in *Gil Blas*, however, and a reference to
codes of this sort may well combine with irony or a reverse sarcasm. "Les
chiens d'hommes!" (VII.7) appears to be an imprecation of the way men
behave, except that it is complemented by: ". . . dit-elle d'un ton à faire juger
qu'elle avait rencontré en son chemin quelque économe."

Love, contrary to what one might expect, appears a rather straight-forward code, the multifarious actions its force inspires all becoming intelligible through reference to commonplaces about the tyranny of passion, the ravages of jealousy, fidelity and fealty (although a phrase like "l'amour rend la servitude si douce" [IV.1] is a pun on the domestic versus the chivalric sense of servitude). That is not to say the understanding of love could not be otherwise than it is here. There is little of the seigneurial and heroic sense of love such as is typified in the works of Corneille; in *Gil Blas* love does not always derive from merit. Especially in the earlier books, its theory follows predominantly a Racinian vein. If there is humor, it is mostly situational, but there is not really much at all directed at the sentiments of love, unless one reads some hyperbole, for example, into: "L'amour est un dérèglement d'esprit qui nous entraîne vers un objet, et nous y attache malgré nous. C'est une maladie qui nous vient comme la rage aux animaux" (II.7). Even in what Laufer considers the "Regency" and the "Louis XV" *Gil Blas* (that is, books VII-XII), little cynicism appears to corrupt this particular code insofar as its lexical components are concerned. Passion seems indeed to play a lesser role, and there is frivolous *sex* related; but the rhetoric of *love* does not appear on the surface to be undermined thereby.

Roland Barthes's suggestion that a character is constituted by repeated attachment of identical connotations (technically, *sèmes*) to the same proper name[37] may help understand why it has so often been maintained that Gil Blas is weak in terms of character portrayal, that even after hundreds of pages covering decades of his life, and told by himself, the reader doesn't "know" him very well. In the "psychological" novel, many clusters of character traits or semes adhere to each prominent individual (there are almost always some secondary roles not so differenciated). In Gil's case, on the contrary, one might say that there just are not enough connotations attached to him--although those present are, to be sure, repeated often enough--to create the complexity we expect of a "character" in the grand psychological tradition. If the self is a mass of texts assimilated and melted together, then it must be said Gil Blas's is spare, even if it does contain allusively the whole body of classical literature, because the human codes to which he gives voice are few in number and mechanistic in their application.[38] Those of a *Princesse de Clèves* are of a quite different order; just to identify a motive is for the heroine a very complicated business. Not for Gil Blas. That is because her "text" is full of subdivisions and nuances, including that one which calls into doubt even the accepted values of the codes and of the language current.

Rhetoric is present in all texts, but it does not always in any remarkable way draw attention to itself. Now *Gil Blas*, being a highly ironical text, depends a great deal on play of language, savored more by the reader who proceeds attentively and has assimilated something of how to read in a particular way. The devices are too numerous to catalog; but to illustrate, there is humor in the partial re-literalizing of an occasional metaphor, such as *mettre à profit* ("je ne m'attachai plus qu'à mettre à profit les moments d'entretien que j'avais avec le duc" [VIII.3]), or in the extension of its forgotten metaphoric value, as in the sexual innuendo Laure draws from "sonder le gué" (see p. 104 above). Nevertheless, *Gil Blas* is not a highly figured text. There are fewer metaphors (in the limited, traditional sense of tropes) than Greco-Roman references, and as such when they occur they rather stand out. A good number have already been cited in other contexts, particularly as they frequently serve to comic purpose, but a few more examples may be helpful here.

At one end of the scale are metaphors encapsuled in popular sayings, similar in impact to proverbs. At the other are those borrowed from epic diction, such as we have seen in other comic novels:

> . . . le sommeil qui m'avait fui la nuit précédente vint répandre
>      sur moi ses pavots. [IX.5]

> . . . la nuit même s'apprêtait à couvrir les arbres de ses ailes
>      noires . . . [VI.1]

> Nous ressemblions, comme aurait dit Homère, à deux milans
>      qui cherchent des yeux dans la campagne des
>      oiseaux dont ils puissent faire leur proie. [V.1]

The episode with Catalina in book VIII is couched in mock-epic terms as a siege; and so forth. A romantic commonplace like the wings of love becomes, in Scipion's persiflage, "La crainte me prêta des ailes pour fuir les prêtres de l'hôpital des orphelins" [X.10]. At both extremes these do play a certain role in characterization. Laure, especially in her story in book VII, abounds in witty metaphors which are saved from purely popular style only by an admixture of theatrical culture: "Phénice . . . faisait la tout aimable et écoutait en minaudant le doux ramage d'un jeune oiseau qui s'était apparemment laissé prendre à la glu de sa déclamation" (VII.7). Fabrice, in his exalted moments, alternates from the popular ("le public était une bonne vache à lait") to the pompous, juxtaposing nicely in this way his origins and his pretentions (VII.13, 15).

It is such little unexpected turns, rather than the mock-heroic alone, which principally characterize *Gil Blas*, and they contribute forcefully to its overall comic tone. Even with banal metaphors--Mergeline is changed from "tigresse" to "brebis" (II.7), Séphora from "agneau" to "tigre" (VII.1)-- there is often a humorous overtone. But along with other animal metaphors one expects, one occasionally comes upon a more pungent and original instance. Gil admiring his fancy new suit: "Jamais paon n'a regardé son plumage avec plus de complaisance" (I.15). Or a standard term can be given a burlesque meaning, as when Gil says of Fabrice: "Il en fut si piqué, qu'il prit une licence poétique. Il s'échappa subtilement de la compagnie, et disparut" (VIII.9). A metaphor like this is further charged by the close relation of referent to context. It might be called a metonymic metaphor: that is, *licence poétique* is suggested by a discussion about poets. Similarly, Gil Blas as doctor bearing with Fabrice's laughter is expressed in these terms: "Je le laissai s'épanouir la rate . . ." (II.3). On another occasion, when Gil is being treated, he is greeted at the end by not only the doctor's bill but in addition the surgeon's, which precipitates a metaphorical series: "Autre plume qu'on me tira de l'aile. Il me fallut aussi cracher au bassin du chirurgien. Après tant d'évacuations, ma bourse se trouva si débile, qu'on pouvait dire que c'était up corps confisqué, tant il y restait peu d'humide radical" (VII.16). "Cracher au bassin du chirurgien" is a reference both to bleeding into the tray and to the necessity of paying him, after which the further metaphor equating bleeding with paying consummates the medical theme.

If we distinguish the thing qualified or compared via metaphor from the metaphoric referent or comparer (in the example just given, Gil Blas and his purse as the first term and bleeding as the second), we usually can see that the humor falls mostly on one or the other side, but not always the same. When Gil says that the two *petits-maîtres* embrace by turns a usurer "comme deux joueurs de paume qui pelotent une balle" (III.3), this phrase alone would contain no humor without its relation to the situation or thing described, which is in itself a typical comic stage situation. Contrariwise, in Gil's comparison of himself, as register keeper for Sangrado, with a clerk booking seats on a coach bound for the other world (II.3), it is the second part which lends humor to the first. And when a character is described as "plus pâle et plus jaune qu'une fille fatiguée du célibat" (III.3), it is the *fille* figuring in the referent who is really the object of the witticism; nothing much has been added to the paleness or characterization of the original descriptee.

If space allowed, samples of numerous other tropes could be shown. A metaphor can hypostatized as parable, the means whereby Gil informs de Lerme of his penury: a "Persian" tale--first level--sets up a conversation between two crows--second level--whereby the metaphor doubles back toward the immediate situation and becomes literal, if slightly transposed (VII.6) There are many apostrophes, especially those addressed to the young Gil Blas by himself; this is perhaps one of the stylistic traits specifically derived from the picaresque tradition, and Marivaux imitates it in *Le Paysan parvenu*. And, although not numerous, there are also instances of personification, antithesis, preterition, hyperbole, chiasmus, and doubtless other tropes as well.

But it is worth pausing a moment here to note a phenomenon which brings several of the levels we have considered into conjunction, namely the appearance of figures whose referent is rhetoric itself. Some concern specifically literary rhetorical exercises like prefaces ("Quoique ce fût un avis au lecteur..." [V.1]) and commentaries ("Il n'en dit pas davantage, et il continua son chemin, me laissant faire les commentaires qu'il me plairait sur un texte si laconique" [VII.7]). But in several instances the referent is more precisely *figures* of rhetoric, in which case the metaphor is a sort of metafigure or metatrope. And they usually become by that right very complicated semantic constructions. In one sentence, figures of rhetoric become *fleurs*--in fact a cliché--but this permits a further metaphor on the level of *fleurs* as literal referent: "nous avions beau l'un et l'autre épuiser notre esprit à semer des fleurs de rhétorique dans ces placets, c'était, comme on dit, semer sur le sable" (VII. 12). Or consider this combination of rhetorical referent with generic parody of the mock-novel variety:

J'aurais, dans cet endroit de mon récit, une occasion de vous
faire une belle description de tempête, de peindre l'air tout en
feu, de faire gronder la foudre, siffler les vents, soulever les flots,
*et caetera*. Mais, laissant à part toutes ces fleurs de rhétorique,
je vous dirai que l'orage fut violent, et nous obligea de relâcher à
la pointe de l'île de la Cabrera. [V.1]

The thrust is parallel to that of the passage on *faiseurs de roman* already
quoted on p. 90, but there is a further, specifically rhetorical (one might say)
irony in that the whole passage is a preterition: "laissant à part toutes ces
fleurs de rhétorique" names precisely an intention that is being honored in
the breech. The first victim of Gil Blas as thief had said: "Je vois bien
qu'avec vous autres, les figures de rhétorique sont inutiles" (I.8), which was
of course meant to make Gil feel too clever to be tricked, thus setting him up
for the ruse which leaves him empty-handed. Thus the word "rhetoric" is
implicated in the matter of deceit (note too that later on, metaphors and
transpositions in a poetic context are linked with obscurity [VII.13]). This
coincides with the notion of rhetoric, in the classical era, as the ornamentation
with which real signification--non-metaphorical--is overlain; rhetoric could
be thought of as a repertory of persuasive mechanisms, irrespective of the
content or truth-value of what it vehicled. On another occasion, the "figure"
represents a bribe: ". . . relâchez-vous un peu de votre devoir en faveur du
présent que ces dames vont vous offrir. Oh! c'est une autre affaire, repartit-
il; voilà ce qui s'appelle une figure de rhétorique bien placée" (II.4).[39]
Discussions of metaphor have always tended to invoke coin and usury; and
here money, so often the metaphor of metaphor, becomes its tropological
signified: that is, metaphor becomes the metaphor of money.

And finally, there is at least one situation where metaphoricity gets
tied up with narrativity. For "Le Mariage de vengeance," the one
heterodiegetic intercalated story and the only one labeled "nouvelle,"
*emerges* from a painting, which is itself narrational. First there is the
painting in Doña Elvire's mansion. By being described, it becomes the
object of a narrative discourse which emphasizes its power through a
rhetorical metaphor: "Toutes ces choses étaient peintes *avec des expressions
si fortes*, que nous ne pouvions nous lasser de les regarder" (IV.3, my
italics). By dint of this pivotal notion that the expressive painting *expresses
itself*, it then in effect narrates itself, becomes the next chapter, which is no

one's *histoire* but its own, the story of how *it* came to be what and where it is. This both establishes and reduces its uniqueness within *Gil Blas*, in that the picture is functionally parallel to the many characters whom the hero encounters and who then relate their stories to him.[40] *Ut poesis pictura.*

So in fact the novel's original proposition about representing life as it is (in the "Déclaration de l'auteur") cannot be taken simply to mean that narration imitates life, for it is no less true that "life" imitates narration. Or rather, things exist only through it; they get their life from being narrated. While this covert message is by no means tantamount to Mallarmé's dictum about everything existing in order to be written in a book, it does assert the inevitable, creative power in human life of narrativity. One does not just tell stories to entertain, nor, as Pascal would have it, because one must be entertained, but because one must tell stories. If it is not they which create value, it is they through which value is created, and no human society is imaginable without them.

## NOTES

Alain-René Lesage (1668-1747), *Histoire de Gil Blas de Santillane*, books I-VI, 1715; books VII-IX, 1724; books X-XII, 1735. Edition: Gallimard "Folio" (ed. René Etiemble), 2 Vols., 1973. References will be given by book and chapter rather than page numbers; but it is important to note that, being based upon the edition of 1732-37, Etiemble's frequently differs from most others, which follow the 1747 version. (Etiemble's Pléiade edition in *Romanciers du XVIII^e siècle*, Vol. I, is essentially identical to this one.)

[1] The term reappears frequently in Vivienne Mylne's article, "Structure and Symbolism in *Gil Blas*," *French Studies*, 15 (1961), 134-45.

[2] Roger Laufer, *Lesage ou le métier de romancier* (Paris: Gallimard, 1971), p. 320.

[3] De Lerme to Gil: "vous avez été tant soit peu *pícaro*" (VIII.2); Gil to Antonia and Béatrix: "Scipion était un vrai *pícaro*" (X.12).

[4] VII.13. Lesage was familiar with Spanish literature of all kinds and frequently translated it, including an adaptation of Avellaneda's spurious sequel to *Don Quijote*.

[5] Cf. Etiemble ed., I, 132, n. 1.

[6] Cf. Laure: "Tu n'as jamais vu de face si hypocrite, quoique tu aies demeuré à l'archevêché" (VII.7). Laufer goes so far as to characterize Lesage as "un des écrivains les moins religieux de l'Ancien Régime" (op. cit., p. 300).

[7] Vivienne Mylne, *The Eighteenth-Century French Novel* (Manchester: Manchester University Press, 1965), pp. 51-52.

[8] "[Les *alguazils*] vidèrent tout doucement mes poches, et me prirent ce que les voleurs mêmes avaient respecté, je veux dire les quarante ducats de mon oncle" (I.12).

[9] In Gérard Genette's terms, this *nouvelle*, like the *histoires*, is intradiegetic (the narrative instance being contained within the larger narrative), but is alone in being heterodiegetic (the narrator is not a participant in the thing narrated). *Gil Blas* in the aggregate is contrariwise extradiegetic and homodiegetic (*Figures III*, pp. 252-56).

[10]Op. cit., p. 303.

[11]Mylne, *The Eighteenth-Century French Novel*, p. 51.

[12]Op. cit., p. 297. Narrative duration is not considered pertinent in reading; that is, the act of producing the primary narrative (Gil Blas writing his story) is treated as an instantaneous act without a temporal dimension (cf. Genette, p. 234).

[13]Laufer, p. 324. His sentence actually concludes: "et renvoient à un principe d'organisation caché," but I wish to avoid adopting his line of rationalizing the structure; more telling, to me, is his use of the word *immédiatement.*

[14]Jacques Proust has also argued the essentially literary nature of *Gil Blas*'s "reality" in an excellent article entitled "Lesage ou le regard intérieur: recherches sur la place et la fonction de la 'description' dans *Gil Blas*," in *L'Objet et le texte* (Genève: Droz, 1980), pp. 75-105.

[15]In his introduction to *Gil Blas*, in *Romanciers du XVIII^e siècle* (Paris: Gallimard, 1960), I, 259; the sentence ends: ". . . et des anachronismes!"--about which I will have more to say later.

[16]Similarly, Diego's sword inspires confidence in him; but, significantly, it flops about and gets tangled in his legs when he walks (II.7).

[17]*Chevalier d'industrie* became a common term for a variety of flimflam activities, but might be too a simple euphemism for a common thief.

[18]See Laufer's tabulations, pp. 292-93.

[19]"Pour le *pícaro*, au contraire, la nécessité ne se laisse jamais séduire: elle garde son caractère élémentaire de *faim*. Et le *pícaro* n'assouvit jamais cette faim, car le monde reste un granit incomestible" (Jean Cassou, "Lesage," in *Tableau de la littérature française* [Paris: Gallimard, 1939], I, 197). See also Roseann Runte, "Gil Blas and Roderick Random: Food for Thought," *French Review*, 50 (1976-77), 698-705.

[20]English Showalter, Jr., *The Evolution of the French Novel, 1641-1782* (Princeton: Princeton University Press, 1972), p. 282.

[21] It is perhaps not unjustified to see in the return of numerous characters in the last three books, as does Laufer, something rather too mechanical, even a certain drying-up of the author's inspiration: "Il reprend les personnages, les situations, l'esprit des tomes précédents en les appauvrissant. . . . Il punit en Laure la luxure, comme il punit en Raphaël l'escroquerie et le vol. Il fait revenir tous les personnages encore vivants pour les punir ou les récompenser" (pp. 359-61). On the other hand, in what better way can the overall odyssey of Gil Blas be brought full circle?

[22] Etiemble's note to I, 298 points out that Hecquet and Andry (Oqueton and Andros in the text) did have a debate over *orgasme*.

[23] "Marguerite, en recevant tant d'hommages confus, devint insensiblement mère. . ." (XII.4)

[24] Pléiade edition, pp. 259, 1514; Folio edition, p. 525.

[25] My calculations come very close, on the contrary, to agreeing with N. Wagner's in "Quelques Cadres d'étude pour *Gil Blas*" (*L'Information Littéraire*, 8 [1956], 29-38). Wagner does not explain in detail why he sets Gil's birthdate at 1590; I would adjust this back some two years only, for reasons which will appear.

[26] In this *Gil Blas* is, like most narratives, in Genette's terms *anisochronic*: that is, the quantity of text and the diegetic time it encompasses do not maintain a consistent proportion. But the characteristic anisochrony, according to him, is an alternation between detailed scenes and summary, comparable but not equivalent to the starts and stops indicated here (cf. Genette, op. cit., pp. 128 ff.).

[27] See *The Eighteenth-Century French Novel*, pp. 64-68.

[28] Preface to Garnier ed. of *Gil Blas* (Paris, 1955), I, viii.

[29] Cf. for example Rotrou's *La Soeur*.

[30] "Point de jalousie, mon enfant! Les jaloux, chez le peuple comique, passent pour des ridicules" (III.10): in comedy, and only in comedy, jealousy is intrinsically ridiculous.

[31] Compare: "D'autres, à ma place, ordonneraient sans doute des remèdes salins, urineux, volatils . . ." (II.2), and: "Un ignorant aurait été embarrassé, et vous eût été dire: 'C'est ceci, c'est cela'. . ." (*Médecin* II.4).

[32] See examples given by Laufer, pp. 355-56.

[33] Id.; cf. Laure's comparable affirmation, further on: "Les femmes de notre profession sont des personnes titrées. Nous ne sommes point responsables des effets que produisent nos charmes."

[34] *The Eighteenth-Century French Novel*, p. 144.

[35] Art. cit., p. 33.

[36] Laufer has tabulated, for the four original volumes, respectively 29, 16, 42, and 25 Greco-Roman allusions (I assume he is including the eight or so Biblical ones in this count). He has attempted to give specific interpretation to this uneven distribution, particularly the bulge in Volume 3: "Ce retour à la culture gréco-romaine, à une époque où la Querelle des Anciens et des Modernes s'est tue, traduit un sentiment profond d'honorabilité bourgeoise. Le précepte de Pythagore y remplace l'examen de conscience chrétien" (pp. 356-58).

[37] Roland Barthes, *S/Z* (Paris: Seuil "Points", 1976), p. 74.

[38] See the harsh but incisive analysis of Gil Blas's moral posture in René Démoris, *Le Roman à la première personne* (Paris: Armand Colin, 1975, pp. 365-75): "La parole du narrateur, comme celle du héros, est creuse, parce qu'elle n'est pas réaction originale d'un être qui veut apprécier son expérience vécue, mais effet second du rôle qu'il joue." Note, however, that Démoris rather arbitrarily chooses to consider the novel as if it terminated at book IX.

[39] Cf. the play on prose (a *billet au porteur*) and poetry (a *billet doux*) in *Turcaret*: "*La Baronne*: [Turcaret] me prie en vers de recevoir son billet en prose. *Marine*: Je suis fort curieuse d'entendre des vers d'un auteur qui envoie de si bonne prose" (I.4).

[40] Tzvetan Todorov has called them "les hommes-récits" (*Poétique de la prose*, Paris: Seuil, 1971, ch. 6), and like them the painting is a narration-in-waiting.

# Chapter 5

## Manon Lescaut

Many of the novels of the late seventeenth and early eighteenth centuries shrug the disjunctive or extradiegetic narrator in favor of "historical" models where an oral (*histoire*) or written (*mémoires*) narrative emanates directly from the protagonist: stories in which, on the surface of the representation, there is, in terms of the fiction itself, no "author." This is the case in *Gil Blas*, except that there the comic tone connotes an author's presence; to be sure, this is deliberate. The novel we are now turning to has frequently been cited as a further advance of realism in that the tone this time is serious and the illusion it creates thereby aspires to be total. Once more, such an assumption calls for some reservations; but the quasi-historical form of the discourse does represent a phenomenon well worth analyzing, both in terms of the history of literature and of the ways it governs the reading of the text.

What is commonly known as Realism is no closer to being *the* representation of "reality" than is any other discourse. Rather, it is the conventional *codification* of reference in particular ways, some of which can be identified--such as the prevalent high frequency of denomination of objects.[1] That is, it does not "copy," but it does *name*. We have become accustomed to thinking of it as in some sense natural, but it can be highly stylized in certain instances. The only thing that language *can* indisputably copy is language. For this reason, the prototype of a realistic discourse in fiction is one where the model is not reality itself but another form of language: the memoir-novel, the letter-novel, or the pseudo-history (for history, like memoirs and letters, is a kind of use that is made of language). The language of fiction that imitates them by pretending to be real memoirs, letters, history[2] is theoretically indistinguishable from them, although its "facts" or its rhetoric may of course betray the camouflage. The ostensibly fictive level has been conjured away. A movement in the direction of such historical models for fiction seems for this reason to have favored the propagation of the novel, at a time when the esthetic prestige of narrative fiction was at best precarious.

The *Histoire de Manon Lescaut* illustrates this doubly, for the subject's relation of his own story (the *histoire*) is then transcribed by its fictive auditor and attached to his own *Mémoires et aventures d'un homme de qualité qui s'est retiré du monde*, of which it forms the seventh and final volume. It is entirely possible that not just every reader would have been aware that the one or the other of these works was fictional. But whether or not he knew this, he was implicitly instructed to read the work *as if* it were not. This constitutes a "mimesis" of a particular order, but it creates its own stock conventions as it goes: paradoxically, a story such as Des Grieux's gives itself away precisely by being framed within another as it is, since such long parentheses were not likely to be found in authentic memoirs. For this reason, *histoire* in the title becomes in practice a fictional marker.

As a consequence of this "embedding" of one story within another, one has every right to question whether "*Manon Lescaut*"[3] can legitimately be read isolated from its parent-novel. It has been maintained, eloquently and forcefully, that it assumes a meaningful place within the *Mémoires d'un homme de qualité*, and that its own reading is conditioned by this context. In that case, one attaches special importance to the listeners of Des Grieux's story, Renoncour (the "man of quality") and his pupil Rosemont: the first because he provides the moral ambiance indicated by *Manon Lescaut*'s "Avis de l'auteur," and the second because he has much to profit from implicit parallels to be drawn between himself and Des Grieux.[4] I have no argument with such a position, which seems entirely justified, provided one retains for the discussion the original text of the novel. Even though the revisions of 1753 were not extensive, they can be significant for interpretation. For example, Jeanne Monty (p. 54) cites as evidence of the "negative qualities" of Des Grieux his remark, "on me comptait pour des vertus ce qui n'était qu'une exemption de vices grossiers," whereas in the revised text this becomes: "on me comptait pour des vertus quelques marques d'aversion naturelle pour le vice" (p. 17), which is a rather different statement.

There remains, however, another valid option, quite aside from the fact that this story comes *after* the rest of Renoncour's adventures rather than being told in its chronological place (which would have been in book vi) and that the "Avis de l'auteur" refers to it as an "addition": for alone among Prévost's works it was carefully revised, and that revision was done for a separate printing of *Manon Lescaut*. It is also true that critics had early singled out this volume for its particular qualities and interest, and that soon after its appearance it was often printed separately;[5] the changes made in 1753 add Prévost's endorsement to this relative autonomy. In reading *Manon Lescaut* as a novel in its own right, therefore, it is appropriate to work with the 1753 version, which has become more or less the standard text.[6]

Like many a younger son of the nobility, Des Grieux has been destined by his family for the order of Malta, of which at seventeen he already wears the cross although he has pronounced no vows. He is thus *chevalier de Malte*, which in general (although not absolutely) meant he should not marry.[7] This detail contained in the novel's title is important because it designates Des Grieux immediately as a man of high birth but little independent fortune. The text is full of allusions to his rank, to which no contemporary reader would have been insensitive, and the mark of privilege accompanies everywhere his adventures as well as his language.[8] Renoncour, who opens the primary narrative,[9] shares with him this fundamental distinction, reflected in such details as the fact that they both travel on horseback, are automatically treated with deference by others, and can invoke their status to command respect ("comptez que j'aurai le pouvoir de vous faire punir" [p. 15]). This common *qualité* underlies and conditions the extraordinarily effective way the story is introduced.

The interpolated *histoire*, it will be recalled, is traditionally the personal story of someone encountered along the road (as in *Gil Blas*; there are others too in the *Mémoires d'un homme de qualité*). In this instance, curiosity is aroused by the juxtaposition of *two* such chance meetings of the same arresting person, the first leaving a vivid impression on the narrator accompanied by very little explanation, and the second, in another city and after an interval of about two years,[10] leading to the chevalier's own story. The sense of story is thus strongly influenced at the outset by the notion of *hasard* (the same chance--which Des Grieux will assimilate to fatality-- causes Manon to arrive in Amiens one day too early for Des Grieux's good [p. 19]), and in addition provides an advance glimpse of Des Grieux as protagonist at a point when his adventure is not yet completed: the scene at Pacy (pp. 10-15) will not become fully clear until Des Grieux recuperates it near the end of his own narrative (pp. 181-82).

Twice Renoncour invokes the "curiosity" of the crowd before what he hears described as a "spectacle . . . capable de fendre le coeur!" arouses his own "curiosity" and leads him to what he at first laconically calls "quelque chose d'assez touchant." Breaking the apparent symmetry of two uniform prisoner-chains of six *filles* each is that *one* ("il y en avait *une* . . .") whose dignified silence announces her own singularity.[11] She appears *socially* miscast: "je l'eusse prise pour une personne du premier rang" (the 1731 edition reads "pour une *princesse*"). The reader's perception of her is firmly controlled by these reactions of respect and pity at the sight of this angel unsullied by her surroundings; even the chief guard, a character by connotation unsentimental, says in awe, "elle vaut un peu mieux que ses compagnes." Des Grieux, who remains anonymous until the second encounter, is for his part first described as "[la] plus vive image de la douleur."

Yet Renoncour's attention is right away riveted on the latter, for the simple but commanding reason that, unlike Manon who *looks* noble, her lover obviously *is*: "on distingue, au premier coup d'oeil, un homme qui a de la naissance et de l'éducation." The real question is not what *she* is doing where she is, but what *he* can have to do with all this--and with her. Quality recognizes quality ("Il se leva") and induces spontaneous sympathy: "je me sentis porté *naturellement* à lui vouloir de bien." If, with hardly any knowledge of the situation, Renoncour concludes that this is a most extraordinary and touching adventure (p. 14) and offers his services, it is precisely because of all the strange social overtones, the egregious disproportion in play: what is extraordinary is that someone so well born ("il était né quelque chose") could possibly be in such a position relative to some fascinating but common woman. After this, the modest and charming Manon is merely "incomprehensible"--not like a mystery, only like a puzzle. This focus on the noble hero already dominates the "Avis," where Renoncour attempts to assess the sense of Des Grieux's experience, and not a word is said of hers.

The simplest understanding of the events in Des Grieux's story depends on awareness of this enormous difference in rank, which Des Grieux himself underscores in relating their first meeting: "Elle voulut savoir *qui j'étais*, et cette connaissance augmenta son affection, parce qu'étant d'une naissance commune, elle se trouva flattée d'avoir fait la conquête d'un amant tel que moi" (p. 22) (The prestige she can offer in counterpart is erotic--"Je m'applaudissais d'être aimé d'une fille que tout le monde trouvait aimable" [p. 126]--and indirectly related to her high commodity value on the market place.) In contrast, Manon "is" not "someone," she is only "called something"; just this once, he calls her *Mademoiselle*: "Mademoiselle Manon Lescaut, c'est ainsi qu'elle me dit qu'on la nommait" (p. 21).[12] Nobles have no forenames in this novel; Manon's is a diminutive form, which no noble except perhaps an infant would use. Passion could not be an appropriate response to such a "girl," however beguiling, and this explains the cutting double sarcasm of Des Grieux's father when he mocks his son's "princess" (p. 34).[13]

The logic of the first brief scene does not apparently anticipate a second: that is, since Renoncour knows that, for whatever strange causes, the young man is bound for America, he scarcely expects him ever to reappear. The second time Des Grieux is encountered therefore, in Calais, the situation is pregnant with drama even before any new data are revealed. Although Manon is not so much as mentioned until his *histoire* proper commences, the fact that he is alone, and that he is in a port city looking poor and drained after a presumably unsuccessful voyage to America, is enough to reinforce the effect of what is already known and set up his narrative, which must necessarily be one of misfortune. Des Grieux's audience of two henceforth remains dimly in the background, reappearing in the first person only briefly at the conclusion of part one.[14]

Now Des Grieux's voice, like Renoncour's, is a marked kind of voice, and some commentators have felt that it dominates rather too much. One can imagine Manon's telling a different version of the events, or for that matter a third person's supplying a different story altogether which could still leave intact Renoncour's opening scenes. But that is beside the point, since we are concerned with what the text actually is. Des Grieux's whole outlook is socially determined, first of all; he is always aware of being able to command more respect than can Manon, and of sharing this quality with his listeners in the novel. What is to him a "simple" life includes a carriage (p. 49); and even when happy, he and she have separate apartments because this is how the properly rich live: in their misery in New Orleans they will have a valet and chambermaid (p. 189)!

In the second place, Des Grieux's narration is suffused throughout with a rhetoric of persuasion, the chief avenue of which is emotive. That this is intentional on his part is clear at the outset; even though he must identify himself as a bad example, he concedes, "je suis sûr qu'en me condamnant, vous ne pourrez pas vous empêcher de me plaindre" (p. 16). Many of the classical rhetorical touches, in a work which is not as a whole highly figured, are subordinated to this end, as Des Grieux attempts to place his hearers in a position where they cannot deny him sympathy without at the same time assuming negative connotations upon themselves:

Un barbare aurait été attendri des témoignages de ma douleur et de ma crainte. [p. 30]

Où trouver un barbare qu'un repentir si vif et si tendre n'eût pas touché? [p. 47]

Il n'est pas besoin de m'aimer autant que vous faites pour en être
attendri. [to Tiberge, p. 59]

Vous êtes bon, vous aurez pitié de moi. [to the superior of Saint-
Lazare, p. 86]

It can be easily seen, when such passages as this are juxtaposed, how
insidious (and compelling) is the rhetoric, which puts all the good
sentiments on one side: with exception of his father and Tiberge, Des
Grieux's enemies have no good motives, or even qualities. He appears to be
asking as a basic condition from his listener not prejudice in his favor but
only a minimum of humanity: "Mais il aurait fallu que j'eusse perdu tous
sentiments d'humanité pour m'endurcir contre tant de charmes" (p. 143).
With that term *charmes*, however, he has permitted himself to slip, as he
does frequently, from one register to another: in principle, "humanity"
should be sensitive to things like suffering, not to "charms," which carries
us into the rhetoric of love, which we shall have a further look at later on. It
can operate through much the same mechanism, but depends also for its
effect upon another, highly structured code. For example: "Donnez-moi un
amant qui n'entre point aveuglément dans tous les caprices d'une maîtresse
adorée, et je conviendrai que j'eus tort de céder si facilement" (p. 129).

Des Grieux admits in numerous instances, moreover, that he has
always effectively slanted things "du côté le plus favorable" (p. 86). He
knows he is good with words and able to manipulate sentiments provided
they are "good" (that is, favorably inclined) to begin with. There are even
times when his own terms suggest that his posturing strains the bounds of
sincerity, that other marked virtue to which his discourse lays claim. One is
tempted, for example, to see something subtly willful in the verb of the
sentence "Je *laissai tomber* quelques larmes en finissant ces paroles" (p.
163), particularly since what follows recognizes the forensic effect achieved:
"[mon père] fut si touché *du tour que j'avais donné* à mes excuses qu'il ne
fut pas le maître de me cacher ce changement"--and his father essentially
surrenders by saying, "tu me fais pitié." Each such success is confirmation
of the justice of all the others. To the concierge of the Hôpital: "vous
marquez de la compassion" (p. 167); of M. de T...: "il me plaignit
beaucoup" (p. 68); to Renoncour himself: "Votre pitié . . . fut ma seule
recommendation" (p. 182).

It is therefore quite possible to maintain that the entire Des Grieux narrative which constitutes the main body of *Manon Lescaut* is merely one further instance of the contrived distortions with which he has related his story numerous times in the past, and no truer than they: why then should we trust him now?[15] The principal objection to this is that no scientific control is possible: there is no autonomous "story" for Des Grieux to pervert. In other words, the reader cannot construct the referential world of the novel on any basis other than Des Grieux's narrative, by which the events of his story are not imitated, but created.[16] To assert even that he has formerly been guilty of slanting it, one can only draw upon the evidence of what he says now: insofar as it identifies their deviations, the present recital in some obvious sense corrects the earlier instances to which it alludes. The reader really has no choice but to "believe" Des Grieux. The alternative is to react subjectively to his account, independently of the text (reading "between the lines") which, although it may itself in a limited manner authorize scepticism, offers no substitute for the data supplied. If one can, for instance, dismiss the motive given by Des Grieux for a particular action, one could equally well--but equally gratuitously--deny the action itself, inasmuch as we have only his word for it that it transpired at all: but in both cases, we have nothing to put in the place of what we are offered, no true story to reëstablish. For all we know, Des Grieux may have concocted the whole adventure, but there is no way to read the *text* on this hypothesis. The way Des Grieux formulates the key to the action--"Manon était passionnée pour le plaisir; je l'étais pour elle" (p. 50)--may not appear satisfactory when measured against some putative "Manon" or "Des Grieux" imagined quasi-historically. But it is the truth of this narrative.

Manon, who not only cannot speak for herself but is infrequently quoted directly, can be perceived by the reader only in ways inherently limited by others' representations. Renoncour himself saw her only once, found her modest, sweet, and charming, and concluded on "le caractère incompréhensible des femmes." Now this word *incompréhensible*, which occurs only here and is not spoken by Des Grieux, has great force by virtue of its location, and has exerted an inordinate influence on all discussions of her "character." Des Grieux for his part never says that Manon is incomprehensible. On the contrary; although her first betrayal is an "enigma" to him (p. 31), and he cannot quite identify her motives when she returns much later (p. 43), he repeatedly insists, early as well as late in the narration, on her transparency: "je ne connaissais pas mieux mon coeur que le sien" (p. 28); "j'ai toujours été persuadé qu'elle était sincère" (p. 110);

"elle est légère et imprudente, mais elle est droite et sincère" (p. 148). He has no doubt whatever, in the face of certain specific situations, how she will react: "Je compris tout d'un coup à quels nouveaux malheurs j'allais me trouver exposé; l'indigence était le moindre. Je connaissais Manon" (p. 53). To him this is the operation of a mechanism which, when particular conditions are fulfilled, empties Manon of all identity: Manon in need "n'était plus rien, et elle ne se reconnaissait pas elle-même" (p. 110). She thus appears as a sort of function without any essense; she cannot, for example, feel "guilty," she can only say, "Il faut bien que je sois coupable, puisque j'ai pu vous causer tant de douleur et d'émotion" (p. 142). This is not to deny Des Grieux's ambivalence towards this person who, at least until the American episode, cannot be brought to share his sense of intense devotion. He can only be flattered, not only by her attentions, but by her great desirability in others' eyes. But she is too much at home in the quantitative world of pleasure to be totally immobilized by someone who, he says, has but love and constancy to offer (p. 137). There is even an unaccustomed brutality in one judgment where he exclaims about her "grossièreté de sentiments" (p. 70).

Thus the whole tradition, inherited from the Romantics, of Manon as the very type of the mysterious woman if not indeed of the femme fatale, and this precisely because she cannot be perceived directly but only via her lover's words, finds no textual confirmation whatever in Des Grieux's actual discourse. It may be replied that he nevertheless presents us with a Manon who seems not to coincide perfectly with his analyses of her, who does not always confirm the knowledge of her he believes he possesses. Doubtless, Manon is pragmatic in a way that he is not, and his love poetry has little purchase on her motivations. His inattention to detail certainly makes it difficult to assess the degree of her duplicity and betrayal.[17] If this is so, then to that degree she could be called mysterious, intangible, or whatever, but that argument would need to be formulated more cogently than it has been so far.

Indeed Manon has been described by one critic as perfectly intelligible in the light of a social situation which poses her an essential choice between prostitution and the convent; she always acts in function of a basic fear of want.[18] To me it is doubtful that such a characterization of her role can escape the accusation of oversimplification. Manon's brother makes it clear that her idea of misery begins with the loss of her carriage (p. 70); the adventure of the young G... M... starts up at a point when Des Grieux affirms that she is lacking in nothing (p. 127). And especially, the one document where she does ostensibly speak for herself on the question is worrisomely suspect. After they are robbed in Chaillot, it is true, she exclaims "Nous sommes perdus!" and panics, striking out within a day in search of better fortunes. But the letter to Des Grieux explaining her intentions is somewhat hyperbolic: "Crois-tu qu'on puisse être bien tendre lorsqu'on manque de pain? La faim me causerait quelque méprise fatale; je rendrais quelque jour le dernier soupir, en croyant en pousser un d'amour. Je t'adore, compte là-dessus; mais laisse-moi, pour quelque temps, le ménagement de notre fortune" (p. 69). Without doubting that she is asking for time ("Je travaille . . .") to serve eventually their common interests, it is difficult to argue here that Manon can confuse dying of love with dying of hunger, which, as far as anyone knows, she has never really been threatened with. Dying of love, besides, is a heroic (and literary) notion that one could not expect to make much real sense to her. She therefore appears to have some investment in a rhetoric of her own, which compromises the picture of her as a lovely urchin on the brink of starvation.

On Manon as a sexual creature we glean rather more information from her other escapades than we do from Des Grieux's reticent descriptions. To be sure he recognizes the existence of desire, even the rather tempestuous one which propels them into their first hotel; but there are only veiled, even equivocal references to their private pleasures: "[j'étais] le seul . . . qui pût lui faire goûter parfaitement les douceurs de l'amour" (p. 61); "nous étions dans le délire du plaisir" (p. 151). And, as has frequently been mentioned in the past, there is something evanescent, abstract about the body of Manon.[19] In part this may be a function of Des Grieux's rhetoric, which emphasizes spiritual over carnal experience. It might also be regarded as an aspect of the text's tendency to stress their common immaturity--they are enough alike to pass as cousins (p. 21), "deux enfants" (p. 25), and brother and sister (p. 71)--rather than their adult vigor.

A correlative of aristocracy is "noble" sentiment; one who is well-born can combine in one breath "la délicatesse de mes sentiments et l'agrément de mes manières" (p. 47), and Renoncour bases his moral explanations in the "Avis" on the generous penchant of "les âmes bien nées." Nobility does not always imply virtue, but virtue implies nobility.[20] Both qualities attach to M. de T...: as "un homme qui a du monde [=social sophistication] et des sentiments," he embraces Des Grieux "sans autre raison que la bonté de nos coeurs, et une simple disposition qui porte un homme tendre et généreux à aimer un autre homme qui lui ressemble" (pp. 100-101). Des Grieux's own sensitivity on the one hand and his sense of noble privilege on the other are closely coordinated; he is willing to accept punishment from heaven--which after all is a grandiose and tragic thing--but withers in despair that it should come at the hands of a "malheureux coquin" like G... M... (p. 156). There is a refinement and elevation of spirit which extends in part to Manon as well: "Nous avons reçu de l'esprit, du goût, des sentiments" (p. 157); but the higher virtues such as fidelity and force of character escape her comprehension. Sentiment is doubtless a somewhat ambiguous category, representing a more fundamental truth than birth, but usually presupposing it nevertheless.

Noble feelings do not descend to grubby matters such as money, by which they can only be tainted. This coincides, in Des Grieux's mind, with that other important "noble" sentiment, love: "rien n'est plus désespérant, pour un amant délicat, que de se voir ramené...à la grossièreté des âmes les plus basses" (p. 109). To him the quest for funds is humiliating, and only a language of passion, on the one hand, and a somewhat forced ironic distance ("*mal* en argent . . . cette fâcheuse espèce de *maladie*" [p. 109]) make it possible for him to cope with it at all. His sarcasm regarding the "honorable marché" concluded with G... M... (p. 68) suggests the repugnance not only of what transpired but of the world of material exchange in general.

In one sense, of course, all this is part of an ideological posturing by which Des Grieux can excuse weakness in the name of extreme sensitivity and crime in the name of passion. He is not necessarily, for all that, "insincere."[21] In a remarkable passage, he analyzes the parallel between this exclusive concept of sensitivity on the one hand, and that of sensory impression on the other:

> *Le commun des hommes* n'est sensible qu'à cinq ou six passions, dans le cercle desquelles leur vie se passe, et où toutes leurs agitations se réduisent. Otez-leur l'amour et la haine, le plaisir et la douleur, l'espérance et la crainte, ils ne sentent plus rien. Mais *les personnes d'un caractère plus noble* peuvent être remuées de *mille* façons différentes; *il semble qu'elles aient plus de cinq sens, et qu'elles puissent recevoir des idé*es et des sensations qui passent les bornes ordinaires de la nature; et comme elles ont un sentiment *de cette grandeur qui les élève au-dessus du vulgaire*, il n'y a rien dont elles soient plus jalouses. De là vient qu'elles souffrent si impatiemment le mépris et la risée, et que la honte est une de leurs plus violentes passions.
>
> [p. 81]

Sentiment thus enters, by analogy, the domain of natural history, and scientific language lends its weight to the qualitative explanation of Des Grieux's exceptional character and destiny. The terminology evidences the admixture of purely affective and genetically or socially determined components. And there is some confusion among *intensity* of sentiment, on which he insists rather more elsewhere, the *strangeness* of sentiments previously unexperienced, and their *complexity*. It is life which appears unworthy of Des Grieux's noble aspirations, because the perspective of the narration necessarily valorizes only the latter, leaving the reader all but bound to experience events in the same (verbal) manner as he does.

To Des Grieux's father, the only sentiment that really counts is paternal/filial affection, and it is firmly subordinated to a much higher sense of honor, or more exactly of social duty. In fact, despite the anxiety his son's disappearance caused, the reproaches addressed to him are not, at first, particularly awesome: he went off without permission, and imprudently committed himself to someone unknown (p. 32). The whole thing is merely a "petite aventure," good for a chastising laugh, and his son a great dupe. It may be a "triste comédie" for Des Grieux, who cannot communicate his passion to his family, but to them he is playing a somewhat ridiculous hero of tragi-comedy. This in itself does not bring on his imprisonment; it is only by his obstinacy in drawing attention to his own recidivous intention that he incurs this precautionary restriction.

The conduct he has been guilty of is simply, in this light, *désordre* (p. 34), a pivotal concept in the novel in that its very presence as a signifier implies the salutary existence of order; *dés-ordre* as disjunction foreshadows a remedy, which is a return to the norm. To *désordre* and *folie* (p. 33) are opposed *guérison* (p. 38), *conversion* (p. 42). Disorder is a temporary and rectifiable deviation, an *égarement* ("Le poison du plaisir vous a fait *écarter* du chemin" [p. 39]) best treated by a competent authority: the father, from the standpoint of social standing and honor; Tiberge, from that of religion and virtue. In time, though, the term *désordre* takes on a more somber coloration (cf. pp. 59-60) as it comes to signify willful disobedience and rejection of right counsel. "Quel remède," his father finally asks, "contre un mal qui augmente tous les jours, tel que les désordres d'un fils vicieux qui a perdu tous sentiments d'honneur?" (p. 162).

Words such as honor do not merely represent "false" values artificially imposed on Des Grieux; it is important to realize that he does not escape his birth, and has internalized them himself. He has no desire to be "la fable de toutes les personnes de ma connaissance, et la *honte* de ma famille" (p. 81) because he too is sensitive to this *honte*. The centripetal force acting on him in opposition to disruptive, centrifugal *désordre* is that of *devoir*. It speaks of a return--*re*calls him literally[22]--to a state of assurance and security which cannot be had in the midst of disorder, where its muted voice occasionally beckons in rare moments of relative calm, and Des Grieux casts his eyes nostalgically towards the distant points which topologically symbolize his former innocence--Amiens, the parental home, Saint-Sulpice (p. 72). "Rentrer doucement dans le devoir" (p. 31) is precisely the condition of his grace, just as it is later when his disorder has become more serious.

The actual, unwilling return to P..., the family domain, is a highly-charged symbolic voyage, in which Des Grieux must retrace his steps through Saint-Denis, undoing the clandestine journey with Manon and, for complete irony, sleeping (this time with three lackeys to guard him) in the same hotel. The extent of the revolution he undergoes in the following months is considerable; he dreams of an idyllic calm which suppresses desire: "je m'occuperai de l'étude et de la religion, qui ne me permettront point de penser aux dangereux plaisirs de l'amour" (p. 40). Love is replaced by the asexuating force of friendship. His joy during his subsequent stay in the seminary, and his inclination for the study in particular of St. Augustine, show how disposed he is basically for the life of denial; he is not even tempted during this absence by the thought of Manon, whom he has all but forgotten (p. 43). But the doors of the seminary are open onto the world, and Manon finds them, precipitating the most dramatized scene in the novel.

Its pivotal position is first underscored by the heavy accents with which Des Grieux builds up to it, culminating in a rare extended metaphor on his own recidivous version of the original Fall: "un instant malheureux me fit *retomber* dans le *précipice*, et ma *chute* fut d'autant plus irréparable, que me trouvant tout d'un coup au même degré de *profondeur* d'où j'étais sorti, les nouveaux désordres où je tombai me portèrent bien plus loin vers *le fond de l'abîme*." Although he will go from anger to tenderness, then to lyrical abandon in the course of the interview (pp. 44-47), it begins with a stunned silence comparable to his dumbstruck passivity when he was captured earlier in Paris: "Le désordre de mon âme ne saurait être exprimé." This is not, to be sure, the only occasion on which Des Grieux evokes ineffably or unnameably intense feelings, but it is the only one in which the very essence of being appears so scrambled:

Quel passage, en effet, de la situation tranquille où j'avais été,
aux mouvements *tumultueux* que je sentais renaître! J'en étais
*épouvanté*. Je *frémissais*, comme il arrive lorsqu'on se trouve la
nuit dans une campagne écartée: on se croit transporté dans *un
nouvel order de choses*; on y est saisi d'une *horreur secrète*, dont
on ne se remet qu'après avoir considéré longtemps tous les
environs. [p. 45]

I insist upon the function of this passage here, not to analyze it anew, but
because it has become so celebrated--particularly through the influence of
Georges Poulet[23]--that one forgets to replace it in its narrative context as a
proof of the exceptional violence of this one particular moment in Des
Grieux's experience with Manon. It is associated in the text with other key
passages--also usually quoted in isolation--which modify and reinforce it.
Confusion invades his terminology, upsetting the neatness of the separate
categories of love and religion which had brought peace to his life, and
creating a spontaneous, phantasmagoric spiritualization of sensuality:
"Chère Manon! lui dis-je, avec un mélange profane d'expressions amoureuses
et théologiques, tu es trop *adorable* pour une *créature*. Je me sens le coeur
emporté par une *délectation* victorieuse." The expression is similar to
Tartuffe's in his attempted subornation of Emilie, but the context is
entirely different and the effect is almost sacrilegious. And this is the precise
point at which Des Grieux receives the sudden, spectacular revelation not
only of his destiny but of a certain kind of sanctimonious lie he has been
living: "Tout ce qu'on dit de la liberté à Saint-Sulpice est une chimère."
Now it is significant that he says this here and not at the time of their first
flight: then, the situation was not yet irreversible; this time, there is a
surrender on his part that cannot be undone. When he is next imprisoned, at
Saint-Lazare, he will not spend six months studying as he did before, but
two months bemoaning his fate. Peace can no longer return to his soul.

It is worth recognizing, though, that in the adventures, however
inexorable, that follow, there are many touches of lightness and even
comedy. It is doubtless appropriate to integrate this fact with the broad
literary movement in the direction of drawing both on traditionally high and
low styles, as Auerbach notably has done,[24] but what interests us most is its
thematic value here. There are elements which come straight from stage
farce: the father's pleasantries about cuckoldry (p. 33); Des Grieux's puns
about sex ("nos deux chairs se touchent de bien proche") and Manon's
departure from the room "sous prétexte d'un besoin" (p. 77); his leaving the

prison without his britches (p. 105). Not only is there much gay laughter from time to time, but many events are characterized in stage terminology: "triste comédie" (p. 34), "ridicule scène" (p. 77), "une scène fort agréable" (p. 129), "une scène bien affligeante" (p. 144).[25] And Manon shows obvious thesbian leanings, notably in the Italian prince episode at the beginning of part two (the staging of which, however, makes Des Grieux uncomfortable), and in their spontaneous repartee based on parodied quotation of Racine (p. 130). But what is all this theatre, and particularly comedy, doing in so tragic a narration? Briefly, I think there are two major effects. One, on the level of diction and representation, has to do of course with the tragic itself. Since Des Grieux's story is billed as the unfolding of a destiny, its emphasis falls on a few critical moments, all of which are laden with both present and future consequences. Yet the plot is not strictly linear, it is more of a broken line of ups and downs. The levity of occasional scenes provides relief in terms of rhythm, tone, and irony, all of which are useful in modulating the tragic impetus. There is a content function too, though, that is often overlooked: these scenes document the less obvious side of Des Grieux's experience, namely its joy. Mere repeated affirmations of happiness with Manon would seem pale beside the continual melodramatic punctuation, and such episodes therefore support our realization that life with Manon was not just ecstatic but spontaneous, lively, even jovial--and a bit fragile.

The heavy accent on destiny translates as inevitable many events which are only marginally credible. The narrative passes rapidly over such gross *invraisemblances* in detail as the fortuitous fact that Des Grieux's own valet opens the door to the younger G... M...'s house (p. 140), and that a man of M. de T...'s station suggests to Des Grieux the kidnapping of his friend G... M... (p. 149). In fact Des Grieux's action follows the characteristically comic pattern of repeated, incorrigeable blunders. But it is notable that, although he understates the degree to which he exacerbates his own plight, he does admit strategic errors: "Je sentis aussitôt la faute que j'avais commise" (p. 153). In particular, there are two with respect to his father: one in not having pled early on in favor of a marriage with Manon (p. 72), and the other in failing to exploit fully his victory at the Châtelet in order to have her included in his pardon (p. 164). In a way, such concessions compromise the inexorable workings of fortune. But destiny, in narrative, is only a question of perspective, and not always a perfectly consistent one at that.

The role of death in this novel illustrates this further. Traditionally, and tragically, a destiny implies eventual death.[26] But not for Des Grieux, to whom it leads only to the grief over someone else's death. And yet it is not *her* destiny which is delineated, but his. Without depreciating the central importance of Manon's death, one can see insofar as he alone is concerned a certain reduction of death as reality. He plays at times with the notion, in rather routinely emphatic rhetorical patterns: "j'étais disposé à souffrir . . . la mort la plus cruelle" (p. 59). But this is also a veiled threat addressed to Tiberge, with even a hint of suicide; hyperbole and blackmail are hard to distinguish. Similarly, when he tells Manon, "vous allez signer ma mort" (p. 144), and when he prophesies to his father of "ma mort, que vous apprendrez bientôt" (p. 172), death of anguish and death by a reckless act or suicide are equally implied. His evocations of death are poetic but objectively somewhat facile. In his father's house (p. 36), exactly as on Manon's tomb much later (p. 200), he thinks that in order to call death to his aid it is enough to throw himself down in despair. He always expects death to come easily; he thinks he is dying every time he faints. Again, though, it is not properly speaking a problem of sincerity: this is all a part of the way he interprets and represents his life.

That he does not have to die is of course central to the structure of the narrative. The forces acting on him have always been different from those acting on Manon. Civically speaking, there is little difference in the nature of the offenses they commit, but an enormous one in the consequences for each. The lieutenant at the Châtelet is perfectly justified in implying that Des Grieux's undoing has less to do with his crimes than with his incredibly poor judgment. Even though he is perhaps weaker than she, he was never as vulnerable, and Simone Delesalle has been right, I think, although she has overstated the case, in drawing attention to what it means in this novel to be *né*, to have a protective father, to be treated like a wayward child.[27] To take one example among many, Des Grieux in the presence of the superior of Saint-Lazare, whom he can call "mon Père," weeps "comme un enfant" (p. 86). Manon never enjoys any of the same indulgences; "quand on n'est pas *né*," writes Delesalle, "on n'a pas d'âge et l'on n'est jamais un enfant."[28] On the other hand, this is not the whole of the matter, for Manon is disadvantaged not just caste-wise but sex-wise as well. That is, the notion of privilege, which attaches of course to nobility, also accompanies the distinction of being male; as a function of this difference also he is judged less harshly than she. No woman, whatever her station in life, could be forgiven as easily for the same conduct as is Des Grieux; conversely there was no masculine counterpart for the expedition of prostitutes to the islands. Manon remains tinged to a considerable degree with the sin of Eve: woman is responsible for man's wrongdoing, and he cannot be recuperated for the good cause until she has been banished.

Des Grieux and his father in fact grope toward compromise, although such hope is illusory. It is less obvious today than it was in Prévost's time why this is so. Certainly, as Des Grieux himself says, the problem is not that having a public mistress is unexampled or even unpermitted. It is rather that he can neither be allowed to marry Manon nor to live with her in defiance of his other social obligations (*devoir*).[29] And we must not forget that even had his father been inexplicably open-minded about this in principle, the original betrayal of Manon has demonstrated to his satisfaction, once and for all, that she is a perfectly unexceptional and unworthy girl of the streets. How could he possibly have thought otherwise? Only in fantasy can Des Grieux imagine an accommodation which will satisfy both himself and his father, and in addition provide income to satisfy Manon (p. 114). When the elder Des Grieux arrives at the Châtelet, he is in fact extremely indulgent and moreover has no desire, whatever the nature of the offenses, to see a son of his stay in jail. But he is happy to be rid of Manon: otherwise, he says, he would rather see Des Grieux dead (p. 171). Indeed Des Grieux *père* and G... M... *père* have little in common besides their reaction to Manon. Obviously she has no trial, no legal sentence; by the same token, there is no legal recourse to save her. Only influence would prevail here too, but it cannot be obtained; Des Grieux's final emotional appeal to his father hits a stone wall and the really last resort--saying that Manon is like mother--is a disaster (pp. 171-72). Patricide is envisioned ("Mon père même eût à peine été respecté, dans une vengeance qui me paraissait si juste" [p. 167]), and discarded principally because it will do nothing to help Manon.

Des Grieux's resolution to follow Manon to New Orleans, and thereby renounce almost all social prerogatives and, more importantly, sever all family ties, is a desperate one (p. 176), a point of no return. But with it, what is first a temptation of suicide--"mourons au Havre" (p. 182)-- gives way to a lyrical vision of happiness. Added to this more thorough sense of commitment is an interesting and highly significant *déclassement*, as Des Grieux spontaneously converts into a bourgeois, closely guarding what little money remains to him as a capital for "le fondement de notre fortune et de nos espérances en Amérique" (p. 183). The events of the New World, although it provides respite from their troubles at first, and the theatre for their new relationship, make it clear that social imperatives have not truly been left behind. Although Des Grieux and Manon can live virtuously there, their attempted marriage shows that they still cannot do so according to social forms, which are those of the Old World. Social cleavage is practically eliminated, yet in the last analysis the family link to power, in the form of Synnelet's claim on Manon through his uncle, recreates the defenseless status of one whose only ultimate right is to serve as an object of desire.[30] God himself seems to reject the obeisance they offer Him, but "c'était sur elle que devait tomber toute la colère du Ciel et la rage de nos ennemis" (p. 194). As this sentence suggests, there is no way to distinguish divine from human intervention; God and the social forces are allies--or, put more abstractly, the gods are social, and overwhelm the unprotected.

A genuine communication seems to have finally been established in this interval between Manon and Des Grieux; it has been noted that she is more frequently quoted in her own voice in this section of the novel. But then, as everything about them suddenly comes unwound, a kind of language dysfunction accompanies Manon's death. For as this "fille délicate" (p. 181) feebly whispers that she is at her last hour, Des Grieux curiously takes this as mere hyperbole, to be largely discounted: "Je ne pris d'abord ce discours que pour un langage ordinaire dans l'infortune" (p. 199), and his own actions at the same time become bizarrely confused with metaphors. "J'échauffai ses mains par mes baisers ardents et par la chaleur de mes soupirs": by interference of the figural and the literal, the tokens of love (baisers, soupirs) absorb as it were the non-metaphoric signified of the conventional trope (ardents, chaleur) and oddly emit heat (échauffer).[31] Also, language transforms this quiet extinction into a complicated death dance. Manon is "à-demi morte" before their flight, is revived ("ma présence la ranima"), then dies again ("elle tomba sans connaissance") only once more to be brought to by someone who is now himself "à-demi mort" (p. 196). Although the narrator speaks of "un récit qui me tue" (p. 199), it is--literally--Manon whom it kills. Finally, he traverses a quasi-death ("sans apparence de vie") on the road back to life.

There are two stories in Manon Lescaut, told simultaneously: a tragedy of passion, and a morality about a prodigal son who returns home. They essentially call for different kinds of terminology, which are woven together here; and this creates the fundamental tension in the text.

Tragedy and passion are of course distinguishable components as well, but in literary tradition they were hardly incompatible. The sense of tragedy is sustained throughout by reminders of Des Grieux's high birth, the pure and elevated diction (often compared to Racine's), and the leitmotif of fate which is first manifested in love and then operates through the mechanism of a plot which grinds inexorably toward Manon's death. Predictions abound because of the way the narrative is cast; that is, Manon is *already* dead when Des Grieux begins: the future, by him who tells, has already been seen. Causality is everywhere, and paradoxically: linkage of one thing to another stresses the inescapablilty of what transpires, but it seems to operate in a minor key, like what was called in events of state *la petite histoire*: great events have petty causes. In marked contrast to classical norms, less than noble thoughts and actions are caught up in this movement; card sharking, for instance, becomes a "cruel" necessity (p. 62). Des Grieux's sustained grandiloquence, in particular the repeated exclamations and tragic epithets, makes everything a cog in the infernal machine. Evident in particular is his use of superlative phrases, with a notably high incidence of the pattern: *le plus* + [adjective] + *de tous les* + [noun]. Referring to himself, Des Grieux is heard to vary the same rigid formula: "le plus infortuné (p. 13)/malheureux (p. 25)/misérable (p. 167) de tous les hommes." The only time it is applied to Manon, it is used with significantly different adjectives: *volage, perfide* (p. 36). The plot itself is "la plus étrange aventure qui soit jamais arrivée à un homme de ma naissance et de ma fortune" (p. 110), "le plus cruel de tous les sorts" (p. 180), and his story in consequence "le plus horrible de tous les récits" (p. 33). but there are many other occurences.

All this relates of course to a certain way of representing events which accentuates the affective, investing the essential truth in feeling and draining raw facts of their indicative value. It is part of this strategy to make his most serious offenses appear trivial, his crimes "friponneries." Since his murder of the servant at Saint-Lazare was not willful and heroic, it must seem inconsequential, unconscious, unintended, un-"true" as an act of the "real" Des Grieux--who alone seems to have imagined that guns are not for killing.[32] What always counts is sentiment, whose intensity is expressed, as Jean Sgard has observed, like an act of faith.[33] Even when the sentiment has no name ("j'ignore encore aujourd'hui par quelle espèce de sentiments je fus alors agité" [p. 69]), the scrutiny brought to bear on it serves to impose it on the reader's attention.

The history of commentary on *Manon Lescaut* makes it clear that most readers fall in empathetically with the rhetoric, highly artificial though it is and in ways whose literariness belies its supposedly oral essence.[34] Des Grieux's discourse abounds in mythical allusions and heroic tropes, varying from light to pompous. Manon is Amour itself (pp. 44, 135), whose presence makes G... M...'s apartment a temple (p. 140). Several other figures are based on similar classical references:

Vénus et la Fortune n'avaient point d'esclaves plus heureux et plus tendres. [p. 66]

Le glaive était suspendu sur nos têtes. Le fil qui le soutenait allait se rompre. [p. 151]

Et puis, tu es une chimiste admirable, ajoutai-je en l'embrassant, tu transformes tout en or. [p. 187]

Objectively speaking, Manon's alchemy works in the opposite direction and makes gold disappear; Des Grieux has recourse to such gallant hyperbole because he is reduced to living in a hovel, which rhetoric alone promotes to a "palais digne du premier roi du monde" (p. 188). These tropes have the effect of lifting events into a higher and literary plane; stylized phrases such as "nous abordâmes enfin au rivage désiré" (p. 184), besides contrasting frequently with the earthly situations to which they apply, are full of epico-tragic connotations. (One of the most original details in Des Grieux's role as lover is his intention to publish his amorous commentary on Virgil [p. 38], which makes him the virtual inventor of a new genre.) The tone is further sustained by the continual epithetic quality of such adjectives, in Manon's case, as *douce, charmante, tendre, belle.*

A given utterance can participate in more than one code at once, and those of destiny and of love, in particular, often overlap. For one thing, destiny itself in this story (as in many others) takes the form of love: "l'aveuglement d'un *amour fatal*" (p. 61); and this association pervades even more banal figures like "je lis ma destinée dans tes beaux yeux" (p. 46). Love can be neither foreseen nor resisted: "destin . . . dont il est aussi impossible à la vertu de se défendre qu'il l'a été à la sagesse de [le] prévoir" (p. 59). It paralyzes will, but not lucidity: "c'est mon devoir d'agir comme je raisonne! mais l'action est-elle en mon pouvoir?" (p. 93). And loss of freedom entails abrogation of guilt. But one should not in any case exaggerate Des Grieux's sense of guilt, which he is capable of shrugging with lyrical abandon: "on se trouve emporté tout d'un coup loin de son devoir, sans se trouver capable de la moindre résistance, et *sans ressentir le moindre remords*" (pp. 42-43). This is one of Des Grieux's most remarkable statements, not just because it implicitly denies the efficacy of free will and grace, but because it rejects conscience of sin while laying claim to complete spiritual fulfillment.

The rhetoric of love operates in powerful but subtle manners; probably no code of discourse is so pervasive in literature, and so insidious even when it is an explicit motif. It is the basis of the manipulations by which Des Grieux attributes his own criminality to forces outside himself: "Par quelle *fatalité* suis-je devenu si *criminel*? *L'amour est une passion innocente*; comment s'est-il changé, pour moi, en une source de misères et de désordres?" (p. 72). How can the pure become impure?[35] And what is the guarantee of its purity? It bears noting that "L'amour est une passion innocente" is not in the nature of a neutral assertion which a reader is free to accept or reject. It is more like an axiom underlying the entire narration, resting on centuries of tradition, and one cannot read the text without it. Only by subjectively standing outside the text and denying Des Grieux in toto can one depreciate it. It is full of ramifications, but they are difficult to identify because they operate invisibly and not in the manner of a syllogism. Straightforward logic, as the quotation shows, immediately runs amok. Montesquieu's often-quoted characterization of the protagonists as a rascal and a whore is too often separated from the rest of his commentary which explains the book's huge appeal by the fact that "toutes les actions du héros, le chevalier des Grieux, ont pour motif l'amour, qui est toujours un motif noble, quoique la conduite soit basse."[36] This is less the affirmation on his part of a value judgement than a recognition of the intransigence of a literary code: *love is always a noble motive*. And Des Grieux in love does not have to depend for exoneration merely on his own specious rationalizations: he inherits the benefit of language and ideological patterns which privilege the love interest.

Love is a socially disruptive force in *Manon Lescaut* because it violates a hierarchical taboo: it degrades Des Grieux socially by causing him to do things unworthy of his rank and offensive to honor and duty. Nevertheless it is always noble, and sentimentally it both redeems his social degradation and raises Manon to his level: if there is any doubt about this, it is only to the extent that Manon's love can itself be impugned. Much of the regal terminology in the book is tied in with this double movement. On the one hand, it makes of Des Grieux a king who has abdicated in order to acceed to a celestial realm: "Aussi mépriserais-je tous les empires du monde . . . pour m'assurer le bonheur d'être aimé d'elle" (p. 104). And on the other, it promotes Manon to princess: "un coeur dont vous étiez la souveraine absolue" (p. 45); "une créature toute charmante, qui eût occupé le premier trône du monde, si tous les hommes eussent eu mes yeux et mon coeur!" (p. 79).[37] Now gallantry is one thing, but Des Grieux slides easily from such light talk to exalted literalism, and builds up to the disarmingly simple transformation of her into a goddess in what has always passed for one of the novel's most sublime phrases: "cette figure capable de ramener l'univers à l'idolâtrie" (p. 178).

Even though nothing in Des Grieux's story, according to him, is commonplace, acceptance by the reader of its rhetorical strategy depends upon the smooth functioning of commonplaces, particularly insofar as this subject is concerned. Despite the emphasis he places on his personal experience, he does not have to go out of his way to explain what it means to be enflamed by love, nor the rapture that leaves him speechless (pp. 19-21). The point is not that the reader knows these things from his own life, but that he knows the code; he will understand what the narrator means irrespective of private analogies. Similarly, Des Grieux does not have to justify the logic of declarations such as "estimer une chose plus que ma vie n'est pas une raison pour l'estimer autant que Manon" (p. 112), which he can invoke as if they were self-evident truths. "Tout l'univers n'est-il pas la patrie de deux amants fidèles? Ne trouvent-ils pas l'un dans l'autre, père, mère, parents, amis, richesses et félicité?" (p. 180). Experience, to be sure, often deflates such certainties and even turns some of them bitterly ironic. "Elle me tient lieu de gloire, de bonheur et de fortune" (p. 112) is a metaphorical truth in terms of the love code, and a literal falsity or counter-truth (particularly with regard to "fortune"). In like vein, true love, one of whose topoi is idyllic, isolated bliss at the ends of the earth, endorses Manon's claim, even though figurative, to be willing to follow Des Grieux "au bout du monde" (p. 144); but the actual event finds Des Grieux instead following her "jusqu'à l'extrémité du monde" (p. 179).

To say that a premise like "l'amour est une passion innocente" in no way operates in the reading as a strange or incomprehensible affirmation does not make it universally valid. It would never occur to anyone in Racine, for example, to assert that love is innocent. In this, the text of

*Manon Lescaut* is firmly aligned with a relatively new tendency in the code to qualify passion as a source of pleasure rather than just pain.[38] "J'étais *heureux* pour toute ma vie, si Manon m'eût été fidèle" (p. 25) sounds like a statement of fact, whereas it is highly relative; if this is not immediately evident, that is only because it is such a strongly coded message. Obviously this sentence bears a secondary, predictive message in the narrative by its negative implication ("*si* Manon . . ."), but it also biases the whole sense of the situation in function of a fixed discourse about love modified by a romantic happiness. There is never any hesitation about this in Des Grieux's narrative: he speaks of "cette *fatale* tendresse dans laquelle je ne me lasse point de chercher mon *bonheur*" (p. 90), and his most obstinate rejection of Tiberge's preachments concerns this very point: "Tiberge a beau dire, ce n'est pas là un fantôme de *bonheur*" (p. 108). There is in his words an almost materialistic persuasion that felicity is present, and that it consists in quantifiable sensation (even if that is sentimental as well as physical). For certain gratifications, Des Grieux is willing to run great risks for his soul. This is expressed materially as a matter of compensation: "je me croirai trop bien payé, par un moment passé avec elle, de tous les chagrins que j'essuie pour l'obtenir" (p. 91).[39]

Much of the antipathy generated for Des Grieux's father is a function of the same language. In the love story, he--and Tiberge--can only be villains because they operate counter to the love interest. Qualitative judgements about characters have never had anything to do with the function of this mechanism, which goes back as far as *Tristan et Iseut*: any enemy of the lovers is, literarily speaking, a villain. Des Grieux's warm praise for his father's goodness does not change that. And this is driven home with particular force early in the narration by the father's explicit rejection of amorous discourse: with him, the whole code is powerless to move, and becomes the medium of what is, to Des Grieux, an excruciatingly cruel mockery reducing his passion to a mere, unadroitely executed gallantry and the hero to an awkward novice: "Tu sais vaincre assez rapidement, Chevalier; mais tu ne sais pas conserver tes conquêtes" (p. 34). But the father's opposition here goes farther than a simple refusal to take the matter seriously. He cannot accept the (etymological) passiveness of "passion"; is totally uncomprehending at the notion of a love which can subsist when esteem is lost. Whereas passion's discourse always predicates the *unique* and irreplaceable individual, his son's he can only interpret as a *general* symptom of a penchant for women, in the plural: "Tu aimes *les* jolies femmes" (p. 37). The remedy should then lie in substitution: "Je t'en chercherai une . . . qui ressemblera à Manon, et qui sera plus fidèle."[40] For Des Grieux's narrative, this is of course a complete nonsense. If he resignedly replies that he no longer makes any distinction among women, it is certainly not because he agrees in principle but because he is attempting to repress in his mind the image of that single woman who alone could ever matter: when there is no more Manon, there are no more women. His father's position is really a kind of blasphemy, an offense of lèse-amour.

For that matter, it might be said that the degree of elusiveness in Manon herself is owing precisely to her failure to subscribe and conform to the love code such as Des Grieux actualizes it. No behavior is comprehensible until we can systematize our perceptions of it, and she fails to answer to any of the codes which Des Grieux recognizes except that of the rather straightforward stimulus-response mechanism triggered by something very generally called pleasure. He is himself the very paradigm of the code of love: he is the *perfect* lover. Manon, needless to say, is by the same criteria hardly the "perfect" mistress. One cannot write, as she does, that "la fidélité que je souhaite de vous est celle du coeur" (p. 147) without sinning flagrantly ("elle n'avait pas même eu le soin de me le déguiser") against that standard which requires total commitment. She is not for all that, however, an enemy of love, which would be structurally impossible. She is saved by the intensity of *his* passion for her, which is rhetorically contagious and helps her participate in his essence: they are "de parfaits amants" (p. 103) together. Thus she attracts adjectives which approach the positive pole while dodging its specificity: she is loving, tender, and so forth. Besides, she does not so much reject the love code as act independently of it; she is perfectly willing to say she loves him; but this does not have for her the same necessary implications as for him. Her ability to violate standard codes innocently is of a piece with our picture of her as flighty and superficial.

In the moral tale of *Manon Lescaut*, however, the father and Tiberge are Des Grieux's friends. It, too, leads to Manon's death, but by a different thematic route. There is never any question of doing anything for the soul of Manon: the salvation, be it moral or spiritual, awaiting Des Grieux is for him alone and in fact depends upon her death, which assumes thereby a sacrificial quality.

The least that can be said of Tiberge is that he is consistent. He is a beacon of virtue (cf. the sunshine metaphor on p. 57), even perhaps a Mentor figure, about whom his friend's feelings are always mixed;

sometimes Des Grieux has recourse to Tiberge first and sometimes last, apprehending his troubling (and troublesome) sermons (p. 111). And even though Des Grieux's rhetoric waxes bold to stand up to him, all the pomp is not on one side. Virtue does not speak with a simple transparent truth unmasking the mythical diction of love; it too has its oratorical periods, traditional in their own way: "il me menaça des châtiments du Ciel, et il me prédit une partie des malheurs qui ne tardèrent guère à m'arriver" (p. 65). This is an oracular function, with echoes of such biblical phrases as "an eye for an eye and a tooth for a tooth" and "those that live by the sword shall die by the sword." Similarly, the father's "Va, cours à ta perte" (p. 172) is a sort of malediction; in a literary text there can be little doubt that it will be fulfilled.

In this context we must return too to the preface where Renoncour introduces the story as a moral treatise. It must be taken as his assessment of its ultimate sense, which once again turns on Des Grieux alone. Renoncour appears to subscribe entirely to the fatality of it all, while leaving in place its fundamental ambiguity. He states that Des Grieux, "un exemple terrible de la force des passions," has acted by choice, without asserting that the "choice" was free--just that it was voluntary: "[il] prévoit ses malheurs, sans *vouloir* les éviter."[41] This seems to suggest that he *could* have acted otherwise, yet that his strength to will virtue was nonetheless sapped away by his willingness to be wrong (which he never denies) in return for specific compensations. Finally Renoncour can do no better than characterize him as ambiguous, a mixture of virtues and vices, good sentiments and evil actions. The question often raised of whether the author is supposedly "sincere" in the "Avis" is particularly irrelevant when we realize how indecisive it is in any case. All of the examples it cites of moral lessons to be gleaned from stories such as this are inapplicable to *Manon Lescaut* itself, and it is difficult to see in what way it could ever serve as "un modèle d'après lequel on peut se former."

If the positive image in Renoncour's eyes is supposed to be that of the repentant prodigal, it is a result only of despair, not conversion. Even Des Grieux's desire toward the end for the sanction of marriage carries no contrition with it: virtue becomes synonymous with marriage ("le goût d'un amour vertueux" [p. 190]) simply as the only form of *devoir* which he can still fulfill. Behind it lurk questions of social station: "qui empêche . . . que nous n'*anoblissions* notre amour par des serments que la religion autorise?" Manon: "Je n'ai point la présomption d'*aspirer à la qualité* de votre épouse"; Des Grieux: "tu serais bientôt *celle d'un roi*, si le Ciel m'avait fait naître avec une couronne" (p. 191). This notion of elevation is hardly a religious inspiration in itself. As long as Manon is alive, there is never a word from Des Grieux about saving his own soul and even less hers. If one views the death scene through Christian binoculars, this will immediately appear shocking: Des Grieux wills his own death without a thought for his state of sin or what would supposedly await him in the beyond. He only wants to join Manon in some pagan paradise, but reality parodies his rhetoric: "Mon âme ne suivit pas la sienne" (p. 200).[42] Only after three months of a violent illness--as it were, the death agony of the Des Grieux who had loved Manon--can he accept the return to life, to earn his salvation, as if despite himself.

Even such a religious message as the end conveys is disconcertingly out of focus inasmuch as it largely coincides with the purely social implications. The light Des Grieux receives from heaven brings back "des idées dignes de ma *naissance* et de mon éducation" (p. 202) and inspires a return to Europe, principally in order to repair the scandal of his former life. There is more of a classical restoration of order here than an orthodox repentance. Synnelet, as Simone Delesalle has noted, stays dead only long enough for Manon to die, then reappears so that Des Grieux can resume his place in society without the major obstacle his murder would represent.[43] Des Grieux's salvation as such does not require him to come back to France, but his social recuperation does. And Tiberge is its agent, coming to the New World to rescue him, and taking Manon's place in Des Grieux's cabin (p. 204) until the ship is ready. But it should be noted that Des Grieux does not go to P..., the family home, as the text closes, as if to say that he has not come full circle, has not relocated the innocent point of origin. In concluding, the narrative remains a trifle off-balance, disoriented (partly by the intervening death of the father) and uncertain of destinations.

Furthermore, the vocabulary of the pagan and Christian axes overlaps in ways which further embroil their relative import. It has oft been repeated that Des Grieux's terminology is tragic, but this is only partly accurate. Classical tragedy does supply much of it, but there Christianity was as a matter of decorum normally unexpressed. Heaven is an abstraction, if not pagan, and one speaks of the gods but not God. It is more ambiguous in Des Grieux's discourse. Where is the demarcation between the Christian and the pantheistic or deistic in pronouncements like these:

J'ai remarqué, dans toute ma vie, que le *Ciel* a toujours choisi, pour me frapper de ses plus rudes châtiments, le temps où ma *fortune* me semblait le mieux établie. [p. 124]

Je levais, en marchant, les yeux et les mains pour invoquer toutes les puissances célestes. O Ciel! disais-je, serez-vous aussi impitoyable que les hommes? [p. 173]

S'il est vrai que les *secours célestes* sont à tous moments d'une force égale à celle des passions, qu'on m'explique donc par quel funeste *ascendant* on se trouve emporté tout d'un coup loin de son devoir . . . [pp. 42-43]?

Aside from the theological implications of the last example, it is important to notice the disparity not just in influence but in essence: *secours célestes*, in the explicitly Christian context of the story, can only refer indirectly to the grace of God, yet *ascendant* comes from astrology. If Tiberge is perplexed by the perverse theology of Des Grieux, what are *we* to make of the implications of his mixed rhetoric? Everything alternates violently in this book: Des Grieux's fortune from bliss to disaster, his temper from submissive to violent, his vocabulary from Christian resignation to pagan insolence. One can take Des Grieux's "ciel" for the ultimate pretext, the absolute unhinging of all personal responsibility, or for the direct intervention of God.[44] He seems to allow himself the freedom to slip and slide between the possible meanings, avoiding commitment to a specific semantic referent and generalizing instead the purely rhetorical effect. Were one to take *ciel* as a specifically Christian referent, then the message is complicated by the content of what the agent so designated does. "Le Ciel" is credited with sending Des Grieux an idea which abrogates his temptation to suicide, but the solution in question is his recourse to *industrie*, or thievery at the gaming tables (p. 53); he also calls the thought of milking Tiberge's purse "un effet de la protection du Ciel" (p. 57)--even though it alters nothing in his plan to turn to *industrie*. And he more than slightly impugns the good intentions of providence: "Mais se trouvera-t-il quelqu'un qui accuse mes plaintes d'injustice, si je gémis de la rigueur du Ciel à rejeter un dessein que je n'avais formé que pour lui plaire? Hélas! que dis-je, à le rejeter? Il l'a puni comme un crime" (p. 191). The only way to reduce all such allusions to a common denominator--and even then one which will have to emphasize dialectic--is to interpret them as formulations of a problem which the text itself, for ideological, historical reasons, could not itself formulate explicitly.[45]

Moral truth does not speak with the urgent, passionate voice of love and has, literally, nothing to put in its place. Nor has it even an antidote for it. The return of Des Grieux is based not upon a repentence which comes only after Manon's death, but upon a failure: the life he had been leading is no longer possible, because Manon is irreplaceable, and that is all. The triumph of virtue is not one of essences. For many reasons, then, the true interpretation of *Manon Lescaut* is an inextricable problem: the ostensible moral lesson has the first and last word, but it lacks clarity; and on the other hand, the subversive message of passion is on a level so different that it is not thereby simply effaced or subordinated. Tension between the different discourses remains a pervasive aspect of the text.[46] Even if explicit statements of meaning did not need to be subjected to a process of interpretation, it would not suffice in the case of *Manon Lescaut* to let the text tell us what it means, for it explicitly enounces contradictory meanings. That is the clearest reason why such disparate interpretations of it are possible. Neither Des Grieux nor even Renoncour seems capable of resolving the matter with any finality.

Des Grieux's is finally a discourse of uncertainty. Abstract on the one side, concrete on the other, Des Grieux is to be pitied because of his fate, because God has mysteriously, for a time, rejected him; but also because he is a modern, the example of "des jeunes gens d'un certain monde . . . dans le siècle où nous sommes" (p. 163)—which is a much more practical sort of justification than the others. These registers do not add up, rationally speaking, to a totality of understanding. A convergence of circumstances seems to offer the choice of various prisms with which to view a given set of events, but Des Grieux does not know which ones are reliable. He has used them all, not because he is a hypocrite[47] but because he has grasped at every straw. His only resting place is in the principle of repatriation, and it would appear futile to go beyond that. The disarray of language which manifested itself particularly at Manon's death but extends its effects throughout Des Grieux's subsequent narrative is largely a paradigmatic or lexical disorder: Des Grieux knows how to compose his sentences, but not how to choose his terms, because he does not know what kind of language he is speaking, or what sort is appropriate to express a meaning which he is not himself fully able to apprehend.

# NOTES

Antoine-François Prévost (1697-1763), *Histoire du chevalier des Grieux et de Manon Lescaut*, 1731. Edition: *Manon Lescaut*, Classiques Garnier (eds. Frédéric Deloffre and Raymond Picard), 1965. This edition is based on the revised and independent edition of 1753, the true title of which is *Histoire de Manon Lescaut*; but it confuses the issue by using all three versions of the title.

[1]Cf. Philippe Hamon, "Un Discours contraint," *Poétique*, 16 (1973), 411-45.

[2]What I am calling here pseudo-history is characterized in part by a third-person narrator, but would not necessarily include what is usually called the "historical novel," which, although it uses history, may be overtly fictitious (such as *Ivanhoe* or *Salammbô*); instead, it claims completely nonfictional status and frequently uses history only incidentally.

[3]I will for convenience's sake use this standard foreshortening of the title; despite it, however, and a tradition which has focused the interest mostly on Manon, there are many reasons for reading the text as the story primarily of Des Grieux.

[4]See especially Jeanne Monty, *Les Romans de l'abbé Prévost* (*Studies on Voltaire and the Eighteenth Century*, vol. 78 [1970], pp. 44-63. This point of view has been renewed by Franco Piva in *Sulla genesi di "Manon Lescaut": problemi e prospettive* (Milan: Vita e Pensiero, 1977).

[5]See Max Brun, "Contribution à la vie d'un roman: *Manon Lescaut*," in Jean Fabre et al., *L'Abbé Prévost* (Aix-en-Provence: Ophrys, 1965), pp. 211-21. Brun notes that the sixth volume of the *Mémoires et aventures* ends with the word FIN.

[6]Aside from the differences in wording, one would seem obligated to acknowledge also, as part of the new text, a vignette and epigraph which figure in it (see p. 9 and note of ed. cit.), the effect of which is to underscore the moral of the story as one in which the hero is wrested at length from the clutches of an unworthy temptress. The implications of this are more fully developed by Raymond Picard in "Le 'Sens allégorique' de *Manon*

*Lescaut,*" in *L'Abbé Prévost* (see preceding note), pp. 119-23. Picard's assimilation of the motif to the Mentor-Télémaque tradition (in which case Mentor here becomes Tiberge) is a valid interpretation, but one which, it should be remarked, is not explicit and has no specific relation to the Horacian epigraph.

[7]On this particular point, his father is willing to offer a concession after his first escapade with Manon, and permit him not to join the order (p. 37). Later he effectively renounces the title when he becomes--also before the fact--*l'abbé* Des Grieux (p. 42); and when that title in turn is discarded he dons "les galons et l'épée" (pp. 47-48), apparently as a simple costume of *noblesse d'épée,* although he continues to be referred to as *chevalier.*

[8]See the explicit references to his station and special treatment on pp. 17, 52, 85, 153, 158, 160, and note 2 on p. 33 concerning the appellation of "Monsieur B..."

[9]The "auteur" who speaks in the "Avis" and at the beginning of the primary narrative has no name in *Manon Lescaut,* but he bore the assumed name Renoncour in the *Mémoires et aventures d'un homme de qualité.* Even without that context, however, this primary narrator is identified explicitly with the author of the "Avis de l'auteur" and neither must be confused with Prévost.

[10]In terms of the chronology of the *Mémoires et aventures,* the first meeting at Pacy would have to take place in about January 1715, the second in July 1716; the internal action of *Manon Lescaut,* however, requires about 22 months' interval between them, and Renoncour speaks of "près de deux ans" (p. 15). Nothing within the text of *Manon Lescaut* provides a fixed historical date. Traditionally, editors of the novel have set the time of Manon's deportation, on comparative historical evidence, in 1719 or 1720, and considered the novel a portrait of the Regency. It would now seem reasonable, on the basis of Jean Sgard's chronology established for the *Oeuvres de Prévost* (Presses Universitaires de Grenoble, 1977-, vols. I and VIII), to abandon that fixation in favor of the dates indicated by the *Mémoires*; in this case the whole span of events in Des Grieux's narrative can be seen with fair precision to begin in June or July 1712 and conclude, with the second meeting with Renoncour, in late 1716.

[11]Italics throughout this chapter are my own, introduced for emphasis; they are rare in the text itself. There is an implicit thematic link between these expressions and those of Des Grieux's own first meeting with her described on p. 19: "Nous n'avions pas d'autre motif que la *curiosité*. . . . Mais il en resta *une* . . ."

[12]Simone Delesalle has justly emphasized this "différence entre *être quelqu'un* et *être appelé quelque chose*" in her provocative article--to which I shall return further on--"Lecture d'un chef-d'oeuvre: *Manon Lescaut*," *Annales*, 26, Nos. 3-4 (1971), 723-40.

[13]Cf. Delesalle: "en face d'un 'fils' [i.e., "de famille"], c'est une 'fille'. Ce qui veut dire qu'elle n'est pas née, qu'elle n'est rien et qu'elle n'a personne. Les deux héros ne sont donc pas deux êtres en face l'un de l'autre, ils sont de deux planètes différentes" (ibid., p. 728).

[14]Renoncour uses only the first-person singular in the Pacy scene, but is in the company of "le marquis de..., mon élève" (p. 15) in Calais; he refers to the two of them with a plural in the last paragraph of part one on p. 116. Unlike most "frame" narratives, this one does not revert to the primary narrative at its conclusion, unless one goes back to book vi of the *Mémoires et aventures*; it is briefly recalled, however, when Des Grieux is interrupted (or allowed to rest) for a meal.

[15]The case is very well put by Jeanne Monty, pp. 47-52. One must have particular reservations, however, about a remark such as the following: "L'enflure de son style devrait nous mettre en garde. . . .Ce n'est pas ainsi que s'exprime l'émotion sincère et désintéressée" (p. 51), because it assumes the possibility of a degree-zero standard for "sincere" diction. But there can be no expression of emotion, sincere or not, devoid of rhetoric.

[16]See Tzvetan Todorov, "La Lecture comme construction," in *Les Genres du discours* (Paris: Seuil, 1978), pp. 86-98.

[17]A good example is the matter of the sequence of events preceding his forced return home at M. B...'s behest. Although his father delivers a relentless calculation to show how few days Manon was faithful, we never know whether M. B... has already written at the time Des Grieux himself proposes to do so, after three weeks in Paris--and whether Manon put him up to it or not.

[18]"L'attitude de Manon est parfaitement compréhensible: contrairement à des Grieux, elle vit dans le monde du véritable risque" (Delesalle, pp. 729-30).

[19]Jacques Proust has boldly carried this inquiry even further in "Le Corps de Manon," *Littérature*, 4 (1971), 5-21, speaking of "la figure de la caresse sans fin refusée, sans fin recommencée, et . . . la représentation récurrente d'un corps qui se dérobe ou d'une vie qui s'épuise" (p. 17) as a constant ontologically determined by the scene of Manon's death: "dans ce système le corps de Manon ne pouvait être ni représenté ni décrit" (p. 15).

[20]Whence the mockery by Des Grieux's father of M. B...'s "noble" motives: "C'est bien d'un homme tel que lui . . . qu'il faut attendre des sentiments si nobles!" (p. 34). See the analysis of these attitudes by Sylvère Lotringer in "Manon l'écho," *Romanic Review*, 63, No. 2 (1972), 92-110: "Les droits de [Marivaux's] Marianne à la naissance sont, bien que laissés en suspens, incontestables puisque d'ordre structural alors que ceux de des Grieux à la vertu témoignent tout au plus d'un effet de différence dû aux interférences abusives du rang sur la morale et surtout à la pression de l'énonciation sur l'énoncé" (p. 102).

[21]Even sincerity, of course, would not mean that he has to be taken as the final authority in such commentary. "Rien dans sa narration," opines Jeanne Monty, "ne permet de croire à une complexité de sentiment qui dépasse la norme" (p. 61).

[22]"La tranquillité où nous vivions servit à me faire *rappeler* peu à peu l'idée de mon devoir" (p. 25); "diverses occasions où mon coeur sentit un *retour* vers le bien" (p. 66); "J'étais disposé à *rentrer* dans l'ordre de mes devoirs" (p. 113).

[23]See the chapter on Prévost in *Etudes sur le temps humain* (Paris: Plon, 1949).

[24]See chapter 16, "The Interrupted Supper," in *Mimesis* (Garden City: Doubleday, 1957).

[25]Auerbach has compared the farewell scene between Des Grieux and his father to *comédie larmoyante* (p. 352). See too the interesting

conjectures about comic structures in *Manon Lescaut* (the son versus father figures, mechanism of repetition, etc.) in Charles Mauron's reading of the book as "une comédie qui tourne mal" (*"Manon Lescaut* et le mélange des genres," *L'Abbé Prévost*, op. cit., pp. 113-18).

[26]This is doubtless why, in part, few tragic novels are related in this manner by the protagonist: Emma could not tell the story of *Madame Bovary*, nor Gervaise *L'Assommoir*.

[27]"Des Grieux a un père . . . une multitude de personnages qui . . . en fait le protègent. Leur fonction à tous, qu'il soient gouverneurs, supérieurs de couvent, capitaine de bateau ou lieutenant de police, est d'interdire ce qui est dangereux"; they are "instruments de sauvegarde pour le héros, barrières qui l'enferment dans une sûreté" (Delesalle, p. 725). Cf. the lieutenant's patronizing and gentle reproach to Des Grieux: "j'avais manqué de sagesse" (p. 160).

[28]Ibid., p. 729.

[29]Duclos's Comte de *** provides some insight into this mentality when he takes his friend Senecé aside in a vain attempt to persuade him to abandon his unworthy mistress: "satisfaites vos désirs, mais qu'une femme ne vous arrache ni à votre famille, ni à vos amis" (*Confessions du comte de ***, p. 103). He adds, further on, after Senecé has been freed from his family and has married her: "J'ai compris par cette aventure qu'il est impossible de ramener un homme subjugué, et que la femme la plus méprisable est celle dont l'empire est le plus sûr. . . . C'est le comble du malheur d'être dans un esclavage honteux, asservi aux caprices de ces femmes qui désunissent les amis, et portent le trouble dans les familles" (p. 111).

[30]See Lotringer, p. 733.

[31]A more "natural" way to interpret the trope involved would be to take "baisers" and "soupirs" as amorous metaphors for *haleine*, which can be used to warm hands all right; the effect would be none the less unusual. There are perhaps other instances too where it would not be out of place to see the functions of Des Grieux's rhetoric as a language disorder, given its discordance with relation to its referents. Take, for example, the moment when he contemplates his two possible sources (*voies*) for money, Tiberge and M. de T...: "je verserais plus volontiers la moitié de mon sang que d'en

prendre une, c'est-à-dire tout mon sang plutôt que de les prendre toutes deux" (p. 112). Camouflaged in his grandiloquence here is a comic arithmetical hyperbole about the "two halves" of his blood, and an ironic contrast (which one is very likely to overlook, and for cause) with the result: after his deliberations, he indeed goes to receive help from *both* Tiberge and M. de T...

[32]Lescaut: "mais voulez-vous tuer quelqu'un?" (p. 95); the superior: "Quoi! mon fils, vous voulez m'ôter la vie . . . ?" (p. 96).

[33]*Prévost romancier* (Paris: José Corti, 1968), p. 240.

[34]Frédéric Deloffre, for one, refers to the decidedly oral style of *Manon Lescaut* as contrasted with the *Mémoires et aventures* (p. lxxxvii), but the few examples he gives are unconvincing. Des Grieux's diction apart, this "oral" aspect is compromised even in terms of the fiction itself by the written mediation of Renoncour, who claims literal fidelity to the original words but also comments that Des Grieux expressed himself "de la meilleure grâce du monde" (p. 17). I find no evidence of such oral qualities --that is, nothing to suggest that the Des Grieux part of the text could not plausibly have been *written* by Des Grieux directly.

[35]Jeanne Monty argues that the sense of this passage alters when it is replaced within the framework of Renoncour's entire story, which denies contextually the premise that love is intrinsically innocent: read in this way, *Manon Lescaut* is less touching (pp. 62-63).

[36]From the *Spicilège*; quoted in the Garnier edition on p. clxiii. A more poetic, and perhaps believing, version of the same idea is to be had from Jean Cocteau: "C'est l'amour qui ne se mélange pas à la crapule et couvre les personnages de cet enduit des plumes de cygne, enduit grâce auquel le cygne barbote dans l'eau sale sans s'y salir" (preface to *Manon Lescaut*, Paris: Stock, 1948, p. x).

[37]Cf. M. de T...: "Pour le lieu, . . . il ne faut plus l'appeler l'Hôpital; c'est Versailles, depuis qu'une personne qui mérite l'empire de tous les coeurs y est renfermée" (p. 104).

[38]Cf. A. Kibedi Varga, "La Désagrégation de l'idéal classique dans le roman français de la première moitié du XVIIIe siècle," *Studies on Voltaire and the Eighteenth Century*, 26, pp. 965-98.

[39]The deeper suggestions of this passage become clearer if one compares it to the diabolic exclamation of Baudelaire's "Mauvais Vitrier" which it much resembles in form: "Mais qu'importe l'éternité de la damnation à qui a trouvé dans une seconde l'infini de la jouissance!" Indeed Tiberge reacts by retreating in fright, quite as if he were in the presence of someone possessed.

[40]The last clause is significant: the very nature of Manon's betrayal of Des Grieux makes her definitively unworthy of his son, and any evidence to the contrary is to no avail; this sequence of events, making Des Grieux the last to learn what has happened, explains his father's certainty that he knows Manon better than his son does.

[41]Cf. Voltaire's similarly ambiguous formula about free will being the power to do what one wants, in his *Dictionnaire philosophique*, article "Franc arbitre."

[42]This may well be an echo of an explicitly ironic use of the same metaphor in La Fontaine's "La Jeune Veuve": " 'Attends-moi, je te suis; et mon âme, / Aussi bien que la tienne, est prête à s'envoler.' / Le mari fait seul le voyage."

[43]Op cit., p. 733.

[44]This is an instance too where editorial decisions concerning the capitalization or non-capitalization of a word like *ciel* cannot be innocent, despite a neutral intent to modernize spelling without influencing the meaning.

[45]Examples tending in this direction are the summaries of Jean Sgard: "l'analyse de la sensibilité débouche sur une description du vide" (p. 251); and Jacques Proust: "c'est Dieu qui d'un bout à l'autre du roman s'offre et se dérobe à la fois au désir de des Grieux-Prévost" (p. 21).

[46]It seems to me unwarranted to speak of duplicity and hypocrisy in his case, as Jeanne Monty has done, since it supposes a possession of the facts on his part and an intention to deceive. The paradox of innocent guilt seems to me rather interior to his discourse then the result of his attempt to confuse and dupe his hearers.

[47]Jeanne Monty sees this imbalance as a product of the 1753 revision: "Des Grieux devient le type du héros préromantique dont la passion, pour une génération sensible, non seulement excuse toutes les fautes mais devient en soi un signe de noblesse d'âme. . . . Les principes de l'Homme de qualité sont vieillis en 1753, ceux de des Grieux ont triomphé. Lorsque Prévost adapte son ouvrage à l'esprit nouveau, il témoigne de la victoire de la psychologie du sentiment" (op. cit., pp. 61-62).

Chapter 6

Confessions du comte de ***

The nobility had for the most part no civil function by the early eighteenth century, and filled many of its idle hours with light verse, cards, and sex. Its eroticism, however pervasive, was in its literary manifestations generally veiled by what Daniel Mornet called "une pudeur apparente, celle des mots."[1] Although the *Confessions du comte de *** is fashioned on a long string of sexual engagements, very little, aside from repeated evocations of "pleasures" reinforced by various emphatic epithets, is said of the physical nature of love. In this novel almost every woman's boudoir has a revolving door, and sometimes another in the rear, yet we see scarcely anything about what transpires within. Even though the procedure involves a kind of euphemism, this fact might suffice to suggest to us that despite the obvious role sex plays as the unnamed center of gravity of the action, it is perhaps less the central concern than a symbolic ground on which various forces of human interaction are played out.

The liaisons of the Comte de *** are so numerous and varied that there is no consensus among critics regarding their objective count.[2] Although one would not relatively speaking call this work structurally complex, there is a proliferation in the detail which is almost vertiginous. It might therefore be useful, for reference purposes, to establish a summary of the Count's main adventures, complete with type characterizations where pertinent, topographical focus, and duration or chronology if it is assignable.

Part One:

1. Marquise de Valcourt (country - Paris).
2. Mme de Rumigny (Paris).
3. Dona Antonia (Spain, 1711).
4. Mme de Grancour (garnison at ***, 1711-1712).
5. The Intendante (garnison at ***, 1711-1712).
6. Marcella (Venice, before 1715, 3 months).
7. Mme de Sezanne (Paris, 2 months).
8. *Petite maîtresse*: Mme de Persigny (Paris).
9. *Dévote*: Mme de Gremonville (Paris, 6 months).
10. *Robe*: Mme de ** (Paris).
11. *Capricieuse*: Mme d'Albi (Paris).
12. *Bourgeoise*: Mme Pichon (Paris).

13. *Libertine*: Comtesse de Vignolles (Paris, 3 months).
14. *Coquette*: Mme de Lery (Paris).
15. *Passionnée*: Miledi B*** (London, 1717-1718, 3 months plus).
16. *Salonnière*: Mme de Tonins (Paris, 1720).
17. *Financière*: Mme Ponchard (Paris).

Part Two:

18. *Caillette*:[3] Mme Derval (Paris, 2 months).
19. Mme de Selve (country - Paris - country).
20. *Petite figure de fantaisie*: Mme Dorsigny (Paris).

This admittedly schematic presentation calls for several additional remarks. First of all, there are other mistresses who remain unnamed; specifically in between numbers two and three, which the Count subsumes vaguely under the purvey of "moeurs de mousquetaires" (p. 15), between seven and eight (p. 45), and fifteen and sixteen (p. 82). Secondly, although these names succeed each other chronologically in terms of the inception of each liaison, the reigns sometimes overlap, as is explicitly the case of numbers eleven-twelve and nineteen-twenty; and their length, of course, varies too, although only three women (9, 15, 19) are overtly credited with more than a three months' stand. Thirdly, while one person on this list is pursued but never possessed (14), at least one is named in the text (Mme de Limeuil, p. 82) yet never accosted. In addition, there is one character (Mme Dornal) who, although not desired by the Count, is nevertheless the focus of an important episode at the beginning of part two. Finally, the novel ends with the definitive return-engagement of Mme de Selve--the only woman by name so privileged.

It will be evident from what precedes that the chronology of the novel is not strictly linear. Not only are there imprecisely chronicled sequences, and others related iteratively (by repetitive actions rather than singular events), there is also a movement--intimately connected to the thematic development--in the direction of overlap of at least partially parallel episodes: mistresses (and other experiences, such as the Senecy-Dornal affair) come to no longer simply succeed each other, but coincide; more than one will be going on at a time. And it is stated too that numerous affairs are omitted entirely, leaving room in the narrative only for those with some formative or typical value. The dates, which I have included where historical events come in close conjunction with the plot, comprise a loose but entirely plausible time frame for the story. With some margin for conjecture, the Count can be said to have been born about 1692, to begin his social initiation with Mme de Valcourt around 1708, ultimately to marry and retreat from society about twenty years later,[4] and to write his *Confessions* about a year subsequent to this, still being under forty years of age (p. 3).[5]

This schema does not in any evident way deliver up to us the structure of the novel. It makes it appear as if almost all the action were concentrated in part one, which occupies about fifty percent more calendar time than part two but is in fact only about thirty percent longer. But that is because it emphasizes only one axis of the narrative, the cumulative history of love affairs. The tempo does seem different in the second part, and this has to do with a more heavily analytical tendency, with a new emphasis on qualitative experience, away from rapid change and toward stability, like the slowing of a caterpillar's pace as it approaches its metamorphosis.

There is another kind of rhythm, although still related to chronology, in the topological organization of the text. This type of novel frequently features a military protagonist, who must divide his time between society and the regiment. Concomitant are many thematic interrelations between these poles, such as the seasonal nature of both high society's and the army's geographical displacements, the juxtaposition of two radically different but metaphorically related kinds of "conquests," and the reciprocal suggestion on the one hand that sex is the diminutive battlefield (*guerre en dentelles*) of once-noble virtues, and on the other that war is a kind of sublimated (or at least displaced) eroticism. Often too, as in this work, the officer's travels justify introduction of an international dimension for the comparative-women motif; the only intensely dramatic episodes occur without exception abroad: one in Spain (Dona Antonia), one in Italy (Marcella), and one in England (Miledi B***). And in each of these countries only one affair is mentioned, which contrasts evidently with the quick turnover during the longer Parisian sojourns. This counterpoint identifies Paris strongly with pure sex and games ("Paris est le centre de la dissipation, et les gens les plus oisifs par goût et par état y sont peut-être les plus occupés" [p. 59]), while great passion is relegated elsewhere. Symbolic of this Parisian function is the fact that the Count first meets Mme Valcourt in the country, but does not consummate the liaison there: her promise to meet him again in Paris for the purpose is coded in a manner that even the neophyte seems able to understand. On the other hand, the alternation from country to Paris does not correspond directly to a thematic polarity opposing rural virtue to urban vice, because it coincides as well with the regiment/leave cycle. At the end, nonetheless, it is obvious that the Count's marriage, withdrawal from *le monde*, and retreat to the country are mutually reinforcing events.

The structure of the text is thus more subtle than at first appears. There would seem to be two essential optics available for organizing the meaning which it apparently disperses; they are not mutually exclusive, but a question of preponderance remains. They might be said to correspond roughly to the division of the novel in two parts. The first is that of *Bildungsroman*: the story of a young noble's worldly education via its masculine (the army) and feminine (the boudoir) quintessences, producing over time the finally formed courtier, something of a tutor to the younger relative to whom his memoirs are now addressed. In this reading we might expect some progression in the nature of the female encounters, even if it is not perfectly rectilinear. The second is that of a moral (or at least wise) tale, leading through disillusion to a kind of enlightenment and conversion: in this construction the conclusion controls the book's overall meaning, and the Count as narrator becomes in effect a preacher.

If the first two pages, which declare his intentions to his addressee, do not exactly decide the matter, despite their somewhat grandiloquent evocation of a "confession fidèle des travers et des erreurs de ma jeunesse qui pourra vous servir de leçon," it is because of the confused motivations on which he founds this act. The reader figured in the text by the second person totally disappears after this point, despite the forceful position he is given in the initial sentence: "Pourquoi voulez-vous m'arracher à ma solitude et troubler ma tranquillité?" Although instigated by this *vous* who presumably has attempted to prod him into a return to society, the narrative quickly takes on the appearance of a self-indulgent mythologization as the Count proffers an unrequested and detailed rendering of his own example. This leaves some confusion too about the fictive status of the text. Who has presumably published it? There is no "editor," and the Count cannot himself have intended a publication, given his commitment to "le silence qu'un honnête homme doit garder sur cette matière" (p. 52). The whole framework, as is frequently the case in first-person narrations, thus implies at some point a scandalous breach of confidence, since publication is the antithesis of "confession," which, it must be remembered, is a religious act, normally private; even Saint Augustine formally addressed his to God.

Later, when Rousseau let it be known that he was writing his *Confessions*, he caused no little discomfort among former associates, precisely because of the flagrant indiscretion implied by the very title. Still, account must be taken here of the effect of the title *Confessions*, which seems to announce a story of *égarement* like Des Grieux's or Meilcour's (in *Les Egarements du coeur et de l'esprit*), and must finally come full cycle via some semblance of contrition, repentence, or conversion.[6] An implicit problem arises if the protagonist then seems to take too much pleasure in his own nostalgia, but it is less fundamental a disparity of principle and tone here than in *Manon Lescaut*.

It is highly significant, even though it may be banal, that the high society in which this discourse is framed refers to itself simply as *le monde*. The term symbolizes at once the closure and the openness of a restricted circle almost completely sealed off from the penetrating eyes of other social classes, but eminently public in the presence of members to each other.[7] This loftiness is neatly indicated by the nature of the Count's reaction at the point in the narrative where Mme de Tonins wants to have a play of his performed at the Comédie Française: rather than being flattered, as one might anticipate, he is appalled, his very rank forbidding on principle any such exhibitionism: "les gens de mon état n'étaient point faits pour devenir auteurs, et . . . s'ils l'étaient par complaisance pour l'amusement d'une société, ils ne devaient jamais se donner au public" (p. 89). Note the opposition here between "*une* société" and "le public": the man of the world lives in *its* gaze but not the public's, and the proposal of Mme de Tonins appears to the Count as inherently vulgar, a kind of prostitution.

His title (and therefore the book's) immediately declare that he belongs to this "world," and this is further underscored when he begins the narrative proper with: "Etant destiné par ma naissance à vivre à la cour . . ." Nevertheless, he is curiously vague about his individual background. "Il est inutile de vous entretenir de ma famille que vous connaissez comme moi, puisque nous sommes parents": by avoiding a pitfall of this form of fiction, which often leads a narrator to tell his addressee things the latter obviously knows but which the reader cannot otherwise have access to, this account also evades any specificity which would textually tie the protagonist into his milieu. For the reader he has no parents, only a title and a fortune; even his name disappears under the conventional anonymity of ***. Despite his family sentiments, he lives in an abstract situation and his relatives appear only accessorily;[8] it is as though he were conceived *in vitro*. And this might be taken as corresponding symbolically to the historically determined position of his social class, which appears functionally as a sort of epiphenomenon in the real world.

The Count bears the mark of his class most obviously in his attitudes towards the other classes, especially those which come into some degree of social contact with his own. There is, of course, not just one, monolithic high society but shifting layers which allow some latitude for manoeuvre amongst them once one has acceded by money or rank to a certain threshold of entry. This world is the *hors-texte*: the context not directly represented, but knowledge of which enables the reader to interpret the text itself. The *intendante* thus comes in for double mockery by embodying both the typical bourgeois and provincial traits: "souveraine en province, elle n'était que bourgeoise à Paris" (p. 33). Her "sovereignty" is tinged with the further sarcasm of noble disdain for the rank of the chief royal officer: *intendance* to the count intrinsically links her to her caste, and this in turn to its constant attributes ("insipide fatuité").[9] Like the other bourgeois in the novel, she aggravates the ridicule by aspiring not only to a rank but also to a polish she does not and cannot possess. The *bourgeoises* can only grotesquely ape the nobility: "D'ailleurs elles sont solides dans leurs dépenses, elles boivent et mangent par état; l'occupation de la semaine leur impose la nécessité de rire et d'avoir les jours de fêtes une joie bruyante, éveillée et entretenue par les plus grosses plaisanteries" (p. 65). In other words, they are inauthentic, borrowed personalities. The case is not quite so hopeless, however, with women of the *noblesse de robe*, who despite their inadequacies seem endowed with a certain degree of perfectibility; the remark: "Les femmes de robe qui ne vivent qu'avec celles de leur état n'ont aucun usage du monde, ou le peu qu'elles en ont est faux" (p. 58) implies that in better company they might acquire some class. They are, in addition, characterized by a certain immaturity ("les plaisanteries de la robe qui tiennent toujours du collège") which suggests snobbery relative to the comparative newness or *parvenu* status of their very titles. Even the expression "leur état" applied to them above is pejorative from this perspective: the Count would never use it with respect to his peers. He notes, moreover, how totally foreign to him are the ways of the robe, and derides them in the first instance for thinking themselves so august--the epitome of proud error. "La hauteur de la robe est fondée comme la religion sur les anciens usages, la tradition et les livres écrits. La robe a une vanité qui la sépare du reste du monde, tout ce qui l'environne la blesse" (p. 57).

The sting in these remarks comes precisely from the implicit put-down; a term like "les anciens usages" is a sarcastic antiphrasis drawing attention to their less than ancient claim to nobility.

Equally symptomatic are the particular aspects of the financial milieu which he selects for satire. Although he explicitly recognizes its social value (p. 93), and celebrates the fine education from which many of its members have benefitted, he would rather, when doing them such honor, suppress all memory of the ladder their families have climbed to their present station. For example, he finds this financial bourgeoisie insufficiently delicate on the question of "la bassesse des premiers emplois" (p. 92); their own honorability seems to depend on the generation that separates them from poverty, and he scorns those who, so to speak, still have dirty hands, that is to say those who made their own fortune: they have known "les plus vils emplois" and remain stained by their "crasse primitive."

But *le monde* is also a matter of conditioning, of apprenticeship; although entitled to enter it, the Count at first lacks "usage du monde" and gravitates toward a woman older than himself (and something of a relative) who can impart that finish he must acquire, "une femme à qui le monde a donné cette liberté et cette aisance que l'on trouve rarement dans un ordre inférieur" (p. 7). Such qualities are, like intelligence in the standard theory, a combined product of innate potential and a conducive environment. The process of initiation will convert him from "petit amant" at this stage to "jeune homme à la mode" (p. 66) some years later, and finally to consummate, unqualified "homme à la mode" (pp. 82, 115). Certainly there is an important symbol as well as humor in his recounting, of Mme de Valcourt, "j'obtins la dernière faveur ayant encore mon épée au côté et mon chapeau sous le bras": the sword, quite aside from parelleling his sexual attributes in action, is the concrete social mark of his rank and title to enter manhood, yet its awkwardness simultaneously indicates his inexperience.

After initiation, the *rite de passage* which he, like Meilcour or Jacob in *Le Paysan parvenu*, receives from an older woman, the Count is introduced to the principle of succession and enumeration in the form of a ritual of regiment. In a process that mirrors parodically the more normal social situation, the turnover of lovers in the small cities where the army is quartered is determined by military mobility; rather than supplanting another lover, one locates a "femme vacante" as one regiment relays another, and all the niches are filled (both figuratively and with an ironic sexual literalness) within three days (p. 29). The only difference really is the motivation of the mechanism, since back in Paris the same fundamental pattern will apply: "Elle ne manqua pas de gens aimables qui s'empressèrent à me remplacer, et qui bientôt le furent eux-mêmes par d'autres" (p. 49). In either instance the tenure would seem to be about equivalent. Never is this so explicit as in the letter he receives later regarding his two-months' occupation of Mme Derval: "un terme si long tient de l'amour, et même de la constance"; justice requires that he return her to circulation, "comme un effet qui devait être dans le commerce" (pp. 114-15). This commercial comparison goes right to the heart of the matter: sex here is the currency of a system of exchange, and lovers like money must circulate. Just as one must possess fortune, one must maintain a liaison; having "nothing better to do" (p. 33) is reason enough for establishing a new one, and reputation suffers from remaining too long out of the market place. And, like spent coins, partners who are passed on are eclipsed by memory and totally cease to exist: "à peine l'eus-je quittée que je n'y songeai plus" (p. 15); "je n'entendis plus parler d'elle" (p. 42); "je la vis même quelque temps chez elle pour la ménager, mais sans . . . le moindre souvenir du passé" (p. 56). Only the institutionalizing act of recording memoires can recreate their existence.

It bears noting that, however much flesh is implicated in all the episodes related, its essence lies in this exchange value rather than in systematic cultivation of erotic intensity. Unlike Casanova, for instance, the Count never places any emphasis on the performative aspect of sexual intercourse, the inexhaustible virtuosity which constitutes the prowess of a Richelieu and the frenzy of Sade's characters. On the contrary: "une femme n'a pas besoin d'être bien pénétrante pour soupçonner des rivales, la multiplicité des devoirs d'un amant les empêche d'être bien vifs" (pp. 111-12). Never would an authentic Don Juan figure make such a concession nor refer to his performance with such a pained euphemism as *devoirs*. Besides, there is no sense of conquest here, although that word is used ritualistically; with exception of the foreign women, who represent real passions, no woman in this story is seduced: they are merely partners in a contract between equals. Tradition in the form of *bienséances* obligates them in principle to conform to certain norms of decency (even then there are exceptions), playing the courted while the men make the official advances; but these are just the rules of the game and should not be mistaken for the structure of what really transpires on a deeper level. However else one qualifies it, the *Confessions du comte de \*\*\** cannot be styled a novel of seduction. It is not even, in the narrow sense, a "roman à liste," although it has that form: his very sense of nobility prevents the Count from advertising foppishly all those he has acquired. He is also much too passive a character for that. No real "homme à liste" could say: "J'ai toujours été plus sensible au plaisir, qu'à la vanité de la bonne fortune" (p. 52). It is perhaps equally or more what one might call a "roman-itinéraire," in that the Count does not just circulate always at the same social level but explores the attractions of women of various conditions.

Even though the nature of his activities remains essentially constant, the Count transforms his narrative to an extent when, between numbers seven and eight, he reduces all such experiences to a uniform pattern--"la plupart commencent et finissent de la même manière" (p. 45)--and rationalizes the remainder of his discourse in terms of types ("je m'attacherai uniquement à distinguer les différents caractères"). Indeed, he never fails subsequently to designate the particular type the mistress represents, and in most cases to identify in some manner as well what impression the encounter left with him. In this way a semblance of gradation is introduced into his experiences, mostly, it is true, in the direction of cumulative formation as a rather jaded man of the world. On the other hand, the sense of their succession must not appear to emanate from any perceptible causality because they are all inscribed under the sign of pure chance: "Le hasard forme ces sortes de liaisons: les amants se prennent parce qu'ils se plaisent ou se conviennent, et ils se quittent parce qu'ils cessent de se plaire, et qu'il faut que tout finisse" (p. 45). Nor is the notion of chance an oblique reflection of the exercise of free will. It is too arbitrary for that; there is no real merit involved even in the process of selection: "[on] ne devait pas être infiniment flatté d'une préférence dont le hasard décidait" (p. 48). Thus, the first representative of this haphazard flightiness is precisely a woman who is characterized by fear of a void and determined in her behavior by the need to escape any hint of boredom: "il était indispensablement nécessaire de trouver de quoi remplir un intervalle qui se trouvait vide" (p. 47).[10] Her lover is a function, a piece of furniture ("un meuble d'usage"), and he gleans in consequence a new cynicism by being purged of his false sense of delicacy in matters amorous.

None of the Count's portraits ever blossoms into a more full-fledged satire, though, than the next one, of Mme de Grémonville. He calls her "dévote par état" to suggest that her civil status is in this case overshadowed by a behavioral trait which transcends class lines. The acquaintance serves as an object lesson in the confusing nature of appearances, as he suggests at the outset in referring to her as an example of "la simple nature ou du moins ses apparences." For it soon comes out that devotion is a disguised sexual signifier, the willful and strategic antidote for a lover; "elle n'avait embrassé l'état de la dévotion, que pour ramener l'esprit de son mari, qu'une affaire assez vive avec un jeune homme avait un peu éloigné d'elle" (p. 50). Dona Antonia had been a *dévote* too, it is true, and had even given him a relic (p. 24), which is a rather extreme form of sacrilege, but that is because she, in her fervor on both scores, confused sacred with carnal adoration.[11] Hardly is that the case with Mme de Gremonville. The satire takes two principal tacks: it designates patterns of conduct shielded by devotion, and reveals the ambiguity of devotional language. In addition, the Count acknowledges, as does Jacob in *Le Paysan parvenu*, the erotic motivation of "l'envie d'avoir une dévote" (p. 53).

On the first of these levels, devotion becomes a pretext machine which provides unassailable cover for behavior which by normal conventions is stigmatized. It thus provides for a kind of license, an exemption from *bienséances*: "Le masque ne donne pas plus de liberté à Venise, que le manteau noir en fournit à Paris."[12] Special rationalizations allow her the use of a *petite maison* (a secret apartment in some neighborhood other than her own); good deeds excuse her going places where one would not otherwise expect to see her. In this way a systematic reversal of ostensible values is achieved: "la vertu, ou ce qui lui ressemble devient la sauvegarde du plaisir."[13] This coincides too with a linguistic dimension, to the degree that a vaguely religious notion like *recueillement* can authorize possession of the *petite maison*. Seduction can operate through the channel of pious language: "J'achevai de la séduire en l'accablant d'éloges sur sa beauté, ses grâces et même sur sa vertu."[14] If this is possible, it is because that language lends itself to sensual use through the ambiguity of its metaphorical structure, which so resembles that of the rhetoric of love:

> On me traitait en directeur chéri. Nous repassâmes dans le lieu de nos plaisirs pour en goûter de nouveaux. L'heure où finit l'office nous obligea de nous séparer. . . . Une dévote emploie pour son amant tous les termes tendres et onctueux de l'Ecriture, et tous ceux du dictionnaire de la dévotion la plus affectueuse et la plus vive. [pp. 54-55]

The transfer of the divine signified to the profane, of which the possibility had already been underscored in *Le Tartuffe* long before *Le Paysan parvenu*, takes place in a pattern of alternation where the *dévote* goes from one "altar" to another.

At this point there is a new modulation but not, as when the Count began to filter out all the routine engagements, in the narrative stance: it is rather on the level of the diegesis, and while it too affects the pace of the narrative, this is for a different reason. The protagonist has shifted his strategy after realizing the isolation in which six months of exclusive attentions to Mme de Gremonville has left him: "Je résolus bien de ne plus tomber dans un pareil inconvénient, et de faire assez de maîtresses pour en avoir dans tous les états, et n'être jamais sans affaire, si j'en quittais ou en perdais quelqu'une" (p. 56). This points the story towards simultaneity and multiplicity, modifying the pattern of succession which allowed for intervals. The object now is to suppress them: "j'avais toujours quelque ancienne maîtresse qui me recevait sans façon, lorsque je me trouvais sans affaire réglée. Ces femmes de réserve sont de celles que l'on a sans soin, qu'on perd sans se brouiller, et qui ne méritent pas d'article séparé dans ces mémoires" (p. 70). Such a passage serves a metadiscursive function: it informs on the status of the narrative text in its relation to the events recounted.

For all their piquancy, not all the subsequent liaisons can be afforded space here for individual commentary. Mme d'Albi is a somewhat special case in that by the extreme nature of her capriciousness she "réunissait en elle tous les caractères" (p. 60). Her character thus appears dispersed, schizophrenic, to some unknown power: there is no self. And in this way she seems adapted to her milieu, which is notable for the shifting value of its signs. This is illustrated by the analysis of the *petite maison* as social institution, the sense of which undergoes a reversal. At first its purpose is secrecy and protection from the public eye, or as the narrator calls it, mystery. But it quickly becomes a fad because, by renting one, an air of mystery can be acquired; and in addition, since the practice begins in the highest classes, it is encouraged by snobbery. So the secret in time becomes public and even ostentatious:

[Les petites maisons] sont enfin devenues si communes et si publiques, qu'il y a des extrémités de faubourgs qui y sont absolument consacrées. On sait tous ceux qui les ont occupées; les maîtres en sont connus, et ils y mettront bientôt leur marbre. Il est vrai que depuis qu'elles ont cessé d'être secrètes, elles ont cessé d'être indécentes, mais aussi elles ont cessé d'être nécessaires. [p. 61]

The equivalency here between secrecy, indecency, and necessity is itself intriguing. Better still, and equally epigrammatic, is the conclusion to which all this leads: "Une petite maison n'est aujourd'hui pour bien des gens qu'un faux air, et un lieu, où pour paraître chercher le plaisir, ils vont s'ennuyer secrètement un peu plus qu'ils ne feraient en restant tout uniment chez eux." Such a description conveys through figuration the vanity of "le tourbillon du monde" as effectively as Solomon's *Vanitas vanitatum*.

At various points the narrator underscores specific lessons or resolutions which grow out of the different experiences: after Mme de Lery, who proves authentically dangerous to him, he swears off coquettes (p. 73). In counterpoint, he then unwittingly inspires in Miledi B*** a passion which very nearly becomes an international incident, and is perhaps equally as frightened as before, particularly when he discovers that her English melancholy has proven somewhat contagious (p. 82).[15] After this, the coquettish Parisian no longer looks so bad to him, and he rebounds towards the flighty and passing woman. But the return to Paris also has another climacteric value because he seems to enter a new phase of his worldly existence; he is now about twenty-six, and is as if inaugurating for the first time a full-fledged mature social presence: "Après un an d'absence, c'était une espèce de début; on était attentif au choix que j'allais faire: de ce choix seul pouvaient dépendre tous mes succès à venir. . . . Un homme à la mode ne doit jamais entreprendre que des conquêtes sûres" (p. 82). This shows him conscious of determining his position purely in function of the *on dit*, which in this society is a kind of self-perpetuating phenomenon: in order to be irresistible, one must have the reputation of already being irresistible. By implication, there is no "being" as such, there is only social credit. Or, as he puts it with some attenuation, "l'opinion nous détermine presqu'aussi souvent que l'amour. Mme de Tonins était à la mode, et dès lors elle me paraissait charmante" (p. 86).

After his affair with Mme de Tonins, indeed, there is yet another "return" to society: "Je rentrai dans le monde" (p. 91). Whether for love or some other motive he cannot really distinguish from it, the Count has in fact a tendency to withdraw into fairly intense relationships for a time, after which some sort of resolution extracted from what he has experienced is codified, and reorients, at least for a while, his worldly presence. This time, deciding once more to try something new (so long as there are still new things to try), he resolves on a plunge into "finance," which of course to him means finding a mistress whose husband is a financier. But as the first part of the novel closes, he declares forcefully the pleasure it gave him finally to be rid of her.

The evolution of the plot is much simpler to analyze in the second part, at least up to the moment where extensive discussion of the role of Mme de Selve accentuates the movement towards a resolution. In the story of Senecé and Mme Dornal, which chronologically parallels some unspecified adventures of his own, the Count excoriates the woman he calls a "vile créature" (p. 111)--a charge one may regard as never really proven by anything concrete--and reproaches Senecé for withdrawing from society (of which he himself has been guilty) and, more fundamentally, for ignoring the public discourse about Mme Dornal: it suffices to know that people think ill of her. Again here there is a lesson, highly explicit:

> J'ai compris par cette aventure qu'il est impossible de ramener un homme subjugué, et que la femme la plus méprisable est celle dont l'empire est le plus sûr. Si le charme de la vie est de la passer avec une femme qui justifie votre goût par ses sentiments, c'est le comble du malheur d'être dans un esclavage honteux, asservi aux caprices de ces femmes qui désunissent les amis, et portent le trouble dans les familles. [p. 111]

After his adventure with Mme Derval, he finally reacts not only against these women "plus jalouses d'être connues qu'estimées" who prize only attention, but by comparison, since the male too is only a cipher in the female's life, against the role he himself has been playing so long:

> Je m'aperçus du mépris que les gens sensés, même ceux qui aiment le plaisir, faisaient d'un homme à la mode, et je commençai à rougir d'un titre que je partageais avec des gens fort méprisables. L'idée d'une vie plus tranquille vint se présenter à mon esprit. Je jugeai qu'elle serait plus conforme à mes véritables sentiments, et je résolus de vivre avec moins d'éclat. Une aventure qui m'arriva alors acheva de me déterminer à céder au penchant de mon coeur. [p. 116]

The standard is still opinion, although the social group which serves as reference is altered: *les gens sensés* is clearly a different subclass than he has consulted so far; and this leads to the discovery of a hitherto unperceived entity called "mes véritables sentiments"--in other words, an independent self. The adventure which then completes his preparation for Mme de Selve is another secondary one, that of Julie, the unwilling but consenting victim he could have taken but was good enough to refuse. It is hard to say whether her example of pure and uncomplicated devotion to her love or his own discovery of potential goodness within himself is the more determining factor in this experience.

It cannot have passed unnoticed that there is much humor in the text, and that is often linked to the social satire: like *Les Egarements du coeur et de l'esprit*--and quite unlike *Manon Lescaut*--this is a very wry book. Not surprisingly, some scenes, for example the classic confrontation at a dinner party with the two mistresses one is seeing separately (p. 153), would be at home in a comedy of manners. For this reason, certain aspects of the narrator's language, especially as they relate to the ironic tone, are deserving of attention by way of preparation for a discussion of the novel's development and conclusion.

Even a rapid survey reveals some interesting traits of diction and figuration. Numerous balanced sentences mark by their cadence a parallelism of signifieds: antithesis is a perfect example: "Je l'avais prise par caprice, je m'y attachai par goût" (p. 114). Antithesis also serves humor, as when the Count says that Mme de Sezanne, being newly married , "n'avait point d'engagement" (p. 43). Portraits are largely composed of such neatly cut aphorisms, and in particular the one of Mme de Selve, where antithesis combines with ternary rhythms:

> La comtesse de Selve avait plus de raison que d'esprit; puisqu'on a voulu mettre une distinction entre l'un et l'autre, ou plutôt elle avait l'esprit plus juste que brillant. Ses discours n'avaient rien de ces écarts qui éblouissent dans le premier instant, et qui bientôt après fatiguent. On n'était jamais frappé, ni étonné de ce qu'elle disait; mais on l'approuvait toujours. Elle était estimée de toutes les personnes estimables, et respectée de celles qui l'étaient le moins. Sa figure inspirait l'amour, son caractère était fait pour l'amitié, son estime supposait la vertu. Enfin la plus belle âme unie au plus beau corps, c'était la comtesse de Selve. [p. 128]

The thematic importance of such regularity of meter is greater than first appears, because it corresponds to and valorizes the two fundamental binarities on which the conclusion is based: *corps/âme* and *amour/amitié*. As if to illustrate that the mentality within which the text functions is locked up in fixed forms of thought, its metaphors are usually clichés: "la Dornal avalait à longs traits le poison que je lui présentais" (p. 107); "elle prend un amant comme une robe, parce que c'est l'usage" (p. 112). The social world itself is repeatedly epigrammatized as a torrent: "entraîné par le torrent" (p. 3); "me livrer au torrent de la société" (p. 45); "entraîné par ce torrent" (p. 150). What few military metaphors there are tend to be humorous; for except on an anecdotal or satirical level, there is no significant relationship between the attack and defense of warfare and what transpires in the story: the case will be quite different in a novel like *Les Liaisons dangereuses*, where the military campaign appropriately figures the overall enterprise of Valmont and Mme de Merteuil, and military metaphors are frequent.

Formulaic knowledge is fundamental to this variety of fiction.[16] It will cause no wonder that a great deal of the encapsulated wisdom on which an understanding of the Count's social world depends concerns women--as formulated, obviously enough, from a masculine perspective. A few examples:

> Chez les femmes du monde, plusieurs choses qui paraissent différentes produisent les mêmes effets, et la vanité les gouverne autant que l'amour. [p. 12]

> Les femmes n'ont pas de plus grands ennemis que les femmes.
> [p. 14]

> Les citations du passé sont un des arts que les femmes de tout état emploient le plus volontiers. [p. 30]

> Les femmes à Paris communiquent moins généralement entre elles que les hommes. [p. 45]

> On peut compter sur la constance des femmes, quand on n'en exige pas même l'apparence de la fidélité. [p. 82]

> Que les femmes ne se plaignent point des hommes, ils ne sont que ce qu'elles les ont faits. [p. 129]

> Les femmes, avec plus de tendresse dans le coeur que les hommes, ont les désirs moins vifs. [p. 165]

Others, though much in the same vein, apply to worldly life more generally; among these are some of the most celebrated passages in the book:

> Les amants seraient trop heureux que leurs désirs fussent entretenus par des obstacles continuels; il n'est pas moins essentiel pour le bonheur de conserver des désirs que de les satisfaire. [p. 139]

Je vois que la constance n'est pas au pouvoir des hommes, et leur éducation leur rend l'infidélité nécessaire. [p. 161]

And more generally yet, there are of course moral truths (especially in part two):

On n'est point vertueux sans fruit. [p. 124]

[Je sentis] quelques remords, et on ne les sent point sans les mériter. [p. 146]

Nous nous contentons quelquefois d'estimer les vertus, au lieu que nous partageons toujours les folies. [p. 156]

Il est sans exemple qu'on ne [soit infidèle] qu'une fois. [p. 161]

Ethnic codes play an important role here by way of contrast. French manners exclude passionate drama, which is relegated according to fixed laws to other geographical foci. The French counterreferent, though, is constantly in mind:

Il n'y a point de pays où la galanterie soit plus commune qu'en France; mais les emportements de l'amour ne se trouvent qu'avec les Italiennes. L'amour qui fait l'amusement des Françaises, est la plus importante affaire et l'unique occupation d'une Italienne. [pp. 34-35]

Je compris que je ne devais pas chercher à Paris la passion italienne, ni la constance espagnole, que je devais reprendre les moeurs de ma patrie, et me borner à la légèreté et à la galanterie française. [p. 44]

Aspects of traditional *romanesque* in this connection attach to Spain: the Duegna leading the Count to a splendid room where a lady awaits him on cushions; a More conducting him to a château; letters dropping at his feet from open windows; rope ladders. (The only such manifestation in France is the grotesque balcony-and-rope-ladder episode with Mme de Grancour [p. 31], which is implicitly part of the satire on provincials, who can only aspire with comic insuccess to such drama.) In England, the decisive characteristic is not just capacity for passion but a temperamental disorder, melancholy: and the combination leads to suicide. It is not entirely clear whether this "sickness" is primarily atmospheric, genetic or moral; but it is pervasive, and again it serves to highlight French traits in return: "Outre les motifs de chagrin qui m'étaient particuliers, on contracte en Angleterre un air sérieux que l'on porte jusque dans les plaisirs; le mal m'avait un peu gagné; l'air et le commerce de France sont les meilleurs remèdes contre cette maladie" (p. 82).

These comparisons already make it clear that the Count does not disbelieve in passion: he simply believes its essence unattainable in the French social climate. Nothing ever calls into question the existence of something which can without inauthenticity be called love. More often than not, the love code appears unexplicitly in indirect allusions, operating in such a way, however, that the corresponding maxim can be reëstablished by deduction. "Trop passionnée pour avoir des remords, mon âme nageait dans les plaisirs" (p. 40): passion overwhelms remorse. Mme Dornal "n'en avait jamais aimé aucun; elle n'en était pas digne" (p. 100): only a worthy heart is capable of love. "Je ne puis exprimer aujourd'hui tout ce que l'amour nous inspirait à l'un et à l'autre dans un instant" (pp. 38-39): love sweeps you off your feet; etc. There is a true language of passion--"les protestations de fidélité, telles que des amis sincères les peuvent prononcer" (p. 76)--and it is spoken by a character like Miledi B*** even when it borrows a timeworn cliché like "voyez si vous voulez me suivre et venir au bout de l'univers" (p. 78) because she restores to it an absolute literalness: she really wants to attempt to realize such a dream of guaranteed exclusiveness.

Overshadowing this accepted potentiality in practice, however, is first a kind of detached generalized observation about the way love seems to operate, including some analytical maxims: "le plaisir imite un peu l'amour" (p. 151), "tout m'était nouveau, et cette nouveauté est l'âme de l'amour" (p. 40); and a more seriously subversive derogation of its language. But the line is thin between the categories. The Count remains lucid enough to make the following analysis of his conversation with Mme de Selve, and yet demonstrates at the same time that continued exposure to such rhetoric tends to corrupt the logical processes:

> Je lui disais que lorsqu'on avait donné son coeur, on ne devait pas refuser à un amant des faveurs dont le prix est moins précieux, quoique le plaisir en soit plus vif. Je lui présentais mes

raisons sous toutes les faces possibles, et je lui débitais enfin ces maximes et tous ces lieux communs que j'avais autrefois employés avec succès avec tant de femmes. [p. 138]

The economics of the first sentence, it can be seen, are a kind of rhetorical fraud: arbitrarily, the code assigns a high value to "heart," and then draws the consequence that once one admits to love the less valuable commodity--sex--cannot be withheld. It is a kind of syllogism, but it only works with the complicity of the partner. In Mme de Selve's case it does not take at all, thus revealing its falseness, its facticious status as mere commonplace without compelling substance.

Indeed, throughout the novel there are hints of a counterrhetoric in the irony of a narrator who has well learned the vanity of love's language, and consistently depreciates what he once calls the "metaphysics" of an elegantly coded discourse which has little relation to the "commerce" (p. 7) or practice of gallantry. The Count's first inklings of desire elicited by the Marquise de Valcourt are quickly cut down by the narrator's voice to their conventional, literary dimensions: "J'avais lu quelques romans, et je me crus amoureux." There is an undercurrent of a cynical love code operating, which refers for example to "toutes les protestations que les amants font en pareil cas souvent de la meilleure foi du monde, et qu'ils ne tiennent jamais" (p. 41), and which practices a systematic reduction of the standard formulas: "je ne laissai pas à la marquise le temps de me parler sentiment, et je crois qu'elle n'eut pas celui d'y penser" (p. 10); "j'avais envie de lui plaire, ou plutôt de l'avoir" (p. 46). In this way he short-circuits the euphemisms and exposes the insincerity or disingenuousness of "tout le langage froid et puérile de la galanterie" (p. 76). What makes that language unworthy, however, is the rift it allows between signifier and signified, or the deception of the displaced signified; such rhetoric itself mocks *true* love, whose validity is maintained in the Count's discourse although its definition may be problematic. A nice formula like "sans amour j'offrais mon coeur à Mme Dorsigny, et elle le reçut de même" (p. 150) can only operate its irony on the use of *coeur* if *amour* has a more or less stable referential value. The novel can come to the conclusion it does because while one kind of love is devalued, another remains possible and can eventually establish its truth.

Remorse has very little place in this narrative, and from the standpoint of sin there is nothing Christian about the Count's eventual conversion. But the beginning had announced that the torrent would eventually be replaced by a tranquillity possible only when the worldly experience has been carried to its utter exhaustion: "J'ai usé le monde, j'ai usé l'amour même; toutes les passions aveugles et tumultueuses sont mortes dans mon coeur" (p. 3).[17] This stage is in fact slow in developing, and seems to depend on a multiphased transformation, first mediated by the experience of Julie, and then passing through three distinct periods with Mme de Selve, where finally the plot joins a deeper thematic development to produce the resolution.

Although he had already evoked "l'idée d'une vie plus tranquille" (p. 116) in quitting Mme Dorval, it seems to take the curious lesson of a disinterested and pure Julie to make the Count dream of really different feelings from those he has previously known. The very spectacle of a pure attachment operating totally outside the framework of worldly life obsesses him with a fascinated meditation, introducing the image of a perfect love; and his own virtue which Julie's devotion elicits compensates him in turn with something that does not fit the habitual concept of pleasure. "Leur état m'en fit désirer un pareil. Je trouvai un vide dans mon âme que tous mes faux plaisirs ne pouvaient remplir" (p. 126): the sense of a lack, which he has never before expressed, clearly anticipates the quest for some new state of being. This new void is, so to speak, active; it empties his life, and impels a break with its usual geographic focus: "L'idée de ce bonheur me rendit tous mes autres plaisirs odieux, et pour me dérober à leur importunité, je résolus d'aller à la campagne." And this transition makes him available to the woman who, to the "homme répandu" he was, offers only a retreat.

It is notable that the person whose life has been preoccupied with what are conventionally called affairs of "love" should on this occasion experience it unawares, because it sneaks up unexpected avenues: "j'en devins amoureux sans le prévoir, et je l'aimais avec passion, quand je croyais simplement la respecter" (p. 128). Mme de Selve too has been "surprised" by love: "J'ai senti pour vous l'intérêt le plus tendre avant que je m'en fusse aperçue" (p. 137). Ironically--and this is much like what transpires in Marivaux's "surprise de l'amour" plays--the language which has been so accustomed to speaking glibly of love becomes by that fact an obstacle to its communication. Because this time the stakes really matter, the Count takes refuge in vague language rather than broach Mme de Selve through the standard vehicle which now seems inadequate. A system of gestures has to take its place:

J'avais fait ces déclarations à toutes les femmes dont je n'étais pas amoureux, et ce fut dans le moment que je ressentis véritablement l'amour, que je n'osai plus en prononcer le nom. Je ne disais pas à la vérité à Mme de Selve que je l'aimais; mais toute ma conduite le lui prouvait, je m'apercevais même que mes sentiments ne lui échappaient pas. [pp. 130-31]

There is still some confusion of domains here, for her uniqueness has not yet been fully revealed. He effects a kind of seduction--at least he calls it that--based not on the deceitful meanings of words, but on their insidious contagion as pregnant signifiers: "Une femme qui parle souvent des dangers de l'amour, s'aguerrit sur les risques, et s'y familarise avec la passion; c'est toujours parler de l'amour, et l'on n'en parle guère impunément. . . . L'amour qui ne révolte pas d'abord devient bientôt contagieux" (pp. 134-35).[18] It is as if the words implanted their signified upon contact.

As this subtle invasion in her is taking place, the Count is realizing that the rules of the game have shifted, that he is no longer himself obeying the normal mechanism when he becomes "constant" without even obtaining a favor; and indeed he cannot explain this to himself, inasmuch as there usually would be no means of keeping him attached for so long (three months), favors or no. When he swears "une constance à toute épreuve" (p. 132) this time it has a different timbre: not because it is "true" in the absolute but because it is sincere, as the offer of his hand soon after--something he has certainly never been moved to before--must prove. He calls it a new kind of life; and yet he falls back on his accustomed formulas. But to no avail: "Mme de Selve ne se conduisait pas sur les mêmes principes que celles que j'avais rencontrées" (p. 138). The protagonist is to be saved from his former manner (as is by implication Meilcour in *Les Egarements du coeur et de l'esprit*) by the totally ungallant woman.

This will come about in parallel to the terminological transition from a predominance of love to that of friendship. Such a shift is far from complete at this stage, but the groundwork is already laid, and for that matter has been from some time. Miledi *** was already qualified as an "ami sincère," and the Count on that occasion had asserted his own incapacity for deceit (pp. 76-77); but her proposal of completely renouncing civil society (like Alceste's to Célimène) could not at that juncture tempt him. Then the experience of Senecé, even though second-hand for him and negative in import, elicits from the Count these prophetic words: "c'est le comble du bonheur, de goûter avec la même personne les plaisirs de l'amour et les douceurs de l'amitié, d'y trouver à la fois une amante tendre et un ami sûr, je ne désirerais pas d'autre félicité" (p. 102).[19] The name of friendship in which he thus implores Senecé to renounce Mme Dornal (friendship--and family--should speak louder than love) reinforces that theme.

And in fact Mme de Selve does not become his mistress until her role as friend has also been sealed: "je trouvai en elle l'ami le plus sûr" (p. 141). The use of the masculine *ami* is interesting, and seems to strengthen the force of the term by making of it an absolute attribute in lieu of the feminine one would normally expect. The euphoria he expresses when finally the relationship is consummated depends indeed on this complexity of sentiments; and the formula "je devins le plus heureux des hommes," despite its banality, is one he has never used before. "Pour concevoir mon bonheur, il faut avoir éprouvé les mêmes désirs. Quoique j'eusse passé ma vie avec les femmes, ce plaisir fut nouveau pour moi; c'est l'amour seul qui en fait le prix. Je ne sentis point succéder au feu des désirs ce dégoût humiliant pour les amants vulgaires. Mon âme jouissait toujours" (pp. 142-43). The terms which stigmatize past experience (*dégoût humiliant, amants vulgaires*) are strong; they set this particular experience apart by its ability to survive immediate satisfaction, and elevate the Count into a new and privileged class of lovers: the soul has finally joined with the body in its *jouissance*. In order to express this novelty, he appeals, in tones echoing those of *Manon Lescaut*, to a higher plane of sensibility, accessible to but a few: "des transports qui ne se peuvent comprendre que par ceux qui les ont éprouvés."

What sounds much like the end of the story is, however, a decoy. The sense of absolute bankruptcy which is the precondition of his transfiguration is only to come after the sad realization that even Mme de Selve does not fulfill him completely. Mme de Selve is a kind of Princesse de Clèves who has given in, and lost her *repos*; and when she exclaims "je vous perdrai!" in the face of the Count's renewed vows, the reader is forced to accept the narrative function (inevitable fulfillment) of the prophecy.[20] The narrator in his own voice foreshadows as much by the disabused universality of his reflection, "Je n'aspire point à changer la condition humaine; mais nos coeurs *devraient* être plus parfaits, la jouissance des âmes *devrait* être éternelle" (p. 144, my italics). Even this glorious new passion falls under the pressure of the *usé*, of time, of the rule which the maxim codifies: "Les amants qui ont usé le premier feu de la passion, sont charmés qu'on coupe la longueur du tête-à-tête" (p. 148). This failure is thus assimilated to a generalized meditation on human limits: constancy is henceforth viewed as a natural impossibility. And so the Count is once more enticed back into the world, even though, in lieu of ennui, it can offer him only constraint, "poisoned" pleasure, and a sense of existential disparity which never before troubled him: "L'état le plus incommode pour un honnête homme est de ne pouvoir pas accorder son coeur avec sa conduite" (p. 151). The woman he elects in this situation, Mme Dorsigny, is not of a higher level than his former mistresses; she, like they, is prized only for her vivacity, "propre à me délasser du sérieux où je vivais avec Mme de Selve."

Out of this crucible comes the new alloy of *amour* and *amitié*. The Dorsigny episode functions as a kind of test, even though Mme de Selve, who has relinquished her claims, has not designed it as such. It helps him discover that his changed heart ("un coeur nouveau") gravitates back to its re-maker; infidelity is more in the mind than the heart.[21] And this burning-out of the first--and physical--passion appears unexpectedly as the necessary precondition for the combination that is to follow: "Mon amour devenu plus tranquille s'était uni à l'amitié la plus tendre." Despite the cooling of ardor, the Count is involved for the first time with someone he regards as absolutely necessary (p. 159). This is doubtless the most original part of the novel, not so much because of the amour/amitié alternation but because it operates through a methodical depreciation of lasting passion. When the Count renews not only his marriage offer but his promise of eternal fidelity (for it is as if he, despite all that has happened, knows no better way to express himself), it is not exactly in bad faith, and Mme de Selve herself accepts the sincerity of his words; but she still cannot credit them either, and therefore is led to draw the same conclusion he has, on the broadest level possible: "la constance n'est pas au pouvoir des hommes" (p. 161). One cannot will constancy, and man (or men) cannot distinguish between novelty and love. The matter of whether sexual infidelity is a consequence of human nature in general or of the social group in particular this novel does not, and indeed cannot, decide: one way or another, its determination in the Count's case is fatal.

It is therefore the sense of love and not fidelity which must undergo some modification. Mme de Selve continues to insist that her "friend" be her "lover," if he is also to be her husband: but she is not speaking the language of pleasure, which in fact she barely recognizes. She is sexually passive: "je suis fort peu sensible aux plaisirs des sens" (p. 165). What she calls love is something more concentratedly affective in character which, given that women have more tenderness than men, and less desire (p. 165), can better become accessible to the male when the intensity of his desire has waned.

The Count accepts this distinction and even feels shamed by the contrast between them, yet unable to effect any change through reason. That is why the parallel adventure with Mme Dorsigny (and perhaps others as well) continues to play a role: only disgust (again, the term *dégoûter* is emphatic) can finally eradicate the attraction of other women:

> Ce n'était pas la raison qui devait me ramener et me guérir de mes erreurs; il m'était réservé de me dégoûter des femmes par les femmes mêmes. Bientôt je ne trouvai plus rien de piquant dans leur commerce. Leur figure, leurs grâces, leur caractère, leurs défauts mêmes, rien n'était nouveau pour moi. Je ne pouvais pas faire une maîtresse qui ne ressemblât à quelqu'une de celles que j'avais eues. Tout le sexe n'était plus pour moi qu'une seule femme pour qui mon goût était usé, et ce qu'il y a de singulier, c'est que Mme de Selve, reprenait à mes yeux de nouveaux charmes. [pp. 165-66]

A conversion is taking place--it is nothing less than that--following the reduction of all womankind save one into a single, necessarily tiresome image which replaces the multiplicity on which inconstancy depended. Variety, even though it would be irresistible, is no longer obtainable; change is sameness and pleasure boredom. To escape this impasse, the Count must decide, in the same movement, both to withdraw from its topological capital, Paris,[22] and to displace the source of meaning, with Mme de Selve as a sort of spiritual guide, from love, the significance of which has been systematically evacuated by the whole social group, and even from the more materialistic and purportedly tangible value of pleasure, to a new and non-mundane concept of friendship, which supplants both of the former even in marriage. Unlike the romantic notion of exclusive passion which idealizes the sexual object as an irreplaceable singularity, this process leads the Count to renounce his usual forms of desire and to fall back on a distinctive person who precisely is no longer his mistress and so can now become his wife--one who, if not romantic, is at least unique in some ways to him.

Mme de Selve's "nouveaux charmes" then emerge as a paradox, possible only because the sense of the terms has subtly shifted: "Ce n'était plus les désirs de l'amour que nous cherchions; un sentiment plus tendre régnait dans mon coeur" (p. 167). The semantic displacement translates a thorough renovation of values. Only after demonstrating to his own satisfaction the impossibility of constancy does the Count find himself able to be constant. It would appear too that he has thereby more or less renounced sexuality; or at least it, like constancy, is now an irrelevant object of discourse. The removal from society is now logical, because Mme de Selve comes alone to repopulate his universe: "Je trouve l'univers entier avec ma femme qui est mon amie." Indeed the two of them are incompatible with the world, to which they would now appear ridiculous. "Le monde est inutile à notre bonheur, et ne ferait que nous trouver ridicules" (p. 167)-- conjugal bliss being regarded not only as a *ridicule* but also as bourgeois. He makes no claim that this is paradise. It is merely, as the urbanely prudent formula which closes the book makes clear, the best of *possible* worlds: "l'état . . . le plus heureux où un honnête homme puisse aspirer."[23]

What we have then from the standpoint of *Bildungsroman* is a kind of novel of futility, turning rather suddenly in the direction of conventional morality which, nonetheless, has its original aspects, not the least of which is that it is not directly in the service of religion.[24] The narrative develops the endless repetition, in the name of variety, of a highly stylized mode of aristocratic existence, yet paradoxically, in the end, collapses that multiplicity into unicity. By the same turn, the rationale of Part One once more becomes ambiguous, since what was justified in the name of character types now evaporates, the various individuals disappearing and leaving in their wake only identity. As a particular court type, the Count is shown to tend toward and finally realize the complete reduction of all experience within the framework of a certain social stratum to circularity and meaninglessness. But the didactic side is also problematic. The overall narrative explains in its way why the Count renounces his former life; but because that does not happen for reasons we would call really moral, it does not necessarily urge the addressee to imitate him. Neither before nor after his transformation, therefore, does his life's story stand *for* anything--not for the worldly life nor even for conversion. It is recuperated in writing despite the project that it should be forgot, and this process in reviving it creates at once all its lessons and all its uncertainties.

## NOTES

Charles Pinot Duclos (1704-1772), *Confessions du comte de \*\*\**, 1741. Edition: Paris: Marcel Didier, "Société des Textes Français Modernes" (ed. Laurent Versini), 1969. Spelling in the quotations will be modernized. The same essential text--that is, one based upon the original edition of 1741 rather than the substantially modified later versions--is available in modernized form in Vol. II of René Etiemble's Pléiade edition *Romanciers du XVIII^e siècle* (Paris: Gallimard, 1965).

[1] Daniel Mornet, *La Pensée française au dix-huitième siècle* (11th ed., Paris: Armand Colin, 1965), p. 19.

[2] Paul Meister tallies about twenty (*Charles Duclos*, Geneva: Droz, 1956, p. 213); Jacques Brengues about twenty-five (*Charles Duclos ou l'obsession de la vertu*, Saint-Brieuc: Presses Universitaires de Bretagne, 1971, p. 36); and Laurent Versini, twenty-three plus (ed. cit. p. xx).

[3] *Caillete*: "personne qui a du babil et point de consistance" (Littré).

[4] Which leads Meister to the remark that the number of the Count's conquests is not so great after all: "Pour un homme à bonnes fortunes, le chiffre semble plutôt modeste" (p. 213); but this is to confuse a mathematical calculation, by which one year per mistress would seem less than a precipitous pace, with the cumulative effect of the narrative.

[5] See Versini's n. 59, pp. xxvii-xxviii. One correction, however, seems in order. Versini objects that Duclos impossibly tries to squeeze too much in between the battle of Villaviciosa (10 Dec. 1710) and the capture of Gironne (25 Jan. 1711). Such a problem disappears if one simply follows the novel's interior chronology without giving absolute value to historical dates: it thus suffices to say that here the taking of Gironne is situated in late 1711. Aside from this matter, I can perceive only one miniscule lapse in chronology: it is when the Count says he saw the Intendante again in Paris a year after Utrecht (1713), at which time he is apparently instead in Venice (p. 34).

[6] In the case of Crébillon's *Egarements*, which was never completed, the "cycle" is of course only virtual; still, the counter movement to *égarement* which the title necessarily implies is unambiguously announced in the opening pages.

[7] For a full general discussion of this literary frame of reference, see Peter Brooks, *The Novel of Worldliness* (Princeton: Princeton University Press, 1969), particularly the chapter on Crébillon and Duclos.

[8] All but one are women, and tangentially affect his love life: both Mme de Valcourt and Mme de Gremonville are friends of relatives; another relative provokes the jealousy of Miledi B*** (p. 76). One could consider this a muted sort of incest motif.

[9] Cf. the remarks of A. Kibédi Varga: "Il n'y a pas de bourgeois dans le roman érotique: le culte exclusif du sentiment aussi bien que le culte exclusif du sens semble être réservé à une classe privilégiée" ("La Désagrégation de l'idéal classique," *Studies on Voltaire and the Eighteenth Century*, 26, p. 992).

[10] Again, one would be entitled here to give a sexual meaning to the terms employed: the literal and the figurative filling of a void in fact coincide. Note that the expression "indispensablement nécessaire" imitates precious speech and thus parodies Mme de Persigny's overemphatic way of talking.

[11] There is another echo in M. de Gremonville's bantering "elle vous convertira" (p. 53), for Antonia in her fanatic devotion had been much concerned about their "difference" of religions (and there is implied humor in Antonia's calling for holy water because this aspiring infidel [protestant] has kissed her hand).

[12] This allusion reflects the notoriety of the conventional anonymity provided by the mask worn during the Carnival, a custom imported from Italy, and more specifically of its continued use in celebrated night spots typified by the *Ridotto* of Venice.

[13] The *directeur*'s role in this is inherently dubious, as writers like Marivaux and Crébillon make clear; Duclos figures the paradox by expressing this situation in the rhetorical (and ironic) form of chiasmus: "ne pouvant pas faire de moi son directeur, je crois que de son directeur elle en fit son amant" (p. 55).

[14]Crébillon's *Le Sopha* of 1742, the year following *Les Confessions du comte de ***,* contains some highly amusing scenes exploiting these confusions with some bad faith; I have discussed them in *Le Masque et la parole: le langage de l'amour au XVIII^e siècle* (Paris: Jose Corti, 1973), pp. 145-46 and 180-81.

[15]There will be mention further on of the English national trait. Although this is hardly what would be considered a "romantic" novel, Miledi B*** may well be, for aught I know, European fiction's first character to commit suicide for love--some thirty-one years before *Werther.*

[16]"A novel directed to an exploration of this worldliness . . . will not describe objects, detail settings, or particularize the world, but rather will focus on language and gesture within a code, and will value forms like aphorism and portrait which transmute experience into language and permit final estimation of the individual's sociability, his adaptation to the image projected by society" (Peter Brooks, pp. 42-43).

[17]It is interesting to compare this expression, so similar in tone but so radically different in import, to Chateaubriand's famous characterization of *le mal du siècle*: "on habite avec un coeur plein un monde vide; sans avoir usé de rien on est désabusé de tout." Here, on the contrary, the idea of *désabusé* can only come as a consequence of the *usé*, worldweariness being the result of experience.

[18]This idea, which Duclos doubtless did not invent, reappears in two celebrated texts posterior to *Les Confessions* which might be noted for comparison: (1) "Sachez donc que le mal que les prudes disent de l'amour, la résistance qu'elles lui opposent, le peu de goût qu'elles affectent pour les plaisirs, la peur qu'elles en ont, tout cela est de l'amour" (Louis Damours, *Lettres de Ninon de Lenclos au marquis de Sévigné*, 1750, Paris: Bleuet, 1798, I, 111); (2) "Or, vous savez assez que femme qui consent à parler d'amour finit bientôt par en prendre, ou au moins par se conduire comme si elle en avait" (Laclos, *Les Liaisons dangereuses*, letter 76).

[19]This theme becomes commoner in the years following publication of this novel: one encounters it frequently, for example, in the works of Mme Riccoboni.

[20]Indicative of the reversal of roles which sets in to some extent is that the formula "je n'avais d'autre volonté que la sienne" (p. 138) reappears later as "elle n'avait jamais d'autre volonté que la mienne" (p. 148). *Selve* might be either a partial anagram of *Clèves* or an evocation of the non-worldly forest (*silva*).

[21]"L'inconstance que j'avais dans l'esprit plus que dans le coeur..." (p. 159); "Votre coeur est bon et fidéle; mais votre esprit est léger" (p. 162).

[22]"Where" they go does not specifically matter--there is no local color involved–except by semantic opposition to Paris: only the earlier identification of "mes terres" with Brittany would indicate the objective place on the map.

[23]I have mentioned the parallel between this conclusion and the one forecast but never written for *Les Egarements du coeur et de l'esprit*: it was said, notes a contemporary who all the same recognizes the substantial differences between the two novels, that "l'auteur des *Confessions* enleva à celui des *Egarements* le seul dénouement qui convînt à son ouvrage" (Nicolas Bricaire de la Dixmerie, "Discours sur l'origine, les progrès et le genre des romans," in *Toni et Clairette*, Paris: Didot, 1773, I, 1ii).

[24]For a discussion of the non-religious conversion in such contexts, cf. Jean Sgard, "La Notion d'égarement chez Crébillon," in *Dix-Huitième Siècle*, No. 1 (1969), pp. 241-49.

Chapter 7

Le Diable amoureux

Little at first suggests to the reader that he will have great difficulty making coherent sense of the story. The element of mystery seems quite undisguised. Don Alvare, after a brief initiation to the occult, intrepidly conjures the devil. After several grotesque manifestations, a beautiful and obedient servant appears, whom Alvare calls Biondetto or Biondetta. She grants his every wish, but refuses to leave him, and he is anxious both at this attachment and at his indebtedness to her. She claims to be a sprite who renounced the spirit world out of love for him, and she begs for a commitment from him. When finally he succumbs and proposes taking her from Italy to meet his mother in Spain to obtain her consent to the marriage, many strange events occur; before they arrive, his defeat is consummated and Biondetta ambiguously disappears, again amid strange apparitions.

Behind this strange but rather simple tale, however, there lurk considerable intricacies to mystify the critic. There will be many question marks in this chapter, because a close reading of the text can only put into relief how problematic it is. Critics have always called attention to its complexities, yet my impression is that they have nonetheless consistently underestimated them by retaining inflexible points of literalism in their readings. According to a modern biographer of Cazotte, for example, there is but little uncertainty; Alvare is finally saved from Biondetta the devil, and the only hesitation is whether the tale is to be taken as an essentially moral or psychological one.[1] Another critic has discussed the ambiguities of the conclusion, and the fundamental doubt as to whether Alvare really escapes or not, but does so only because Cazotte wrote two different conclusions: neither the identity of Biondetta nor the definitive nature of the truth pronounced at the end by Quebracuernos is questioned.[2] Everyone seems to notice, in the Epilogue's assertion that "l'allégorie est double," the significance of the word *allégorie*, but no one mentions *double*, which is what creates the real dilemma: what is the *second* (and for that matter the first) allegory? One is simultaneously mystified by allusion to the work in the Epilogue by the diminutive terms "petit ouvrage" and "chimères agréables," which would seem to undercut the weightiness of the allegory.

First, however, we must deal briefly with two problems regarding the status of the text, conditioning the manner in which it is appropriate to read it. The first concerns the option to adopt the revised 1776 text rather than the 1772 original, in which notably the ending was almost entirely different.[3] My principal reason, in line with the general rule that the author's definitive version is normally preferred, is that Cazotte explicitly recognized the revised text as superceding the former one by his discussion of their differences in the appended epilogue. He states there, furthermore, that his original intention was to complete a diptych, of which only the first part was published: this limits in any event the claim of that earlier edition to status of integral text. An important consequence of this choice for the reading which follows is that only the conclusion of the adopted version can be taken into account: we are only reading one text at a time, and are respecting its autonomy. By the same token, however, one must accept the Epilogue as fully a part of the new text, even in its discussion of the alternative versions: but they are then present only by representation. That is, one is not entitled to refer to the first version itself qua independent text, but only to what is said about it *here*; and at the same time "part two" of that version, although never published (and indeed still unknown), also exists on the level of *allusion*. But this is itself an ambiguous status, for in that supposedly suppressed supplement is to be found a major assertion not present elsewhere in the text: the devil is explicitly identified as Alvare's actual possessor. But at the same time that is signified precisely *as a variant*, as something suppressed; it stands, indeed, as an alternative, but not as *the* truth of the narrative--which in this instance has none.

Also, since this work differs in important ways from others discussed in this book, account must be taken of its particular generic affiliations. There can be little doubt, in the light of recent work, and especially of Todorov's on the fantastic genre, that *Le Diable amoureux* should be classified neither among *merveilleux* narratives nor among the fairy tales, both of which had long traditions before Cazotte, but as a *récit fantastique* of which he is in fact one of the creators. Despite similarities, the fantastic differs from them by characteristics which can be defined with some precision. It does not take place amidst an other-worldly suspension of the ordinary laws of nature:

> Dans un monde qui est bien le nôtre, celui que nous connaissons, sans diables, sylphides, ni vampires, se produit un événement qui ne peut s'expliquer par les lois de ce monde familier. Celui qui perçoit l'événement doit opter pour l'une des deux solutions possibles: ou bien il s'agit d'une illusion des sens, d'un produit de l'imagination et les lois du monde restent alors ce qu'elles sont; ou bien l'événement a véritablement eu lieu, il est partie intégrante de la réalité, mais alors cette réalité est régie par des lois inconnues de nous.[4]

In *Le Diable amoureux* we are certainly not in the merveilleux where absolutely anything may transpire. The physical and psychological laws of the real world govern the narrative with only exceptional violations which are easily identified, notably the frightening and spectacular wonders of Alvare's night in Portici with which the story commences, and which posit the existence of the enigmatic Biondetta. Otherwise, all progressions follow normal logic, and the narrative space-time is quite coherent. Except for the voyage from Turin to Estramadura (pp. 92-117), the action takes about six months, from Carnival season to July (p. 86; Biondetta says twice, pp. 82 and 92, that she has been incarnated for six months).

But it is unclear how to *interpret* these violations of the natural order, and this hesitation is inscribed in the text itself in that the narrator shares it. Such hesitation may be, in Todorov's terms, between the real and the illusory (the events happened, but are ill understood), or between the real and the imaginary (whether or not they really transpired). Both possibilities could apply, at different levels in the interpretation, to *Le Diable amoureux*. Note too that there is a difference between inscribing the reader's *perspective* in the text and figuring the *reader* in the text (as Renoncour does in *Manon Lescaut*, for example). The former depends only on, in this case, the fact that all the reader's perceptions come via those of the combined narrator-protagonist; allusions direct or indirect to the reader--"je continue ma route dans la situation que *l'on peut imaginer*" (p. 89, my italics)--are, however, rare.

The two radically opposed faces of Alvare's experience with Biondetta are of course incompatible, as Todorov remarks, but equally convincing: "La façon dont cet être est apparu indique clairement qu'il est un représentant de l'autre monde; mais son comportement spécifiquement humain (et, plus encore, féminin), les blessures réelles qu'il reçoit semblent, au contraire, prouver qu'il s'agit simplement d'une femme, et d'une femme qui aime" (Todorov, p. 28). But even when we allow that the gamut of the fantastic extending from the *étrange* to the *merveilleux* is continuous, there is no clear placement along it for this text, as further discussion will show. To the extent that what has happened to Alvare can be entirely explained as a dream, the story leaves the mixed "fantastique-merveilleux" to enter rather the domain of the "fantastique-étrange," where events which previously appeared supernatural are at the end given a rational explanation, as in Jean Potocki's *Le Manuscrit trouvé à Saragosse* (Todorov, p. 49). But that very interpretation--which indeed belongs to the natural order--can here succeed at best only partially.

The narration's first sentence provides "facts" which, besides their expository function, offer several levels of meaning. "J'étais à vingt-cinq ans..." for one thing suggests immediately, to anyone familiar with Dante's famous beginning, "Nel mezzo del camin di nostra vita," the strategic situation of a revelatory experience at somewhere near life's midpoint.[5] Both a military orientation and a social one are connoted in the next words: "...capitaine aux gardes du roi de Naples." The former might imply an optic for viewing the struggle of good and evil, or on another and less metaphysical but still metaphorical plane, relate the protagonist to Duclos's Comte de*** as a man of gallant pastimes; the latter tends to assimilate him to Des Grieux as one whose rank predisposes him to extraordinary and fateful adventures. Nor is Naples an indifferent location. Alvare's *gaieté* (p. 62) makes of him an adoptive Italian, whereas his seriousness and his sense of honor lean towards the somber Estramadura as the other geographical pole.[6] Occult secrets, like religious truths, seem to emanate from Italy (the devil answers in Italian: "Che vuoi?"); but the existence of Rome is merely implied, while Naples hints of a more uncontrolled and dark region symbolized by the ruins nearby and their role in the story.

The rest of the opening sentence ("nous vivions beaucoup entre camarades, et comme de jeunes gens, c'est-à-dire, des femmes, du jeu, tant que la bourse pouvait y suffire, et nous philosophions dans nos quartiers quand nous n'avions plus d'autre ressource") specifies three resources whose thematic role will be important throughout the narration: women, gambling/play (*jeu*), and philosophy. Since the major part of the plot is concerned with seduction, and a mistress of Alvare's makes an important intervention in it, little need be said for the moment about the first of these. *Jeu* figures prominently both as plot element and also as symbol: Alvare's whole enterprise in invoking spirits is a kind of game of chance involving his taste for risk; even gambling, "que j'aimais passionnément" (p. 65), loses its attraction without that element. Moreover, at just the time when he is trying to come to grips with the problem of who is Biondetta and what to do about her, he is immersed in *jeu*; unaccustomed gains and sudden losses lead to the first secrets divulged to him by his genie: "on apprend les jeux de chance, que vous appelez mal à propos jeux de hasard. Il n'y a point de hasard dans le monde: tout y a été et sera toujours une suite de combinaisons nécessaires que l'on ne peut entendre que par la science des nombres" (p. 64). Thus, through *jeu, hasard* becomes a doctrinary key, the frontier separating knowledge from ignorance: in short the very concept by which the philosophical domain is engaged.

The role of philosophy is of course evident in that it initially introduces the discussion of cabala which soon leads Alvare to his encounter with Biondetta. It continues thematically to underlie the events, corresponding to their ambiguities inasmuch as it primarily concerns the question of *secret* truths, known--and accessible--to only a few: of the five involved in the early debate, only one speaks up for the "science" which the others stigmatize brutally as "un amas d'absurdités, une source de friponneries propres à tromper les gens crédules et à amuser les enfants" (p. 33). There is no indication whether that singular voice is an initiate or on the contrary someone whose credence is based on mere hearsay. Soberano's continued silence suggests he has no truck with this person, and so we might conclude he is an outsider *if* Soberano himself represents the truth: but this, as we shall see, is uncertain also. Alvare's "j'ai deviné cette sphère élevée" (p. 35) qualifies him not merely as curious but as favorably predisposed, intuitively in contact with what is to be revealed.

Knowledge specifically mediates the relationship between matter and spirit, as Soberano makes clear by the bipolar nature of his test question to Alvare: "Croyez-vous qu'il puisse exister une science qui enseigne à transformer les métaux et à réduire les esprits sous notre obéissance?" (p. 34). (The exact place to assign in this schema to astrology, which seems to have some access to truth when invoked by the gypsies--witches?--on p. 104, seems undecidable.) That these two registers, which imply each other and must be linked, remain nonetheless distinct and irreducible to Alvare as the story goes on is suggested even in the language he uses to describe his own behavior, for example: "Je me promène à grands pas dans mon appartement, cherchant la tranquillité de l'esprit dans l'agitation continuelle du corps" (p. 70). Even his attempt to believe that his imagination is troubled, which would leave material existence unshaken, succumbs to the invasion of the real by the dream; the signifiers, linguistic and other, no longer can separate them: "Tout ceci me paraît un songe, me disais-je; mais la vie humaine est-elle autre chose? Je rêve plus extraordinairement qu'un autre, et voilà tout" (p. 80). The rational faculty, which in profane science is in contact with the material, loses its hold in this temptation of the spirit: "Le résultat de mes réflexions fut de me livrer encore plus à mon penchant, en croyant consulter ma raison" (p. 81).

The thirst for secret knowledge is in itself reminiscent of the tree of the knowledge of good and evil by which Satan tempted man to his Fall. It takes on a further dimension as temptation, however, when it is coupled with that of power: Alvare, predicts Biondetta, "nous soumettra, avec les éléments dont j'aurai abandonné l'empire, les esprits de toutes les sphères. Il est fait pour être le roi du monde, et j'en serai la reine, et la reine adorée de lui" (pp. 79-80). The Biblical text recalled here is not that of the Fall but the temptation of Jesus by Satan, which also amounts to the exchange of worship (note the ambiguity of *adorée de lui*) for earthly dominion. Thus when Alvare, who up to this time has wanted to avoid discussion of Biondetta's secrets, brings up again later on his own initiative her promise to impart knowledge (p. 82), the *connaissances* he demands are tinged with this further, although unexpressed connotation.

Soberano at first appears to be the instrument of Alvare's initiation,[7] the tutor who will soon be eclipsed by his more gifted pupil. Everything about this relationship, however, is ultimately questionable. Calderon, Soberano's personal genie, is to all appearances a benign spirit (he says that in any event only our weakness can give the spirits power over us), but that really depends upon the reliability of Soberano himself. Soberano's identification of himself with "natural religion"--a highly charged term in the eighteenth century--could be read, depending on contextual factors which appear insufficiently strong here to determine the position, as either a negative or a positive marker. Alvare describes Soberano's two friends as being "d'une physionomie peu prévenante" (p. 37), and suspects they are all "mauvais plaisants" (p. 39). Their designs, according to Biondetta (p. 78), are even darker than that suggests; but we have then only her word for it, just as we have only her assertion for the accusation of necromancy which makes Alvare flee Naples, and for the insidious persecution of Alvare (or Biondetta, or both) by Bernadillo. (Alvare *thinks* he spots Bernadillo and recognizes his voice [p. 74] in Venice: objectively, he never knows.)

Be that as it may, Alvare is unwise, or more exactly foolhardy, from the "philosophical" standpoint (the novice risks loss of control) as well as from the Christian perspective represented by Quebracuernos (he is fooling with the devil). Playing with words--ultimately magic ones--comes rather easily to Alvare. With the bravado of a captain of the guard he says of the spirits, "Ah! je les commanderai!" (p. 37) just as he has the arrogance to intone pompously, about arrogance: "Voilà, disais-je, le pouvoir du temps sur les ouvrages de l'orgueil et de l'industrie des hommes" (p. 37). Alvare assumes with regard to the spirits a facile kind of assurance: "S'il ne tient qu'à ne pas les craindre, je les mets au pis pour m'effrayer" (p. 37). But this formulation of the problem is misleading, first because it is essentially tautological, and secondly because it fails to foresee that the devil can seduce as well as cower. Nor, for that matter, does Soberano give him a clear reply: "si vous êtes si sûr de vous, vous pouvez vous risquer" is ambiguous, and promises at most that he can assume his own risks. The rapid undoing of Alvare (who likens himself to the *fanfaron* of comedy as soon as he finds himself alone in the ruins of Portici) is signaled by the disparity between word and deed. The devil seems to put him to an immediate test of literalness, which he fails: he who had boldly exclaimed, "Je tirerais les oreilles au grand Diable d'enfer," now finds himself confronted by a grotesque apparition defiantly characterized precisely by its available ears ("surtout elle avait des oreilles démesurées" [p. 39]) as is its successor form, the spaniel ("les oreilles traînantes jusqu'à terre" [p. 41]). Alvare unwittingly betrays his own (perhaps repressed) awareness of the challenge he is avoiding, in that he was free to specify the second form the spirit would take, and himself elected--even among all possible dogs!-- the spaniel.

As at birth, of which we have a figure when Alvare steps outside the circle or *pantacle* protecting him, the novice is not so much delivered into a new sphere of knowledge as engulfed by an uncertainty which can nevermore be dispelled. It cannot even be determined whether he owes his spectacular success on this occasion to a particular spiritual adeptness (Biondetta will speak both of his "imprudence" [p. 54]--of course she in so saying is trying to trap him between a past and a future "imprudence," since in the same passage she says, "Si vous méconnaissez mon zèle par la suite, vous serez imprudent" [p. 55]--and of "la vigueur de votre âme" [p. 78]), or, on the contrary, to his unexampled and reckless presumption (he calls it "curiosité vaine" and "témérité" [p. 48]). Every utterance becomes henceforth ambiguous: "Vous nous donnez un beau régal, ami," says Soberano, "il vous coûtera cher." Bernadillo's words likewise seem both flattering and ominous; he alludes to "la plus céleste vision" but also suggests Alvare is burning his candle at both ends: "à votre âge on désire trop pour se laisser le temps de réfléchir, et on précipite ses jouissances" (p. 47). All the visual signs Alvare now records are laced with paradox, as in for example his description of Fiorentina:

> Elle prend sa harpe, prélude avec une *petite* main longuette, *potelée*, tout à la fois *blanche* et *purpurine*, dont les doigts insensiblement arrondis par le bout étaient terminés par un ongle dont la forme et la grâce étaient inconcevables. . . . On n'a

pas, avec plus de *gosier*, plus d'âme, plus d'*expression*: on ne saurait rendre *plus*, en chargeant *moins*. [p. 45, my italics]

Even when the sense is not apparently contradictory here, the referent is evasive: can one picture what is meant by "doigts *insensiblement* arrondis par le bout"? Biondetta proper (although Fiorentina is Biondetta)[8] also in many ways obscures all the signs, with increasing confusion towards the end of the story, which she leaves with both a diabolical *Che vuoi?* and a "frightening" (?) *human* laughter (p. 115).

Alvare is instinctively concerned, once the magical banquet of Portici is over, about the risk of entering into (or worse, of having already done so inadvisedly) a pact with the devil. He neglected to ask Soberano how to put an end to the spell and send the spirit away, then exacerbated his own vulnerability by leaving the protective circle. Yet on the way back to Naples he makes a silent vow to his mother to desist his experiments, as if unaware that even this first episode is not over yet, that while thinking this he is still riding in the carriage he ordered up from Biondetta. After that first evening he asks no more services of Biondetta; but he continues, somewhat passively, to accept the favors politely proffered. Uneasy about the persistant presence of this ambiguous creature who may be the devil or one of his emissaries, he still knows not how to dispel it, and his attempt to do so now brings an ominous yet ambiguous reply:

> "Biondetto, vous m'avez bien servi, vous avez même mis des grâces à ce que vous avez fait pour moi, mais comme vous étiez payé d'avance, je pense que nous sommes quittes...
> --Don Alvare est trop noble pour croire qu'il ait pu s'acquitter à ce prix... [p. 49]

There is something too facile about this approach, for to what does "vous étiez payé d'avance" refer? The gnawing, dreadful fear of an unholy obligation is explored again in terms of a debt:

> --Si vous avez fait plus que vous ne me devez, si je vous dois de reste, donnez votre compte, mais je ne vous réponds pas que vous soyez payé promptement. Le quartier courant est mangé; je dois au jeu, à l'auberge, au tailleur...
> --Vous plaisantez hors de propos... [p. 49]

The reply, once again, does nothing to dispel the doubt: it can mean either "you own me nothing" or "surely you don't think it is that simple." When Biondetta renders him the service (if it is that) of warning of the supposed plot against him, the debt, now disguised as a loan, increases, and is modified by implications of a league between them (Biondetta: "vos intérêts et les miens" [p. 54]). Alvare, wary of an imprecise sort of indebtedness to his page lest it implicate him in ways unsuspected, insists on the faithfully executed I.O.U. Even were Biondetta to disappear at this moment, Alvare would doubtless have to be concerned about this: a promissory note to the devil is not a happy thing to have hanging on one's conscience. Instead he takes measures to acquit the debt: "[Biondetto] m'a donné de l'argent; je veux le lui rendre" (p. 59); but the attempt only proves it cannot so easily be done, since unbeknownst to him the new money he puts to the purpose also comes from the same (or a related) source.[9] In fact, every time he pays Biondetta (in restoring the capital she has advanced for his gambling, for example), it is with money he again owes to her. Biondetta's manner is not insistent, but the implications of her presence and the debt are.

Yet Alvare commits once more the same mistake as before by attempting to drain words of their power, referring depreciatively as "les mots qui lui semblaient si importants" (p. 56) to the oath—affiliating her definitively with him—which complaisance leads him to pronounce. In time, these terms are eclipsed by a language of love; but then his terms of devotion to Biondetta continue to hint via another register at the debt, the league all but forgotten: "je me lie par des liens indissolubles" (p. 76). Whatever binds--*lier*--is in some sense a debt (cf. the etymology of the English words *lien* and *liable*). While it thus becomes ostensibly a question of giving and not owing, Biondetta steadily pushes in the direction of words which will bind irrevocably: "il faut que vous vous donniez, et sans réserve et pour toujours. . . . Il me faut un abandon absolu" (p. 82); this total commitment is to be motivated out of desire and willfulness rather than indebtedness or obligation, which offends the rhetoric of love.

There is thus, of course, confusion about the true nature of the stakes. Biondetta emphasizes not his degree of engagement, but hers; it is she who is depicted as a prisoner of what has been once sealed: "la folie est faite" (p. 91), "j'ai balancé pendant des siècles à faire un choix, il est fait, il est sans retour" (p. 110). "Une imprudence plus grande que la vôtre" (p. 50) maintains her in a position which is apparently doubly inferior to his, in that she is a servant-spirit, and in that she is a woman and subject to woman's frailty. He is the "master."[10] Neither her language nor his can be taken on the surface as a reliable gauge of their relative status. She confirms Soberano's assertion that mortals have power over the spirit world and that he can protect her; yet at the same time he needs her knowledge to reign over "les hommes, les éléments, la nature entière" (p. 112). The gypsies seems to reinforce this promise: "La terre en vous voit son maître" (p. 105); but note that Biondetta has upped the ante and now pictures Alvare ruling on an even greater scale.

What exactly has been promised, after all, and what is required in return? There is something Kafkaesque about the engagement, insofar as it is nowhere explicit just how the game is played. Yet it must be played. Are the rules (are there rules?) followed? It seems that, unable to lure Alvare by vice, or pass a Faustian contract with him in exchange for something desired (even sex, which apparently is not particularly his weakness), Biondetta must have recourse to direct, personal sexual seduction, which paradoxically must take the guise of modesty, as the Epilogue asserts: "son adversaire, pour le tromper, est réduit à se montrer honnête et presque prude, ce qui détruit les effets de son propre système, et rend son succès incomplet" (p. 124). The devil is accustomed to ruse, but perhaps not to feigning virtue; it would seem then that this is a form of cheating, a strategic error which somehow compromises his/her victory.

No matter where he turns, Alvare is surrounded by ambiguity. Attempts to solicit valid information from Biondetta procure oblique and conditional answers, even when he demands "clarté et précision" (p. 55). He continues to be disturbed about the monster and the spaniel who preceded her appearance at Portici (p. 78); it was he after all who gave her the same name as the dog, thus recognizing their continuity. He defers to her as to a woman, and retains her out of a certain sense of gallantry. But in fact he does not know what code to apply, whether to treat her like a spirit or like a lady. A worldly man inculcated with a strong concept of honor--plus some sentimental or sensuous inclination--prefers to opt for the lady. Yet if she is human, this affects his own nature, making of him the cruel monster ("je suis un tigre, un monstre" [p. 76]) perhaps responsible for her death. For it must be remembered that Alvare is not purely and simply seduced in this story, he is mislead also by his sense of compassion: "Ah! chassons des idées qui me feraient manquer à la reconnaissance, à l'humanité" (p. 76). Sex may be among the most obvious of temptations, but what if one's sense of humanity cannot be trusted either?

On the other hand, Alvare does not try very hard to get at the truth. He would rather have reassurance than revelation: "Achevez de rassurer un coeur tout à vous, et qui veut se dévouer pour la vie" (p. 78). He is lulled too by his own passive tendencies, which hardly hasten to come to terms with the problem: why indeed need one expedite her withdrawal, if an act of will at any time will suffice? But the ability to will itself wanes, and finally, for lack of it, Alvare flees--first into worldly life, later towards Estramadura. And added to this is an important aspect of the plot construction: between pages 50 and 113, nothing unambiguously supernatural transpires. There are to be sure things which are strange, even eery: the bed which breaks, (p. 52), his dog pulling at his leg (p. 83), the violent obstacles placed in his way by nature and man during the voyage to Spain (pp. 92-95); the gypsies whose significance hovers at the border of the natural world. What is original about *Le Diable amoureux* is not so much the supernatural it contains as this unclear distribution: the long suspension which coddles the mind into a certain inattention, even into a certain sense of security, before the stability again begins to crack.

Everything Alvare can perceive about Biondetta makes her difficult to identify. She is associated with music, first in the Fiorentina scene, then with the harpsicord and song; her voice, "à la douceur de laquelle la plus délicieuse musique ne saurait se comparer" (p. 112), could be that of a Siren or the vestige of her origins as sylphid, pure spirit of air. There is something ephemeral about the prism effect which seems to make of her an image of an image: "Je n'avais pas besoin de me retourner pour la voir: trois glaces, disposées dans le salon, répétaient tous ses mouvements" (p. 61). And the rhetoric of love comes as quickly to her lips as to his. Her vulnerability, as evidenced by the wound inflicted on her through the apparent ministry of Olympia, not only lowers his defenses, it also assuages his suspicions because of the carnal mortality it implies: "Elle avait la vie comme je l'ai, et la perd" (p. 76). She claims that she has contracted life--and thus mortality--in order to obtain their corollary, which is sensation (p. 79); she thus illustrates this paradox: immortals do not live. It is nonetheless uncertain that she can die: she misses a good chance; and there is no clear explanation for her curious suspension of animation just previous to her victory over him.[11]

And it is just that: a conquest of the male by the female. It operates through the medium of sex, but is expressed in a way which curiously asexualizes her: "la révolte de mes sens subsiste d'autant plus impérieusement qu'elle ne peut être réprimée par la raison. Elle me livre sans défense à mon ennemi: il en abuse et me rend aisément sa conquête" (p. 114). Many indices in the earlier parts of the story, however, prepare this confusion and this ambiguity about the sensual nature of the whole experience, beginning with his description of himself as "affamé d'idées nouvelles" (p. 36): could one of the allegories of *Le Diable amoureux* concern initiation to, and contamination by, the female? In this perspective the ugly camel's head could symbolize the animal nature of sexual appetite. This much is conjectural, but there is nothing subtle on the contrary about the way the spaniel disarms his aggressive urge by baring her sex to full view: "je fais un mouvement pour lui tirer les oreilles, il se couche sur le dos, comme pour me demander grâce; je vis que c'était une petite femelle" (p. 41)! He sees Biondetta indeed as a woman ("l'élégance, l'avantage de la taille se faisaient beaucoup plus remarquer sous l'ajustement de femme que sous l'habit de page" [p. 45]), and she tells him as much ("vos soldats, vos gens m'ont vue et ont deviné mon sexe" [p. 50]), but he tries to repress this knowledge of her femininity. And she immediately, symbolically, invades his bed: "la scène finit là pour le moment; mais elle recommença bientôt dans mon lit" (p. 51). He continues for a long while to alternate between masculine and feminine designations for her, made more plausible by the prevalence of the masculine term *mon page*. But why should he swear on his honor (which he surely does not take lightly) that Biondetta is *not* a woman, when Olympia confronts him with this fact? Here, as in the philosophical sphere, there is an opposition between penchants and principles, and when he finally decides that only his mother can authorize such a relationship, Biondetta mocks his filial dependence: "Est-ce un homme destiné à la haute science qui me parle, ou un enfant qui sort des montagnes de l'Estramadure?" (p. 84). She insists more and more overtly on her sexual identity and sensuous nature: "Je ne suis pas devenue femme pour rien" (p. 85); "je suis femme, enfin, . . . je ne suis pas de marbre. . . . Mes sensations sont d'une vivacité dont rien n'approche, mon imagination est un volcan" (p. 91). The volcano as organic metaphor might well frighten him, and even more so her taking his hand and placing it on her breast (p. 96). Once possessed, he is "honteux, immobile" (pp. 111-12); and his last memory of Biondetta is haunted with the grotesque phallic forms both of the snails' gleaming horns and the camel's enormous tongue (pp. 114-15). In his mind as he heads homeward the next day are the twin resolutions to take the frock and renounce women, as if both were aspects of repudiating the devil.[12]

The force in him most strongly resisting the attractions of Biondetta is, of course, the idea of his mother. She, if not more specifically the uterus, is symbolized by the *pantacle*, the magic circle, inscribed with mysterious characters which Alvare, as in a state of preconsciousness, cannot fully apprehend. Nor does he grasp the danger of emerging from it; does not the spaniel say, "le cercle redoutable qui vous environne me repousse" (p. 41)? After the banquet, his thought reverts instinctively to his mother robed in her dual attributes, "la femme la plus religieuse, la plus respectable" (p. 48), anti-devil and anti-sex at once. It is evident that she represents, among other things, the Faith, and the scene where he sees her image on a tomb is coupled with a penitence for his long absence from church.[13] But the rivalry between her and Biondetta is not limited to this plane. To begin with, Biondetta engages Alvare to keep her by exploiting an injunction made by his mother on the subject of gentlemanly behavior: "Quand ma mère me donna ma première épée, elle me fit jurer sur la garde de servir toute ma vie les femmes, et de n'en pas désobliger une seule" (pp. 50-51). It is as if his mother had armed him--at birth, but also as an act of sponsorship and initiation--with a phallus; but in the back of his mind, she also forbids its unauthorized use, despite the ambiguous order to "serve" women. His masculinity is both affirmed and compromised at the start, just as his mother both forbids and then approves (in his mind) Biondetta.[14]

When tempted by Biondetta, he regularly alternates between her image and that of Doña Mencia, which also exercises a magnetic attraction; a return to his mother for counsel is the only resolution he seems to have the force to frame. He *talks* to her:

O ma mère! disais-je . . . [p. 48]
Digne femme! m'écriai-je: que fais-je ici? [p. 62]
Tendre mère! m'écriai-je, vous ne m'abandonnez pas . . . [p. 76]
O ma mère! est-ce pour m'avertir . . .? [p. 87]

And, on two occasions, she talks to him too in absentia: during the first dream (p. 75), and at the church (pp. 87-88). In the dream, of course, Biondetta is ambiguously represented as a danger and the mother as salvation: but there is no way of knowing whether the dream speaks with the voice of Providence or the superego. *Respect* is generated by the mother image as a function of protection, and his fear of violating respect is identical with his fear of sexual involvement: as he says to Biondetta after nearly succumbing to her enticements, "Nous avons, lui dis-je, pensé faire hier une folie dont je me fusse repenti le reste de mes jours. . . . Vous regardant déjà comme ma femme, chère Biondetta, mon devoir est de vous respecter" (p. 83). Between the two sentences, he speaks of his mother.

When he thinks he sees her image in a church, he addresses her like an unfaithful but repentant lover: "votre Alvare vous a conservé tous vos droits sur son coeur. . . . Si je dois la bannir, enseignez-moi comment je le pourrai faire" (p. 87). She is, in short, asylum from whatever it is that beseiges him; "si je puis me mettre sous la sauvegarde de ma respectable mère, fantômes, monstres qui vous êtes acharnés sur moi, oserez-vous violer cet asile?" (p. 117). The mother is *inviolable*. And if he has caused her death he must be symbolically buried himself: "Je *m'ensevelirai* dans un cloître" (p. 117). But she is also the life principle, and in finding her again he is at once uplifted spiritually, and reborn: "J'*élève* la vue et reconnais ma mère *sur le balcon* de son appartement. Rien n'égale alors la douceur, la *vivacité* du sentiment que j'éprouve. Mon âme semble *renaître*: mes forces *se raniment* toutes à la fois. Je me précipite, je *vole* dans les bras qui m'attendent" (p. 118, my italics). Finally, the summation of Quebracuernos at the end concludes that the only safe form of sexuality is that over which the mother presides: "Croyez-moi, formez des liens légitimes avec une personne du sexe; que votre respectable mère préside à votre choix" (p. 122).

By tracing some of these important filaments in the text we become aware of their polyvalencies, resisting any reduction of the meaning to something straightforward. There are too many variables, too few constants to fix a clear path of navigation. No literal reading of the text, not even the one which states that Biondetta "is" the devil, can be adequate if absolute coherence is the criterion for judging it. This will be more apparent, I think, if we look at the problems inherent in the three theses which are specifically inscribed within the text itself: (1) Biondetta is Beelzebub; (2) Biondetta is some lesser kind of perhaps beneficent spirit who has been definitively metamorphosed into a human form; (3) part of Alvare's experience is-- "literally"--a dream. It will be noted that neither the first nor the second is necessarily incompatible with the third (Doña Mencia and Quebracuernos would seem to accredit both one and three), and that all will likely contain supernatural elements (the first two by definition, since they suppose a spirit world) and to that extent be incapable of recuperating the entire experience for the realm of the natural. Let us now examine these theories one by one.

(1) This is the most obvious reading, which the title itself suggests (imposes?). If Biondetta is Beelzebub, she is then unreliable, a seducer who will use any means of deceit; and her effort is only counterbalanced by the maternal-religious force which indeed (and not Alvare's own efforts) saves

him. Biondetta's first and last appearances are framed by the name of Beelzebub, and she does say, in shedding her sylphid-human identity, "Je suis le diable, mon cher Alvare" (p. 112). In particular, this identification gives meaning to the marriage scene, which prefigures the possible union of Alvare and Biondetta under the patronage of a host whose colors evoke a satanic image: "il est vêtu d'un pourpoint de satin noir taillé en couleur de feu" (p. 100); his home is also associated with a forge. Biondetta's passion for the dance evokes a long association of witches' festivals and medieval images of demonic dances. Almost no critic has ever doubted that Biondetta was the devil.[15] And yet there are numerous objections to this assumption:

--Biondetta's "je suis le diable," if *anyone* is right about the dream (third theory), is a part of that dream.

--Biondetta manifests at least four physical traits which extraterrestrial incarnations and other supernaturally endowed beings are often traditionally considered not to possess: she blushes (pp. 49, 60), she weeps (pp. 56, 71, 111), she bleeds (p. 74), and she is reflected in mirrors (p. 61).

--It is not evident why she should fear the gypsies, who say nothing contradicting her own assertions and even evoke, as she did, the reign of Alvare; yet she appears ready to reverse any plan of action they seem to have approved.

--Why should the devil maintain a language of emotion even after the successful seduction of Alvare (pp. 111-12)?

--If she is Beelzebub, then Soberano and his friends are presumably right, since they were the ones who told Alvare to summon a spirit by that name. But then why should Biondetta claim they are out to get her, and why is Bernadillo implicated in her stabbing?

--Numerous other details remain perplexing: for example, why should Biondetta have had the attention to see that his coach is repaired before she disappears from the farmhouse (p. 116)?

--Where is the "act of will" on Alvare's part which makes the devil depart (unless the devil lied about this)? Hiding himself under the bed? On the contrary, he has just reached a complete abdication of will, not only sensually but also in renouncing the trip to Maravillas (and why should

Biondetta then reverse stance also and insist on continuing?). And what then has saved Alvare, if indeed he is saved (what are the "secours extraordinaires que vous avez reçus" [p. 121] of which Quebracuernos speaks)? The devil's defeat, after his victory, and his retreat remain unsatisfactorily explained. The Epilogue says ambiguously: "[Alvare] aurait sans doute fait de certaines pertes, mais il sauverait l'honneur" (p. 124).

--Quebracuernos himself does not explicitly identify Biondetta as an incarnation of the devil himself, although Alvare has to him been the target of the devil's plot. Nor does the Epilogue, which refers to her only as "son adversaire."

--A theological problem remains: the devil can invade (possess), but it is not clear that he can be genuinely incarnate (only Jesus fully realized this assumption of human form); even Bekker, whom Quebracuernos cites, is skeptical about assertions concerning impersonations by the devil.

(2) Biondetta is the sylphid she claims to be; in this hypothesis, she is the reliable witness about herself. Readings which treat her straightforwardly as the devil fail to take into account the fact that she argues in the text an alternative version of why she appears where and when she does. She is a good spirit who, however, has passed definitively into the mortal life. There is no question, in that case, that the living are more powerful than the spirits. Her persecution by Bernadillo is explainable because he is in league with the evil spirits who spitefully want to punish her. The devil may exist, but he is not directly involved in her story and Alvare's. Hers is the voice of science and realism--"Je ne le craindrais pas [= le tonnerre], si je le connaissais moins: je me suis soumise pour l'amour de vous aux causes physiques, et je les appréhende parce qu'elles tuent et qu'elles sont physiques" (p. 95)--and Alvare is not amiss in seeing in her "la nature même" (p. 92). Her resistance to Doña Mencia is at least partially comprehensible, then, on practical and psychological grounds--the very ones she invokes. Objections:

--She says she is the devil, and attributes to herself the name Beelzebub, reverting to the horrifying camel's head just before she vanishes. The objection is weighty, but lends itself to solution if the dream hypothesis is also true: in that event, her statement does not belong to the realm of authentic experience, and nothing identifies her as the devil.

--Her sudden disappearance also seems uncalled for if she is the transformed sylphid; but this objection yields to the same rejoinder as the first, if this part of Alvare's narrative is a dream. (There is still, however, no evident reason why Biondetta should disappear at all.) The plausibility of our second hypothesis then rests largely, it appears, on that of the third; unfortunately for it, the third cannot itself be applied coherently.

(3) Alvare has just emerged at the end from a dream (or hallucination). This is his own explanation (p. 119), to which his mother subscribes although she classes it under the more general category of *mensonges* which govern the overall experience. The problems in fully adopting this line, however, seem unsurmountable:

--Alvare invokes the dream comparison much earlier: "Tout ceci me paraît un songe" (p. 80). Moreover, when he is awakened by the host of the farmhouse, he raises the question of dream in the present ("Dormirais-je?") before he applies it to the past ("Ai-je dormi?"). He thus becomes a dubious source for drawing the lines between the domains because of this generalized confusion, and more specifically because he cannot locate the point at which the dream definitively terminated.

--When did it begin? Our first impression is that it began with the snails; but then we see that it began earlier, since Biondetta had in fact retired to another room; then Doña Mencia says he has dreamt the whole farm. He calls his dream "[le] plus long . . . que l'on puisse faire" (p. 119), which suggests that it goes all the way back to Portici. But if the conjuring of Beelzebub in the first place was part of it, what danger has Alvare incurred?[16] And if the farm does not exist, which Doña Mencia declares categorically, then Don Alvare has not slept with Biondetta, devil or not! (It is evidence of the many seductions of this text that no critic seems ever to have noticed this consequence.)

--When did it end? There is an unexplained continuity between the dream and reality, quite aside from that which exists in Alvare's mind and narration, for he emerges from the "dream" into the world via an unbroken chain of events. The mule-driver, for instance, may have vanished, but he existed in Doña Mencia's world and indeed in her town: he may belong to the spirit world, but does not seem to be just part of the dream (unless Doña Mencia also is!). Alvare himself immediately raises this objection: "Ah! madame, repris-je, le muletier qui m'amène a vu cela comme moi. Il a dansé à la noce" (p. 120). The man's disappearance makes him useless as a witness before Doña Mencia, but not before the reader, for whom he was indeed "there." Perhaps this is the "particularité" which makes Doña Mencia hesitate when she says: "Il y a, dans la fin de votre rêve, une particularité qui m'embarrasse" (p. 120). But in that case her hope is vain that Quebracuernos will explain it.

--Quebracuernos' own version of the dream theory is very obscure; or more exactly he does not espouse the theory as such, speaking rather of a much more general state of confusion or illusion where sleep and wakefulness are muddled: the enemy has mixed "le mensonge à la vérité, le repos à la veille" (p. 122). But what on earth can Quebracuernos mean by the following: "vos intentions, vos remords vous ont préservé à l'aide des secours extraordinaires que vous avez reçus; ainsi son prétendu triomphe et votre défaite n'ont été pour vous *et pour lui* [my italics] qu'une *illusion* dont le repentir achèvera de vous laver" (p. 121)? If the enemy is also under an illusion, nothing more about the nature of the illusion or dream can be controlled; language seems to have lost its hold on the situation. Could Quebracuernos' broken horns (quebrar 'break' + cuernos 'horns') be those of his own knowledge? His speech (and the book) end on a note of arresting platitude.

In short, this must be one of the most underdetermined texts in narrative literature, which means it must be interpreted, as "l'allégorie est double" suggests, to give it a unified reading. Such non-literal versions would include: (1) the mythic: the text symbolizes the battle of good and evil as primal forces; (2) the psychological: it figures the urges and inhibitions of the psyche, and the efforts of the conscious to cope with them;[17] (3) the religious: it is a parable about faith and sin;[18] (4) the polemical: it is anti-philosophe propaganda;[19] (5) the ontological, or the epistemological, or the ethic: the search for various forms of grounding and signification; (6) the marxist: the story in some way reflects social cleavages or structural tensions. Any standard grid can be applied, as to any other text, with more or less satisfactory results, but this one does seem to invite them as few others, given the flaws in its literal surface.

If we now turn to aspects of the figural language in *Le Diable amoureux* for other indirect clues to meaning, we encounter further ambiguities there too. For one thing, the context confuses the levels on which the identification of a metaphor normally depends: even a banal one like "je devins son ombre" (p. 36, referring to Soberano) becomes charged here with various connotations, hinting for example at the spiritual if not ephemeral nature of Alvare, prefiguring Biondetta's attachment to him, and so forth. But too the metaphorical aspects of the text become unreliable or inconsistent in the same way as do the literal ones, from which they cannot ultimately be distinguished. The messages relayed by light, for example, are difficult to organize. Beelzebub first appears accompanied by a light brighter than day, and a frightening brilliance fills the room too just before Biondetta disappears (pp. 114-15); noonday sun, on the other hand, marks Alvare's next moment of awareness, which he does not at first, in his sleep, distinguish from the preceding one. Biondetta herself has been named (by Alvare) for her light-like hair ("soies fines et brillantes" [p. 41]) and is associated with soft light: with the full moon (pp. 40, 96); with dawn, to which she is compared as her ivory hand combs her blond hair (p. 53). She even glows with a light of her own: "au passage, la lumière de la lune ayant frappé sur sa cuisse, avait paru gagner au reflet" (p. 52). The phosphorescent brilliance of the snails Alvare sees above him have an obvious other-worldly quality, but the vision (?) of his mother's tomb also possesses luminescent properties: "Toutes les figures étaient de marbre blanc, et leur éclat naturel, rehaussé par le contraste, en réfléchissant vivement la faible lumière de la lampe, semblait les faire briller d'un jour qui leur fût propre, et éclairer lui-même le fond de la chapelle" (p. 86)--this, moreover, on a stormy day. Supernatural suggestions of similar kinds appear thus on both sides of the register.

The largest group of metaphors, aside from those that derive from well-known aspects of the love code (for example: "figurez-vous l'Amour en trousse de page" [pp. 43-44]; "je sacrifierai à vos pieds le reste de ma vie" [p. 88]), serves to describe Biondetta: her hand is compared to ivory, her face to spring dawn (p. 53) and so forth. But are "metaphors" metaphoric for a sylphid? She is a sort of metaphor herself, for instance of noble birth: "je m'élevais," says Alvare like an ambitious suitor, "quand je venais à me flatter sur le brillant de son origine" (p. 81). But there is also the "brillant" of her fluorescence. "Pourquoi une femme ne serait-elle pas faite de rosée, de vapeurs terrestres et de rayons de lumière, des débris d'un arc-en-ciel condensés? Où est le possible?... Où est l'impossible?" (pp. 80-81): and where is the metaphor in this poetry, when she is a pure spirit of the air?[20] One can no longer distinguish; there is even a sense in which the metaphoric idea of dew and so forth is reliteralized here. Or consider this example:

Ses cheveux étaient renfermés dans un filet cramoisi: on n'en voyait que la pointe, c'étaient *des perles dans du corail.* Son visage, dépouillé de tout autre ornement, *brillait de ses seules perfections.* On croyait voir *un transparent* sur son teint.[21] On ne pouvait concevoir comment la douceur, la candeur, la naïveté pouvaient s'allier au caractère de finesse qui *brillait* dans ses regards. [p. 57, my italics]

The first instance italicized is clearly enough a metaphor founded on color; but the others? Does she "shine" by virtue of perfection, or by her supernatural radiance? Similarly, the reader cannot know whether it is more appropriate to interpret "literally" or "metaphorically"--or really to distinguish between them--when he finds "un nouvel enchantement s'empare de moi" (p. 99); and still less, after Biondetta's victory, this satanic evocation doubled with amorous rhetoric: "Laisse couler dans tes veines un peu de cette flamme délicieuse par qui les miennes sont embrasées" (p. 113).

That is an important dimension of the problem of comprehension for Alvare too: words are almost inept as interpretive and investigatory tools. This narrative necessarily poses the question of the power of language as incantation, if only implicitly. For example, the charm by which Beelzebub is conjured in the first place is signified ("Alors il me donne une formule d'évocation courte, pressante, mêlée de quelques mots que je n'oublierai jamais" [p. 38]) but not transcribed as a signifier, because words (even nonsense or magic words) cannot be "represented," they can only be repeated:[22] and to do so would be to actualize their performative power. And yet Alvare despite his disturbing success does not exactly believe in the binding power of words; he thinks formulas are empty--pure form. Only later does the search for signification seem paramount to him. The word binds, nevertheless, the order of the spirits; and when Alvare says, with regard to Fiorentina, "j'oubliais presque que j'étais le créateur du charme qui me ravissait" (p. 45), he recognizes implicitly but incredulously that he has duplicated the original act: the *fiat.* Still he does not realize the full import of what is said to him, either the dark warnings of Soberano and Bernadillo, or Biondetta's thinly veiled declaration of intention--"de vous désarmer et de vous plaire" (p. 42).[23] Indeed Alvare will never know-- among other things--what the secret characters inscribed in the magic *pantacle* mean; he never learns the signifieds. He also says, with respect to Biondetta's *combinaison* for winning at cards, "je n'en devinai pas les principes" (p. 65). He has entered, to anticipate Baudelaire, a domain of "confuses paroles":

L'homme y passe à travers des forêts de symboles
Qui l'observent avec des regards familiers.

In fact he will have learned no secrets at all, departing his friends first, and then Biondetta, very nearly as ignorant of their impenetrable (inter)-connections as ever.

But the need to escape ambiguity leads him all the same to scrutinize words, at least up to a point. Long after he first demanded an answer from Biondetta "avec clarté et précision" (p. 55), he chides the gypsies on their indirectness: "Là, je les supplie de me dire, en prose, sans énigme, très succinctement, enfin, tout ce qu'elles peuvent savoir d'intéressant sur mon compte" (p. 107). But he never finds out whether such truth can be delivered, as he puts it, "en prose." And he cultivates the reverse illusion: that evading the *name* is equivalent to escaping its signified; to Biondetta's revelation of her identity with the devil he replies: "Cesse . . . de prononcer ce nom fatal et de me rappeler une erreur abjurée depuis longtemps" (p. 113). This suggests again that he is at once desirous and fearful of knowing.

For that matter, the intents of the devil, if devil there be, are hardly clearer. Is not Biondetta's explanation, "Je désirais ta possession, et il fallait, pour que j'y parvinsse, que tu me fisses un libre abandon de toi-même" (p. 114), a gigantic pun on the conventional amorous sense of "possession"? Demon possession, at least conventionally construed, hardly operates this way; it is as if the devil were out to demystify certain abuses of language in everyday contexts. To Biondetta, who seems to know what to do with words, it is writing, "ces lettres écrites de tous côtés" (p. 98), which seems to represent a particularly grave threat; yet that fear, viewed either from her perspective or from Alvare's, is objectively insubstantial, for Doña Mencia has received, as far as we can ascertain, no letters at all from Venice denouncing either him or her, and has herself written him only good news (that he has inherited his brother's regiment). On this level, all the mystifications evaporate, but they have served to heighten the general apprehensiveness which trickles down from the original experience of the power of the word. Essences seem to float, in this text, like spirits, and "le diable amoureux" might be imagined after all less as "le *diable* 'amoureux' " than "le 'diable' *amoureux*." Is this a story about love using a fairy-tale "devil," or a story about the devil pretending to be in love? Or just a mystifying conflation of the two possibilities? Language, with its incantatory powers, proves to be a satisfactory magical medium, full of fearful resonances, but an inadequate tool for pinning down the essence of things. It seems unable to capture objective truth, yet able perhaps to furnish a glimpse of the unknown.

# NOTES

Jacques Cazotte (1719-1792), *Le Diable amoureux*, 1772. Edition: Gallimard, Collection "Folio," 1981. Essentially the same text, that of the revised edition of 1776, is available in Vol. II of the Pléiade *Romanciers du XVIII<sup>e</sup> siècle* (Paris: Gallimard, 1965); the very similar 1788 text is to be found in the Garnier-Flammarion edition (1979).

[1] Edward Pease Shaw, *Jacques Cazotte* (Cambridge, Mass.: Harvard University Press, 1942), p. 60. Shaw does allow, though, that Biondetta's principal adversary is not Alvare but his mother.

[2] Max Milner, *Le Diable dans la littérature française de Cazotte à Baudelaire* (Paris: José Corti, 1960), I, 88-102. In his introduction to the Garnier-Flammarion edition, however, Milner has given more emphasis than any other critic to date to the ambiguities of the text.

[3] In the edition cited above, the earlier conclusion is given in note as a variant on pp. 322-24.

[4] Tzvetan Todorov, *Introduction à la littérature fantastique* (Paris: Seuil, 1970), p. 29. Cf. the distinction made by Jacques Barchilon in *Le Conte merveilleux français de 1690 à 1790*: "Dans le conte de fées, les personnages ne sont guère surpris de ce qui leur arrive: ils sont eux-mêmes merveilleux. Mais les personnages des contes fantastiques sont épouvantés par ce qui les confronte et ils nous communiquent leur angoisse. Le fantastique est donc une sorte de surnaturel dans lequel l'imagination s'attache à combiner l'irréel avec la *sensation* du possible" (Paris: Honoré Champion, 1975, p. 116).

[5] The last paragraph of the Epilogue echoes this beginning: "On se souvient qu'à vingt-cinq ans..." (p. 125). This seems to apply to the "author" of which it speaks, but in a manner twice removed: first by the third-person *il* used throughout the Epilogue, and second by the substitution of *on* in the final sentences.

[6] Inasmuch as Biondetta later says to him, "C'est à Paris, c'est à la cour que je voudrais vous voir établi" (p. 93), there is a sense in which the putative *devil's* other pole is not Spain but Paris, his consummate worldly capital and temptation. But my point here is that Naples stands for the otherworldly, not for the satanic.

[7] Soberano's identification with smoke from the beginning suggests his relation to the spirit world, and could also be regarded, as Robert O'Reilly has remarked, as "a pun on the traditional association of the devil with fire and the alchemist with his furnace" ("Cazotte's *Le Diable amoureux* and the Structure of Romance," *Symposium*, No. 31 [1977], p. 232).

[8] But why should Fiorentina lie (although transparently) to Alvare: "je n'étais pas prévenue que vous eussiez compagnie" (p. 44), and refuse his request/order for a second song? Any interpretation would be hard pressed to account for every detail of the story.

[9] The banker says it was delivered by Pimientos, his mother's squire. But later, on p. 120, Doña Mencia says Pimientos died eight months earlier, or about (perhaps precisely?) the same time this takes place.

[10] Any derogation from "mastery" in terminology thus implies the precariousness of the situation, as when he says of his passion, "il m'est impossible de m'en rendre maître désormais" (p. 87). Even an expression like "cette proposition un peu brusque de me donner un maître" (p. 64), although it refers primarily to tutoring in the science of chance, takes on a further significance in this light--and Alvare says he shuddered at the thought.

[11] "La respiration l'embarrasse, les yeux sont à demi fermés, le corps n'obéit qu'à des mouvements convulsifs, une froideur suspecte s'est répandue sur toute la peau, le pouls n'a plus de mouvement sensible, et le corps paraîtrait entièrement inanimé, si les pleurs ne coulaient pas avec la même abondance" (p. 111): it is as if the devil/sylphid could not become human but could only feign human traits one by one and, concentrating on the tears, forgot to maintain the others. On another occasion (p. 96), it is the heartbeat which is singularly pronounced.

[12] None of these remarks is essentially predicated upon the application of Freudian binoculars to the reading, although the text could easily be subjected to further interpretation along those lines: the erotic elements evoked here are a perfectly patent constituent of the text itself.

[13] This aspect has been most often emphasized in the past. Milner, for example, interprets her importance as follows: "Son amour pour sa mère survit à toutes les tentations et symbolise, avec une profondeur inattendue, la

foi du chrétien, qui reste intacte dans le péché et offre à la grâce un point d'appui où s'exercer" (p. 100). O'Reilly, reading the novel as a Fryeian romance, sees in her the good pole which rescues Alvare from evil (he being drawn instinctively to both): she opposes "such higher social and spiritual values as chivalry, wisdom, family loyalties, and religion to the more primal concerns of the libido" (p. 236). Georges Décote multiplies the meaning even further: she is tradition, family, conscience, faith, the Virgin Mary, the Church ("Logique et fantastique dans *Le Diable amoureux*," *Revue des Sciences Humaines*, 119 [1965], p. 313).

[14]"Ma mère veut absolument que je me marie. Je ne saurais être à d'autre qu'à vous, et ne puis point prendre d'engagement sérieux sans son aveu" (p. 83). There is of course the objection that Olympia represents a separate sexual involvement on Alvare's part; to this there are two answers. First, quite aside from the matter of Biondetta, Alvare has been guilty in his mother's eyes (or so he believes) of a dissipated life, and Olympia would come under that condemnation in any event. And secondly, he desexualizes the role of Olympia in the narration in several ways: by making her the rival not of a woman but of a boy page, by associating her with a milieu which represents less the libido than "une liberté réelle dont j'aimais à jouir, une gaieté bruyante qui pouvait m'étourdir" (p. 66), and finally by insisting that he flees to her arms *without desire*: "Elle me laissa bientôt apercevoir du goût qu'elle avait pour moi, et, sans en avoir pour elle, je me jetai à sa tête pour me débarrasser, en quelque sorte, de moi-même" (p. 66).

[15]The only one I am aware of is Todorov, whose frame of reference has the value of focusing on uncertainties of interpretation: "Alvare est amené plus tard à coucher avec cette même femme qui *peut-être* est le diable" (op. cit., p. 29).

[16]The dream theory undercuts part of the plot's status-as-event but not necessarily all, and the Portici scene may be real, in which case the supernatural still exists. It would be possible to encompass the whole Portici apparition too in the interpretation that the whole of the story was a dream (the way Golding does in *Pincher Martin*), but that point of view is not represented within the text unless Alvare's adjective *long* suggests it. And even then, the problem of continuity cited below remains, at the beginning as well as at the end: where does the (chronological) distinction between reality and dream fall? Something in the story frame has to provide an anchor.

[17]The text in fact suggests oddly that Alvare's visions are prepared by movements within himself, for instance just before Beelzebub appears: "Un frisson courait dans toutes mes veines, et mes cheveux se hérissaient sur ma tête (p. 39): it is as if the spoken formula had produced a transformation in him rather than in the atmosphere. The ambiguity is even stronger in the case of the "message" from his mother in the church, for he does not even say it comes positively from without: "Je réfléchis maintenant, ce que je n'étais pas en état de faire alors, que dans toutes les occasions où nous avons besoin de secours extraordinaires pour régler notre conduite, si nous les demandons avec force, dussions-nous n'être pas exaucés, au moins, en nous recueillant pour les recevoir, nous nous mettons dans le cas d'user de toutes les ressources de notre propre prudence. Je méritais d'être abandonné à la mienne, et voici ce qu'elle me suggéra." But it seems much as if Doña Mencia has delivered "la réponse que j'étais presque sûr de recevoir"; and the "Je réfléchis maintenant" at the beginning of the passage suggests that he originally believed that to be the case (p. 87).

[18]Robert O'Reilly has probably combined these possibilities as successfully as anyone: "On its allegorical level the story depicts a dialectic between the forces of good, as embodied by the Church, and the forces of evil incarnated as the devil. On the anthropomorphic level, the Church has its homologue in the mother figure and in the theme of filial duty. The devil finds its counterpart in the seductive female Biondetta and in the theme of lust. At the center of the tale is the psychological drama of mortal man, Alvare, who combines in himself the mythic struggle between man's lower instincts and higher social and spiritual values" (op. cit., p. 232). Cf. also Max Milner's introduction to the Garnier-Flammarion edition, particularly his Freudian interpretation pp. 39-41.

[19]"Cazotte a probablement voulu nous montrer l'importance d'une vie spirituelle et religieuse, dans un siècle imprégné par contraste d'esprit philosophique et rationaliste" (Décote, p. 313).

[20]Cf. this passage: "En voulant tarir la source de cette rosée précieuse [=larmes], je me suis trop approché de cette bouche où la fraîcher se réunit au doux parfum de la rose." More telling here, though, is the hint of the octopus which, in its conclusion, remains just below the surface: "et si je voulais m'en éloigner, deux bras dont je ne saurais peindre la blancheur, la douceur et la forme, sont des liens dont il me devient impossible de me dégager" (p. 111).

[21] The term *transparent* comes from the realm of painting: a shiny coating based on wax and turpentine, used to heighten the colors (Littré).

[22] I am assuming when I say this, of course, a practical equivalence between speech and writing; in another sense, writing is itself a kind of "representation" of spoken words.

[23] *Plaire* has a coded meaning in the language of love; cf. *Les Confessions du comte de ****: "j'avais envie de lui plaire, ou plutôt de l'avoir" (p. 46).

# Chapter 8

## Les Liaisons dangereuses

In more ways than is the case with any of the other novels discussed in this book, *Les Liaisons dangereuses* comprises the story of a story. For even within the fiction, the "project" of the main characters is conceived from the outset in terms of literary models. Cécile's first letter gives the false impression that it is to be the story of a marriage, which is also what Mme de Volanges believes; but Mme de Merteuil quickly substitutes for this another plot:

> Je veux donc bien vous instruire de mes projets: mais jurez-moi qu'en fidèle chevalier vous ne courrez aucune aventure que vous n'ayez mis celle-ci à fin. Elle est digne d'un héros: vous servirez l'amour et la vengeance; ce sera enfin une *rouerie* de plus à mettre dans vos mémoires: oui, dans vos mémoires, car je veux qu'ils soient imprimés un jour, et je me charge de les écrire.

The book that is to be, which this passage banteringly envisions, is rich in implications. *Aventure*, a perfectly banal metaphor for a love affair, is recharged by Merteuil and Valmont with a new sense of daring escapade which resorbs it, not without irony, in a vocabulary of knighthood and heroism. Such "adventure" hesitates, as Merteuil's terms show, between fact and fiction, memoir and romance—Cécile is called "l'héroïne de ce nouveau roman." The novel is a project in waiting, and its "authors" are to be Merteuil herself and her accomplice Valmont, without whom, indeed, she has little hope of "writing" the story she has in mind. But he, in his reply, proposes instead another story, "le plus grand projet que j'aie jamais formé," which he later assimilates to "le genre héroïque" (115).

The future is regularly projected thus as the story to be told; to plot and execute is to write.[1] Terms like "mon ouvrage" and "mon chef d'oeuvre" are frequent.[2] Merteuil's reduction of Prévan, as project, is pre-written: "Quant à Prévan, je veux l'avoir et je l'aurai; il veut le dire, et il ne le dira pas: en deux mots, voilà notre roman" (81).[3] And because she knows he plans to tell a different version of the same basic events, she frames her claim of victory in terms of his own projected narrative: "je suis curieuse de savoir comment vous raconterez la fin de l'aventure" (85); this is capped off with a letter to Mme de Volanges illustrating "cette histoire telle qu'il faut la raconter" (85). Besides the main plots, the letters of Valmont and Merteuil are studded with micronarratives; they refer to assorted episodes as *récits* and *histoires* or *historiques*. The celebrated "triple aventure" of Prévan is one of these encapsulated narratives, as Valmont's terminology playfully insists: "Ici, comme vous le jugez bien, les preuves manquent à l'histoire; tout ce que peut faire l'historien impartial, c'est de faire remarquer au lecteur incrédule que . . ." (79). Their failure to renew their own liaison becomes a *récit manqué*, or as Merteuil puts it, the "simple récit d'un projet impossible" (134). She precipitates the end of her's and Valmont's actual "story" by telling her little parable (141) about themselves, to which, in his answer, he requests "the ending."

Their inspiration is in the first instance literary: Mme de Merteuil says she studied "nos moeurs dans les romans"[4] and learned to combine the talents of author and actor (81); Valmont tries to cull ideas for his seductions from novels and memoirs (110). There are many references to literary sources, a characteristic of their letters alone. Both of them quote frequently in prose (Rousseau, Marmontel) and especially in verse, from theater and opera above all (Racine, Regnard, Voltaire, Gresset, Piron, Favart, Sedaine, Belloy);[5] there are allusions to the Bible, Livy, *L'Astrée*, La Fontaine, Voltaire, *Le Sopha, Clarissa* (Valmont suggests an explicit parallel between Clarissa and Mme de Tourvel) and--particularly interesting in that they represent epistolary models--to Mme de Sévigné and *La Nouvelle Héloïse*.[6] This is both an aspect of their general cultural sophistication and a confirmation of the literary grounding of their project/novel.

There is both jest and solemnity in such language. The chivalrous register participates in an ironic depreciation of gallant commonplaces--the willful mock-heroic tone such as Merteuil manifests in her admonition to Valmont: "Venez donc, venez au plus tôt m'apporter le gage de votre triomphe: semblable à nos preux chevaliers qui venaient déposer aux pieds de leurs dames les fruits brillants de leur victoire" (20). Yet as Malraux pointed out in a famous article (given as a preface in the edition cited here), they think of themselves in mythological terms, and the grandiose imagery corresponds to a real inflation of ego. Thus *aventure* is used in many contexts, both positively and negatively (but usually the latter), the better to maximize the sense of conquest while minimizing any suggestion of serious involvement;[7] the "heroes" and "heroines" of the various "adventures" are generally derided by such appellations, especially Cécile and Danceny --"ce beau héros de roman" (57, 63), "Céladon," "le héros de cette aventure," "ce beau berger" (51). The *romanesque* is their way of belittling grand sentiments; Merteuil applies the term to Belleroche ( 10), for instance, and, after chiding Cécile by saying, "vous figurerez à merveille dans un roman" (105), she upbraids Danceny for using jargon to be found "dans le premier roman du jour" (121). Likewise, she taunts Valmont for what is reputed to be his "amour romanesque et malheureux" (113), an expression which sticks in his craw sufficiently to be quoted back to her six weeks later (114). Yet they model their own exploits, like the Prévan and Vressac episodes, on the most flamboyantly romantic scenarios they can imagine: the Prévan affair is dependent on that archetypal romantic device, the hidden stairway; the Vressac one on kicking in a door in the middle of the night--not to mention the purloined key in the Cécile adventure. Thus they give life to their own, more challenging sense of the *romanesque*. "Conquérir est notre destin," intones Valmont (4).

When the counterpoint is not romantic, it is theatrical. Valmont in particular uses dramatic language to highlight or satirize numerous "scenes," comparing himself to the hero of a drama (21) as he does Azolan to a "vrai valet de comédie" (15). Both refer to their exploits in terms of acting on the world as theater (81, 99); Valmont once designates a piece of furniture which will serve as "théâtre de ma victoire" (125). The stage also plays a diegetic role in that Valmont picks up Emilie at the Opéra and the new play Mme de Merteuil ostensibly goes to see at the Théâtre Français is eclipsed for her by the presence of Prévan. This creates a whole interplay of esthetic versus actual expectations which Valmont expresses in his rhetorical question, relative to love, "Eh quoi! ce même spectacle qui vous fait courir au théâtre avec empressement, que vous y applaudissez avec fureur, le croyez-vous moins attachant dans la réalité?" (96). Madame de Merteuil makes repeated word-plays on roles, reversing her terms for example, after declaring Cécile unfit for playing *secondes* (106), to jest deceptively to Danceny about her own intentions: "Quand l'héroïne [Cécile] est en scène, on ne s'occupe guère de la confidente" (146). But once again we must note an ambivalence in the terminology. The allusion to drama helps Valmont to pass off his tearful performance with Tourvel as ironic mastery, whereas its real meaning is just the opposite if he is repressing or disguising an awareness that it was uncontrolled and spontaneous: his "drama," rather than feint, might have been a realization on the stage of experience of a sentiment previously supposed to be purely romantic. The novel then becomes, like *Le Fils naturel*, not just *a* drama but the story *of* a drama.

It also fulfills this function in another sense, for the creation of the book is itself an outcome of its own plot. Proof, as numerous of the letters remind us, must be in written form, and it is through their letters that Valmont and Merteuil ultimately furnish each other and their other enemies with the means of destroying them. The thematic richness of this theme has been admirably summarized by Tzvetan Todorov:

> Ces lettres ne racontent pas seule l'histoire qui est dans le roman; elles racontent aussi l'histoire du roman lui-même. Et c'est là leur dernier rôle, leur sens ultime. . . . L'histoire de cette publication commence au moment du dénouement. . . . [Laclos] intègre la signification de l'existence globale du livre au réseau d'axes significatifs, sous-jacent à l'histoire racontée dans *Les Liaisons dangereuses*. . . . Le roman se termine par une sorte de double suicide, chacun d'eux rendant publiques les lettres de son adversaire et causant ainsi sa ruine, morale ou physique. . . . L'imperfection de ces personnages forts consiste, littéralement, à avoir rendu possible la création du roman.[8]

This dénouement resolves the long tension between the intimacy and secrecy connoted by personal letter and the broadcasting function of the rake's life. Danceny first "publishes" two letters (81, 85) in the sense that he copies and circulates them. Then he confides the rest to Mme de Rosemonde who promises them "l'oubli qui leur convient" (172): even at this stage, the material publication of the book represents an unexplained breach of contract on the part of someone, presumably an heir of Rosemonde after her death.

The "Avertissement de l'éditeur" and the "Préface du rédacteur" also deal with the literary status of the text, but in ways which only seem to further embroil their divergent connotations. The latter appears soberly realistic and moralistic, but, coming second, has in effect already been undercut by the irony of the "Avertissement"'s "nous avons même de fortes raisons de penser que ce n'est qu'un roman." Yet they seem to agree, despite the difference in tone, on the double import of its story focusing on Cécile and Mme de Tourvel:[9]

> . . . nous ne voyons point aujourd'hui de demoiselle, avec soixante mille livres de rente, se faire religieuse, ni de présidente, jeune et jolie, mourir de chagrin. ["Avertissement"]
>
> On y trouvera aussi la preuve et l'exemple de deux vérités importantes qu'on pourrait croire méconnues, en voyant combien peu elles sont pratiquées: l'une, que toute femme qui consent à recevoir dans sa société un homme sans moeurs, finit par en devenir la victime; l'autre, que toute mère est au moins imprudente, qui souffre qu'un autre qu'elle ait la confiance de sa fille. ["Préface"]

These enunciations have the effect of underscoring the parallel between the two principal victims of the "scélérats" (9, footnote), and also of integrating the sense of the ending in the beginning, since both, standing at the head of the story, concern its outcome. The "Préface," furthermore, seeks to ground the whole in a (conventional) discourse about sources in the *rédacteur*'s functions, but at the same time obfuscates that very role ("je n'étais pas le maître") by invoking nameless others whose criteria for decision are supposed to be simultaneously *vraisemblance* and *vérité*.

This ambiguity of even the fictional stance of the fiction, the "Préface"'s ironic allusion to the "auteur qui se montre derrière le personnage," and the way it draws attention to the supposed "style trop simple et trop fautif de plusieurs de ces lettres," all are reminiscent of Rousseau's *Nouvelle Héloïse*, the preface of which manifests the same characteristics and, to make the rapport more explicit, furnishes the epigraph to *Les Liaisons dangereuses*: "J'ai vu les moeurs de mon temps, et j'ai publié ces lettres." This quotation in effect declares an intention which is extrinsic to the letters as such. Rousseau's studied ambiguity, however, does not simply reinforce that of this new context, inasmuch as it now constitutes in its own right a properly *literary* referent. For all its roundabout patter, the "foreword"-matter of *Les Liaisons dangereuses* grounds the text in literarity.

The title is linked to the text by a whole series of occurrences of the term *dangereux*: Valmont, Merteuil, Tourvel, Volanges, and Danceny all evoke danger(s), and the specific expression *liaison dangereuse* appears in both mocking (Merteuil, 63) and sober (Mme de Volanges, 32, 175) contexts. Each such occurrence brings us naturally back to the title, uniting in one movement the separate claims of moral (via semantics) and literary (via functions) paradigms. Danceny and Valmont agree, for different reasons, on the danger of Merteuil; Valmont speaks of "vos liens dangereux" (115) and Danceny calls her "réellement dangereuse" (169). Merteuil, who delights in producing situational ironies for her own, and sometimes Valmont's, gleeful consumption (but which, of course, often turn against her), tells Danceny that it is dangerous to write (150). It is symptomatic of Mme de Tourvel's innocence that to her a notion as heavy with implications as *liaison dangereuse* really cannot attach to Valmont but rather to his own undesirable associates: "M. de Valmont n'est peut-être qu'un exemple de plus du danger des liaisons" (22) means that he has been swept away, as he says, by the *tourbillon* (52). In her reply, Mme de Volanges expressly takes up the same term again in an effort to make it stick: "Quand il ne serait, comme vous le dites, qu'un exemple du danger des liaisons, en serait-il moins lui-même une liaison dangereuse?" (32).

There are throughout the novel many webs of words which thus appear and reappear with constantly changing yet constantly reinforcing value. Space forbids commenting on the entire text in this way, but the principle can be illustrated with some examples from the very earliest letters. Cécile's silly anecdote about "cet homme à mes genoux" (1) who turns out to be a cobbler has a counterpoint effect as parody-in-advance for a whole series of dramatic, amorous, and humorous occurrences of *genoux* and its semantic equivalents. Just as love was--falsely--connoted in Cécile's initial interpretation of the scene, love is both connoted and held at a distance by irony in Merteuil's summons to Valmont, "vous devriez venir, avec empressement, prendre mes ordres à genoux" (2).[10] Valmont's reply agains picks up the metaphor, but connects it to a discordant--and perhaps already fatal--designation of Merteuil as a *femme facile* (4). Literally, Merteuil falls to the knees only of Belleroche (10), and Valmont to those only of Tourvel (23), but the figure is frequent in his letters--mostly hyperbole and irony, translating both subservience and domination ("Je la verrai encore à mes genoux" [100].

Allusions to slavery, equally a conceit of conventional love rhetoric, also take on from the start a wide range of connotations. Mme de Merteuil, for all her cajolery, begins her first letter with a firm imperative: "Revenez, mon cher Vicomte, revenez. . . . Partez sur-le-champ; j'ai besoin de vous." Which Valmont, for all his, rejects with persiflage of the same language: "Vos ordres sont charmants; votre façon de les donner est plus aimable encore; vous feriez chérir le despotisme. Ce n'est pas la première fois, comme vous savez, que je regrette de ne plus être votre esclave; et . . . je me vois forcé de vous désobéir" (4). The veiled tension present in these exchanges soon will mushroom into an endless series of sarcasms about their respective intentions, often pointed in this manner by the reprise and turnabout of specific phrases. She calls his design a "ridicule caprice," a "ridicule aventure" (5, 10); and the next time she says *revenez* it is in the form of "revenez à vous" (5)--"vous qui n'êtes plus vous" (10). He refutes her snide remark about Tourvel's heart tripping mostly from fear of the devil (5, 6), making it clear that a man in her place would have been challenged over such remarks, and returns some sarcasms of his own about Belleroche's "despair."

Exasperated by his refusal, and its tone, Mme de Merteuil ridicules Valmont in essentially two ways. The first is methodological, pointing up the unwonted slowness of his procedures: "pour qu'elle finisse par se donner, le vrai moyen est de commencer par la prendre" (10); "pour Dieu, avancez donc" (20); "dépêchez donc votre présidente" (38). The second is to suggest that the reason for this creeping pace is, in fact, a sentimental involvement which Valmont's principles do not allow. "Cette femme, qui vous a rendu *les illusions de la jeunesse*, vous en rendra bientôt aussi les ridicules préjugés" (10).[11] Ridicule is one of everyone's vulnerabilities given the way the social codes function. She calls him a slave, "un homme à terre"; and he retorts, with reference again to Belleroche, "Vous le croyez dans vos chaînes! C'est bien vous qui êtes dans les siennes" (15). As Valmont implicitly, for the moment at least, prefers Tourvel to Merteuil, she will flaunt her preference of Belleroche (10); she underscores the parallel of the two cases by setting the one as a deadline for the other (20). At the same time, she notes another parallel, the one between his seduction of Tourvel and hers of Cecile, by the prediction: "j'aurai fini avant vous" (33). As the irony of the plot will have it. Valmont himself in fact accomplishes her side of this double seduction, doubtless exacerbating her anticipatory jealousy over this particular sexual role (she had said: "je suis presque jalouse de celui à qui ce plaisir est réservé" [38]).

Neither imagines that the time factor will be great; Cécile is to be married soon, and Valmont expects like others of his milieu to return to the city in the fall. But everything conspires to delay on all fronts, creating a time bomb whose fuse is built into a comment Cécile overhears and reports in her second letter: "Il faut laisser mûrir cela, nous verrons cet hiver" (3). The four months' interval that presupposes ("mais alors ce ne serait donc que dans quatre mois!") corresponds closely to the chronology of the novel (all but the last two letters are written between August 3 and December 16),[12] and what is promised ultimately is not a marriage but a "maturation," whose ominousness is further prepared in Mme de Volange's expressed wish that Mme de Tourvel attend the ceremony (9). Gercourt is sent off to Corsica until October. At the same time, Merteuil defers her renewal with Valmont (20) until the Présidente is dispatched; but as August wears into September and then October, she loses patience and finally absents herself from Paris for some six weeks. When the due date of this first cycle is approaching, Gercourt writes (October 10) to extend his absence for another six weeks to two months, the Président de Tourvel remains inexplicably in abeyance, and Merteuil's lawsuit begins to wind toward its conclusion: all converge for a countdown to December.

The structure of the epistolary exchange in *Les Liaisons dangereuses* has been studied many times; without pretending to any great originality I want to deal with it briefly here because I do think it helps both reveal the intricacies of the novel and expose some of the patterns which are otherwise disguised in its subtle workings. The table below, by my count, summarizes the flows of letters by sender and recipient.

Numerically, it can be seen that Valmont as writer dominates the text in ways that most critics of recent years, almost unanimously considering him the weaker of the two principal characters, cannot account for. Also numerically, Merteuil, Tourvel, and Cécile come out about even. On the other hand, Merteuil's and Valmont's relations to Cécile and Danceny are almost perfectly balanced. The empty spaces are of course significant also. These data can be usefully complemented by a summary chronological distribution of the letters which, for simplicity's sake, I will give only graphically, and in terms of the novel's four-part division. The axes of communication in the successive parts (with Valmont and Merteuil marked in the central positions) are shown on the following pages:

## Table I

### RECIPIENT

**SENDER**

| | Valmont | Merteuil | Tourvel | Cécile | Danceny | Volanges | Rosemonde | Other |
|---|---|---|---|---|---|---|---|---|
| Valmont (51) | -- | 33 | 12 | 2 | 2 | | | 2 |
| Merteuil (27) | 21 | -- | | 2 | 2 | 2 | | |
| Tourvel (24) | 9 | | -- | | | 5 | 9 | 1 |
| Cécile (25) | 2 | 4 | -- | | 8 | | | 11 |
| Danceny (19) | 4 | 3 | | 9 | -- | 1 | 2 | |
| Mme de Volanges (13) | | 1 | 2 | | 1 | -- | 9 | |
| Mme de Rosemonde (9) | | | 6 | | 1 | 1 | -- | 1 |
| Others (7) | 2 | 1 | | | 1 | 1 | 2 | -- |
| Total recd. | 38 | 42 | 20 | 13 | 15 | 10 | 22 | 15 |

## Tables II - III

Active Axes in Part I (11 vectors)                                           Total:  50

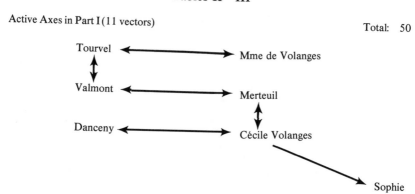

Actives Axes in Part II   (6 new vectors)                                    Total:  37

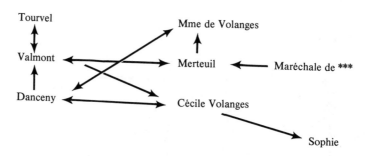

## Tables IV - V

Active Axes in Part III (11 new vectors)                    Total:   37

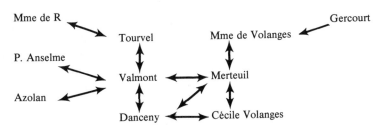

Active Axes in Part IV (8 new vectors)                    Total:   51

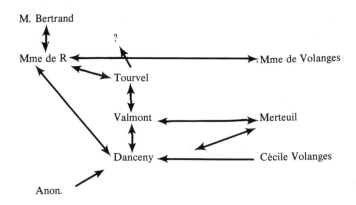

The symmetry of the part one diagram has no significance in itself, since it results from the way I have arbitrarily arranged the names; it is nonetheless useful as a figure of the simple and well-ordered schema of communications in the first stage of the novel, to which that of the subsequent parts can be compared. What such charts thus reveal is a constantly increasing complexity in each part, and also the steady decentralization and fragmentation of the control evident at the outset. This structure thus figures the mainspring of the plot in a manner that Todorov describes by the common quality of "infraction à l'ordre."[13] Other observations: Certain potential axes remain vacant throughout: Merteuil-Tourvel, Valmont-Mme de Volanges; Tourvel has no epistolary contact with either Cécile or Danceny. And Cécile has none with her mother: the lack of letters between them, when added to Cécile's remark that her mother "ne me dit rien du tout" (27), symbolizes of course their total lack of communication. The only axes occupied in all four quarters are Valmont-Merteuil and Valmont-Tourvel (each in both directions), and Cécile to Danceny. It is notable that the Volanges-Tourvel axis is dormant after part one (for reasons which in terms of the plot are obvious, and are even commented upon by Valmont in letter 110), and of course the inert Sophie drops out of the picture after part two. There are also some relative silences which these charts do not immediately show, such as Valmont's, with regard to Mme de Merteuil, after the Prévan affair (September 18 to October 1), and Merteuil's when she goes unseasonably off to the country (November 11 to 24): in part three, they exchange only seven letters, compared to 16, 14 and 17 in parts one, two and four respectively.

There are many permutations of the straightforward letter from A to B, which give the novel its technical dazzle. For one thing, there are numerous copies of letters and draft letters floating about, many to be read by eyes other than those of the ostensible addressee. Letter 24 is never sent to Tourvel, and letter 35, sent to her, is never read by her; letter 36, on the other hand, which she tears up, she reads. Several letters are dictated, notably two of Cécile's by Valmont for his ironic pleasure. The missives to Tourvel mentioned in letters 108 and 149 are not given in the text of the novel, nor is the one mentioned in 154. Particular juxtapositions in the order of presentation of letters in the text (not always chronological) can create additional effects. The whole unsavory spice of letter 48 is relative to the context from which it emanates: one can hardly be more materialistic than is Valmont in the choice of writing desk for this famous letter which is read by both Emilie and Merteuil and sets up Tourvel as the laughing-stock "femme à la lettre" (138). Rosemonde's letter 125 to Mme de Tourvel produces stark situational irony following Valmont's letter detailing Tourvel's defeat. Sometimes, as again Todorov has set forth, the letter is significant as a material object, aside from its value as message: the altered hand in which Mme de Tourvel has copied Valmont's first letter before returning it has its own independent meaning, as does the trace of tears (44). And, of course, not to write can itself be heavy with meaning; Danceny gives this thought a superficial rhetorical charge in letter 28, but there is much dramatic value in the long and ominous silence of Mme de Rosemonde regarding Cécile's involvement in the affairs of Valmont and Merteuil once her mother has written, "je consens à vous laisser en effet ne vous expliquer que par votre silence" (173).[14]

The life of the letter extends from before its completion until after its reading. Danceny, with some lyricism, voices the feeling that its value does not reside merely in what it "says": "si on ne la lit pas, du moins on la regarde... Ah! sans doute, on peut regarder une lettre sans la lire, comme il me semble que la nuit j'aurais encore quelque plaisir à toucher ton portrait..." (150). The activity of writing too affords a certain euphoria which Danceny expresses in his paradoxical conclusion, "Il me serait impossible de vous quitter, si ce n'était pour aller vous revoir" (31). Letters are a mode of existence, and not a mere, inadequate substitute for presence. In its own absence, the letter must be imagined: "je ferai mes efforts pour me dire ce que tu m'aurais écrit" (150). The written, as a mode of experience, takes precedence over others. The letter is not, in any case, a simple reflection or derivation of action occurring independently of it: of this, in addition to the novel/memoirs project of Valmont and Merteuil mentioned earlier, Danceny himself provides one of the most intriguing examples. His first letter to Cécile refers to certain gestures of his which are supposed to connote, and communicate, love: "qu'ai-je à vous dire, que mes regards, mon embarras, ma conduite et même mon silence, ne vous aient dit avant moi?" (17). But these signs he evokes have been manifested, as Cécile relates (16), just previous to the moment when Danceny places his letter in her harpcase: in other words, the behavior which is Danceny's "referent" is produced only *after* he has *written* the letter calling attention to it; the action is an effect and not a cause of what is written.

"*Oui, Monsieur, je vous ai écrit*" (25): writing becomes both a circumstantial metaphor for, and an aspect of, the seductive process which is one of language. For one thing, as Valmont says, a correspondence already implies, indeed already constitutes, a deception of the husband (40 *suite*)—his letter postmarked from Dijon, demanding "les mêmes droits que le mari" (34), is a form of rape—but also, more fundamentally, *répondre* is already an act, a ceremonious participation, both in the context of epistles and in that of ritual love. The verbs *écouter, entendre,* and *répondre* become involved in a whole series of utterances symbolizing the degree of Tourvel's reluctant involvement with Valmont:

> Vous m'avez tenu des discours que je ne devais pas entendre, vous ne vous seriez pas cru autorisé à m'écrire une lettre que je ne devais pas lire. . . . Hé bien, Monsieur, le silence et l'oubli, voilà les conseils qu'il me convient de vous donner. . . . Je serais vraiment peinée qu'il restât aucune trace d'un événement qui n'eût jamais dû exister. [26]

> Je m'en tiens à vous prier, comme je l'ai déjà fait, de ne plus m'entretenir d'un sentiment que je ne dois pas écouter, et auquel je dois encore moins répondre. [50]

> . . . je ne veux ni ne dois y répondre. . . . Cette lettre est la dernière que vous recevrez de moi. [56]

> Quittez donc un langage que je ne puis ni ne veux entendre. [67]

> Fuyons surtout ces entretiens particuliers et trop dangereux, où, par une inconcevable puissance, sans jamais parvenir à vous dire ce que je veux, je passe mon temps à écouter ce que je ne devrais pas entendre. [90]

A less elaborate cluster of similar pronouncements is to be found in Cécile's letters to Danceny.

In fact, Valmont does not place his entire wager on the written medium, oscillating strategically instead between the presence of speech and the absence of the letter. Merteuil, of course, chides him for his foolish correspondence with Tourvel, who, as she puts it, can viably defend herself in writing and even "defeat" Valmont (33); Valmont for his part places greater stress on the degree to which the Présidente has betrayed her true feelings in writing. He replies that he has no choice; but he is on secure ground in his undertaking, for the written trap proves quite insidious. "Sûrement, Monsieur, vous n'auriez eu aucune lettre de moi, si ma sotte conduite d'hier au soir ne me forçait d'entrer aujourd'hui en explication avec vous" (26): forcing the explanation is the strength of Valmont's incredible epistolary mastery, another of the ways in which he dominates the novel. He can twist and turn reasoning so that it always slants in his favor, and Mme de Tourvel, though aware of this, is drawn into a spider's web of inextricably sticky threads.

Nothing she can summon to the aid of her verbal defense can stand in the face of his onslaught: "Ce qui n'eût été que de  la candeur avec tout autre, devient une étourderie avec vous" (43); "les choses qu'on vous demande de ne plus dire, vous les dites seulement d'une autre manière" (56). She can see what is happening, and yet is not only sucked into explanation after explanation but finds herself posed incongruously in the aggressive role:

> Je ne voulais plus vous répondre, Monsieur. . . . Cependant je ne veux vous laisser aucun sujet de plainte contre moi; je veux vous convaincre que j'ai fait pour vous tout ce que je pouvais faire. . . . Quand vous faites tout ce qu'il faut pour m'obliger à rompre cette correspondance, c'est moi qui m'occupe des moyens de l'entretenir. [67]

> Je veux bien entrer encore une fois en explication avec vous. [78]

Valmont's guileful devices include this sort of transfer which seems to place the burden of proof on her. "Quel dommage que, comme vous le dites, je sois *revenu de mes erreurs!*" (68) he writes, for example, thus imputing to Mme de Tourvel a phrase which is his own, as shows the passage from her previous letter: "Si, comme vous le dites, vous êtes *revenu de vos erreurs*, n'aimerez-vous pas mieux être l'objet de l'amitié d'une femme honnête, que celui des remords d'une femme coupable?" (67). Conversely, Valmont "defends" himself from her (83), and precipitates the final victory by exclaiming, "Il faut vous fuir, il le faut!" (125) although it is she who has repeatedly spoken of flight (Valmont is perhaps recalling the first line of *La Nouvelle Héloïse*: "Il faut vous fuir, mademoiselle . . .").

Tourvel can no longer sort out who is quoting whom, nor who the aggressor is. The power over his language, which he ostensibly confers upon her—"vous ne parviendrez point à vaincre mon amour, mais vous m'apprendrez à le régler, en guidant mes démarches, en dictant mes discours . . ." (24)--is liquidated by his own skill in playing the ventriloquist. "Le mot le plus indifférent vous sert de prétexte pour ramener une conversation que je ne voulais pas entendre" (78). The clearest example of this is use of the word *reconnaissance* in her first letter (26) which, as Merteuil remarks (33), leaves the door ajar for further incursions; yet in letters 41 and 90 she repeats the same process, which Valmont of course can exploit. If we assume, whatever her secret desires, that she would like to win the argument with Valmont to put her mind at rest, then part of her anguish is the impossibility of doing so; Valmont is one of the deftest masters of contorted reason known to literature. As long as the game is one of words--and for a while, even if only as a delaying action, it is that--the Présidente hasn't a chance.

There is another sense, however, in which the firmness of the distinction between the written and the oral is tempered by the mediation of the letter--not just in the usual sense that in literature even conversation is transcribed into a written medium, but in terms intrinsic to the specific fiction: all diegetic action here must pass through a letter. Even *paroles* are a part of the written record, ingested by the letter mill. The whole intrigue commences with accession to the power of language: Cécile's first letter announces, "je tiens parole"; instead of dolls she now has a secretary with a key, the instrument of private correspondence, and her new life is marked by the twin rights to do nothing and to write. Music too provides a double means of access to verbal media,[15] without which the rest of her story is inconceivable. Initiation into active society is effected largely through the acquisition of certain polished forms of discourse, the lack of which at this stage sets Cécile's style markedly apart from that of the other characters. And that society's organizing components are intensely verbal. Reputation, which is of such central importance for Tourvel, Volanges, Merteuil and Valmont, exists only in words and evidences this fact in its great plasticity. Valmont's prestige consists precisely in being much talked about (Merteuil was "séduite par votre réputation" [81]); but when Merteuil writes him that "on commence à s'occuper de vous à Paris" it means something quite different, namely that his reputation is beginning to suffer from under-nourishment and negative inferences. The consequences of this, she goes on, are serious in their milieu, precisely for the reason that his "irresistibility" is not a personal attribute as such but a quality invented and maintained purely in discourse: "Songez que si une fois vous laissez perdre l'idée qu'on ne vous résiste pas, vous éprouverez bientôt qu'on vous résistera en effet plus facilement" (113).

The characters which lend themselves to Valmont's and Merteuil's manipulations obviously do so partly because of their innocent attitude with respect to language. Danceny provides a clear example: to him, words are a form of substance ("un mot pour l'autre peut changer toute une phrase" [92]); their nominating power can confer essential qualities. "Emané de vous, sans doute [mon amour] est digne de vous être offert; s'il est brûlant comme mon âme, il est pur comme la vôtre" (17): to call something pure shields it from corruption. (Valmont of course imitates and exploits this sort of rhetoric in his letters to the Présidente: "Quel mal peut-on craindre d'un sentiment si pur . . . ?" [83]). Such straightforward confidence in words and things alike makes Cécile vulnerable to a subversive education in "complaisances" and "mots techniques" (110): "elle ne s'imagine pas qu'on puisse parler autrement." Tourvel's fear of words would seem to arise from an uncomplicated assumption of natural equivalence between signifiers and signifieds; she doesn't want to hear the "name" of love spoken (50), and her first letter to Rosemonde apparently represses the name of the loved object with its classical, intransitive "j'aime," as Mme de Rosemonde in her reply points out (102, 103). But it is more complicated than that, as if Mme de Tourvel felt no compulsion to name in order to possess; it is possession instead which delivers the freedom to name: "pourquoi craindrais-je de le nommer?" (104)[16]

Words have, on these "victimized" characters--especially Mme de Tourvel--a sort of insidious power via the text, whether they as characters are confronted with them or not. The association of Tourvel with a tomb begins ironically and metaphorically in the letters of Merteuil: "Vous vous enterrez dans le tombeau de votre tante" (5), "le tombeau où vous vivez déjà depuis si longtemps" (113); and of Valmont: "la saison morte dans laquelle est venue cette aventure" (133); "faire expirer sa vertu dans une lente agonie" (70), "lui fermer les yeux sur le danger, car si elle le voit, elle saura le surmonter ou mourir" (110). But this sets in motion a process which infects her own language and gradually modulates into a death pact:

Cet empire que j'ai perdu sur mes sentiments, je le conserverai sur mes actions . . . . fût-ce au dépens de ma vie . . . . Mais devenir coupable! . . . non, mon ami, plutôt mourir mille fois. [90]

Il vaut mieux mourir que de vivre coupable. [103]

Si quelque jour [Valmont] en juge autrement . . . , il n'entendra
de ma part ni plainte ni reproche. J'ai déjà osé fixer les yeux sur
ce moment fatal et mon parti est pris. [128]

La funeste vérité m'éclaire, et ne me laisse voir qu'une mort
assurée et prochaine, dont la route m'est tracée entre la honte et
le remords. [143]

Elle ajouta qu'elle n'en sortirait *qu'à la mort*: ce fut son
expression [Mme de Volanges, 147]

Only in literature do people die of love, for only there does its "poison"
(124), which is strictly discursive in nature, attack in a purely homogenous
cultural medium which can oppose it no resistance: it is a corrosion of words
by other, parasite words.

Valmont and Merteuil, on the contrary, treat words like wild cards.
She tells Danceny that letters must be sincere, and Cécile that they must
not. "Comme s'il était bien gênant de promettre," exclaims Valmont,
"quand on est décidé à ne pas tenir!" (66). But this very virtuosity
prevents Valmont and Tourvel from elaborating any consistent theory of
their own with regard to language. There is, to be sure, a certain firmness
manifested in Merteuil's letters to Valmont. She detects in Mme de Tourvel
a fuzziness of perception of the limits between words and things: "Je prévois
qu'elle [épuisera ses forces] pour la défense du mot, et qu'il ne lui en restera
plus pour celle de la chose" (33). Tourvel's *irrévocable* is soft while
Merteuil's is hard.[17] Valmont is again in this regard very flexible,
sometimes pressing for "the" word and sometimes not; he says first that "je
ne me dissimule pas que ce titre [d'amant], qui ne paraît d'abord qu'une
dispute de mots, est pourtant d'une importance réelle à obtenir" (70),
and later: "nous ne disputons plus que sur les mots. C'était toujours, à la
vérité, *son amitié* qui répondait à *mon amour*: mais ce langage de
convention ne changeait pas le fond des choses" (99). And he then
dispenses her from the word, asking only for a look.

Most of the language Valmont and Merteuil use to refer to themselves
is tinged with humor and irony. There are two principal terminological

categories, the first consisting in the divine constellation assimilating their practice to faith and their powers to those of gods; it includes most of the relatively few extended metaphors in the novel, among which the following:

> Depuis que . . . nous prêchons la foi chacun de notre côté, il me semble que dans cette mission d'amour, vous avez fait plus de prosélytes que moi. Je connais votre zèle, votre ardente ferveur; et si ce Dieu-là nous jugeait sur nos oeuvres, vous seriez un jour la patronne de quelque grande ville, tandis que votre ami serait au plus un saint de village. [Valmont, 4]

> Je vis en effet cette femme adorable à genoux, baignée de larmes, et priant avec ferveur. Quel Dieu osait-elle invoquer? en est-il d'assez puissant contre l'amour? En vain cherche-t-elle à présent des secours étrangers: c'est moi qui réglerai son sort.
> [Valmont, 23]

> Me voilà comme la divinité, recevant les voeux opposés des aveugles mortels, et ne changeant rien à mes décrets immuables.
> [Merteuil, 63]

> Je suis pour vous une fée bienfaisante. Vous languissez loin de la beauté qui vous engage; je dis un mot, et vous vous retrouvez auprès d'elle. Vous voulez vous venger d'une femme qui vous nuit; je vous marque l'endroit où vous devez frapper et la livre à votre discrétion. Enfin, pour écarter de la lice un concurrent redoutable, c'est encore moi que vous invoquez, et je vous exauce. [Merteuil, 85]

There are many other examples, which have induced critics perhaps to overemphasize the mythological imagination--not to mention the Satanism --of the characters because, out of context, one too easily forgets the degree of self-mockery involved in such classically-laden terminology. Not that these statements aren't serious in their way; but they are not entirely literal. The humor in the other constellation, that of military metaphor, is perhaps more evident. Valmont consistently compares his campaign to that of a general, likening himself first to Alexander (15), then to Turenne and Frédéric II (125); he sends the *bulletin* (25)[18] of his "petite guerre" (34), which terminates in a triumphal battle: "J'ai forcé à combattre l'ennemi qui ne voulait que temporiser; je me suis donné, par de savantes manoeuvres, le choix du terrain et celui des dispositions; j'ai su inspirer la sécurité à l'ennemi, pour le joindre plus facilement dans sa retraite . . . [etc.]" (125). Love, he says in his first letter, hesitates for his crown between myrtle (for happy lovers) and laurel (for conquerors). But Merteuil does not leave to him exclusively this kind of language, which from her vantage point becomes more of a joust: "il se rabattit sur la délicate amitié; et ce fut sous ce drapeau banal, que nous commençâmes notre attaque réciproque" (85). She declares, "je fus vaincue, tout à fait vaincue" (the language in use will hardly permit her to reverse subject and object in such a sentence) with as much satisfaction as Valmont does, "La voilà donc vaincue." Although all jest is gone by the time they sign off with "une véritable déclaration de guerre" (153), the hyperbole which has dominated much of their exchange must be taken for the grim kind of black humor it is.

Indeed the observation least often made about *Les Liaisons dangereuses*, an unfair omission, is that it is replete with wit. Cruelly funny, to be sure; but the winsomeness of the central couple, to the degree that a reader empathizes with them (and virtually all critics have allowed that one must to some extent), comes not just from their analytic mastery, their intelligence, but also from their sheer cleverness. Their letters teem both with parodies of others' styles and vocabularies and with witticisms and word plays. Expressions like "remplir de vin ce petit tonneau à bière," referring to Emilie's new protector (47),[19] are child's play to Valmont, most of whose jokes touch on things which are important to him, principally sex. They translate a basic ambivalence: sex is both valorized as the medium of their exploits, and depreciated as a mere accessory; it is central to "pleasure" but subordinate to "glory." Many euphemisms and metaphors concern sex acts: "une [des trois femmes] se trouva prête à éclore près de quinze jours avant les autres" (79); "J'ai d'abord été tenté d'aller plus avant, et d'essayer de passer pour un songe" (96); "nos entr'actes" (110); "je ne tiens plus à elle, que par le soin qu'on doit aux affaires de famille" (115). There is at least one such pun by Merteuil, referring to Danceny and Cécile: "Ils doivent répéter beaucoup de duos, et je crois qu'elle se mettrait volontiers à l'unisson" (5); as for Belleroche's "hommages réitérés" (10), usage had pretty much deprived the euphemism of its metaphoricity.

The sexual pun[20] is a particularly appropriate instrument of expression for a libertine who delights in bivalent utterances, and the famous letter 48 is but one gigantic *équivoque* of this sort based upon a fundamental semantic vulnerability of the conventional language of passion. It leads Joël Papadopoulos to speak of an "homologie de l'érotisme et de l'écriture dans Laclos,"[21] which in fact is perhaps more profoundly revealed in other passages. When Valmont writes, "Je déguisai mon écriture pour l'adresse, et je contrefis assez bien, sur l'enveloppe, le timbre de *Dijon*. Je choisis cette ville, parce que je trouvai plus gai, puisque je demandais les mêmes droits que le mari, d'écrire aussi du même lieu" (34), one can really speak of absolute homology: the husband's sexual prerogatives correspond to his writing. Or again, Merteuil's teasing musings about what the written proof of Tourvel's defeat will actually contain: "je suis curieuse de savoir ce que peut écrire une prude après un tel moment, et quel voile elle met sur ses discours, après n'en avoir point laissé sur sa personne" (20). Another instance concerns Valmont's reconciliation with Mme de Tourvel after the scene outside the Opera: "dans un moment, j'irai moi-même faire signer mon pardon: car dans les torts de cette espèce, il n'y a qu'une seule formule qui porte absolution générale, et celle-là ne s'expédie qu'en présence" (138). *Formule*, a verbal expression, is here the metaphor for sexual intercourse, which is wrapped up with writing (*signer* mon pardon) in one ironic utterance.

Love and sex constitute such a pervasive mythology in the novel that one can hardly create a separate category for the language devoted to them. But it is problematically related to language conveying a rather different mythology, that of pleasure and knowledge. Most of what Valmont and Merteuil have to say about love is depreciatory; from Valmont's fear of "le ridicule d'être amoureux" (4) to "les nausées de l'amour" (115) in which Merteuil wants to drown Belleroche, all "discours sentimental" (10) is parodied and mocked. Partly this is due to a rejection of the conventionally overblown rhetoric which to them is good only for comedy, but which a character such as Danceny naïvely rehearses with his fulsomely redundant "malheur éternel" (28), "désespoir éternel" (46, 93), "éternité d'amour" (93), "éternellement heureux ou malheureux" (17), of which their "éternelle rupture" is their mocking antithesis.[22] And partly it is owing to their materialistic theory of sex, which views love, though without denying its existence, as a kind of epiphenomenon generated by pleasure, to serve as its pretext: "Quelque pressée qu'on en soit, encore faut-il un prétexte" (10);

"l'amour, que l'on nous vante comme la cause de nos plaisirs, n'en est au plus que le prétexte" (81). Other people, to them, behave in ways that virtually are entirely determined, which is why they can be so easily manipulated by these human engineers. Sex is a particularly mechanistic aspect of such automatous behavior;[23] seduction is accomplished through the application of known laws.

In this, Mme de Rosemonde's indulgent but disabused judgment corroborates theirs. Her first response to Mme de Tourvel (103) admits that, after much reflection, she has no better counsel to proffer than an effort at valiant defense; no more than Valmont does she see any sure way out for the victim under attack.[24] This is to say that she takes love dead seriously as a passion, although she has no weakness for its dreams, which she qualifies as "idées chimériques d'un bonheur parfait, dont l'amour ne manque jamais d'abuser notre imagination" (130). Mme de Merteuil characterizes in much the same way the personal fantasy Stendhal was to call "crystallization": "ce charme qu'on croit trouver dans les autres, c'est en nous qu'il existe; et c'est l'amour seul qui embellit tant l'objet aimé" (134). And yet, this position is not totally without ambiguity either. Her stern diatribe in letter 104 to Mme de Volanges against love and its "dérèglements" must doubtless be filtered through an awareness of who is being addressed, and to what end (to ensure Cécile's marriage to Gercourt, and thereby the fruition of her own vengeance); but there is no letter which is not in some degree conditioned by these factors, not even those to Valmont. Everything in the novel is ostensible only, and one can never know whether what is said is "true": there remains only discourse. Merteuil idealizes Danceny, as one "in love" might, in letter 113, but this may be only the better to needle Valmont. Is Valmont sincere or not when he declares to Merteuil: "vous posséder et vous perdre, c'est acheter un moment de bonheur par une éternité de regrets" (115)?

The semantic problem is that in insisting on their very uniqueness as superfigures standing outside the general purview of laws, Valmont and Merteuil are appropriating a vocabulary of exclusiveness which overlaps with the ordinary rhetoric of love. It is in the name of this superiority that Valmont rejects the first call to effect a seduction when "vingt autres peuvent y réussir comme moi" (4), and that he justifies his exceptional procedures with Tourvel: "me traîner servilement sur la trace des autres, et triompher sans gloire!" (110). "Il est peu de femmes qui se sauvent alors du piège" (76): this remark by Valmont about Prévan, which assimilates

Mme de Merteuil to the general rule governing women, is part of the context in which she forges her affair with him as a demonstration that she is "au-dessus des autres femmes" (81). Although it is doubtless with some humor that Valmont pronounces, "Plus je vais, et plus je suis tenté de croire qu'il n'y a que vous et moi dans le monde, qui valions quelque chose" (100), the remark is perfectly consistent with the attitudes they express throughout. But there is already a breach in the solidarity, which began the minute Valmont, however jocularly, classed her with the "femmes faciles" (the category, in her mind, which Cécile represents); and when she is inclined to humiliate him, she in turn has recourse to observations which undermine his superiority: "dès que les circonstances ne se prêtent plus à vos formules d'usage, et qu'il vous faut sortir de la route ordinaire, vous restez court comme un écolier" (106). This trend continues on both sides, all their proliferating sarcasms by turns exalting and depreciating each other's and their own exceptional stature.

In contrast, the general rule is a comfort to the more conventional characters because, as Mme de Rosemonde puts it somewhat tautologically, "la vérité générale a pour garant la voix publique" (130). Even the admitted inconsistency of Mme de Volanges's public and private attitudes toward Valmont is rationalized as a general rule--"c'est une inconséquence de plus à ajouter à mille autres qui gouvernent la société"--whereas Tourvel is behaving in deviation from the norm: "Il était réservé à [vous] . . . de donner l'exemple de cette inconséquence" (32). Consistency, or, otherwise put, integrity of character, is not the principal criterion of acceptability, but rather the community standard. In this respect, Tourvel belongs to the special class of characters who claim exceptional status, repeatedly insisting she not be confused with *elles*--the other women in Valmont's past (11, 26, 41). Valmont implicitly accepts this claim, and much of the bile manifested in his exchanges with Merteuil has to do, in one way or another, with whether it is justified.

From such a vantage point all other people are interchangeable, part of a circulating system like money and having their "price." Emilie has her "prix convenu" (47), and even Tourvel, whose special nature is as often affirmed as denied by Valmont, is referred to in jest as "payée d'avance" (21). It is the necessity of reaffirming the exchange value of the Présidente that leads Valmont, in the same sentence in which he concedes the high "price" he places on this particular "adventure," to insist that it "ne m'empêchera pas d'en courir d'autres, ou même de la sacrifier à de plus agréables" (133). But this is another instance where the vocabulary of *badinage* progressively darkens into an intense point of contention. Valmont's "reward" (106, 110) is consistently referred to by both him and Merteuil in mock-economic terms, she calling it a "renouvellement de bail" (20)--raising some ambiguity about whether it is to be a single occasion or a more durable arrangement--and he as a promissory note: "Cela me fait songer que vous m'avez promis une infidélité en ma faveur, j'en ai votre promesse par écrit. . . . Je conviens que l'échéance n'est pas encore arrivée; mais il serait généreux à vous de ne pas l'attendre; et de mon côté, je vous tiendrais compte des intérêts" (57). It is interesting to note the ambiguity with which Valmont combines this register with that of (mock- ?) love rhetoric (*empire*) when he writes: "revenez donc au plus tôt jouir de votre empire sur moi, en recevoir l'hommage et m'en payer le prix" (144). It is perhaps because the "prix convenu" (131) has thus lost its connotations of spontaneity and generosity to the specificity of a demand for payment that she eventually repudiates the debit ("celui à qui on ne doit rien") and adds, sarcastically, "je ne vaux pas que vous vous donniez tant de peine" (152).

It is part of this pretention that, while being oneself irreplaceable, one can freely substitute for others--as did the Greek gods, and particularly for sexual purposes. Valmont stays in the Dutchman's stead with Emilie, occupies Vressac's with the Vicomtesse de M***, offers to replace Belleroche (in fact, however, Merteuil substitutes Danceny for Valmont), and, of course, substitutes for Danceny (and Gercourt) with Cécile: "ce jeune homme fit pour moi ce qu'il comptait que je ferais pour lui. Cette idée doublait, à mes yeux, le prix de l'aventure" (96). He takes special pleasure in recounting his virtuosity in this regard; he supplants Merteuil as stylistic and amorous tutor to Cécile, and dictates her letter to Danceny[25] in consummation of his Proteian performance: "Que n'aurai-je pas fait pour ce Danceny? J'aurai été à la fois son ami, son confident, son rival et sa maîtresse!" (115). And, of course, he usurps the husband's prerogatives with Tourvel--not to mention God's: "Les ferventes prières, les humbles supplications, tout ce que les mortels, dans leur crainte, offrent à la Divinité, c'est moi qui le reçois d'elle" (96). Merteuil makes similar claims,[26] although she is not free to demonstrate them so flamboyantly. But Valmont, in her eyes, loses his identity in the course of things, yields to an inferior version of himself: "Au vrai, vous accepter tel que vous vous montrez aujourd'hui, ce serait vous faire une infidélité réelle. Ce ne serait pas là renouer avec mon ancien amant; ce serait en prendre un nouveau, et qui ne vaut pas l'autre à beaucoup près" (152). There are thus other than economic overtones to Bertrand's declaration (relating to inheritance) after Valmont's death that "ce malheureux événement finit la substitution" (163).

Infidelity versus constancy forms one of the rhetorical axes of the novel, raised in Valmont's first letter: "Souvent même je désire . . . de finir par donner, avec vous, un exemple de constance au monde." The "amitié inviolable que nous nous sommes jurée" is a scaled-down version of "cet empire où je régnais seul" (15), and which Merteuil likewise evokes in nostalgic/ironic terms as "le seul de mes goûts qui ait jamais pris un moment d'empire sur moi" (81). *Fixer* is the concept around which not only Mme de Tourvel but also the central couple organize their discussion of the dilemma represented in the desired yet feared, indefensible and impossible ideal of constancy. Although humiliated by Belleroche's "insultante confiance"--"Il me prise donc bien peu, s'il croit valoir assez pour me fixer!" (113)--Merteuil asks Valmont, "comment vous fixer?" (131). Valmont: "Vous me fixerez. . . . Ai-je donc jamais cessé d'être constant pour vous?" (133);[27] "je veux me consacrer à vous tout entier" (144). But Merteuil, whatever her intentions with respect to the "reward," seems by this time to have renounced any hope of a durable liaison with him. In any case, the "empire" she insists on now has something tyrannical about it.

The inference that Valmont "really" loves Mme de Tourvel, and Merteuil Valmont, is plausible. But it remains an interpretation. The nature of the language will not reveal the presumed truth, because it has no clear purchase on exterior reality, even fictional: there is no reality, there are only versions of it. The interpretive freedom to ascribe love to a character is too unrestrained because love is a function of so many intertwined, and such ambiguous, codes. Is the criterion for love that the subject admits to it, or that someone else perceives it? Valmont says he loves Tourvel to Tourvel, and says the opposite to Merteuil. There are no grounds for privileging the first of these affirmations over the second, although in recent years most critics, including Rousset and Poulet, have done so. Just as good an argument can be made for the proposition that Valmont loves Mme de Merteuil.[28] If we can say with a lesser degree of interpretive subjectivity that Mme de Tourvel loves Valmont, it is a question of textual consistency: in other words, there is no countervailing evidence; she rarely gives any sign of disguising her thoughts, and she says, to him as well as others, that she loves him. But the person who affirms that someone else "loves" can really say just about anything, for the concept has no objective correlative. Love is discursive, and all we can do is to examine the way it makes its claims in discourse.

Love does not speak with any single style or vocabulary, but Valmont does give the impression of some lyricism when he calls Mme de Tourvel "céleste" and "angélique," says she reanimates his "charmantes illusions de la jeunesse," and admits to "un sentiment inconnu" and momentary loss of control over his sentiments. He himself has raised from his first letter the suspicion he is in love ("le ridicule d'être amoureux") with which Mme de Merteuil continually taunts him as "l'amant langoureux." But *amoureux* is hardly a translucent term in Valmont's hands, and may refer exclusively to the public judgment that is made on the basis of certain conventional exterior signs, which it calls *être amoureux* and which are, in Valmont's perspective, a *ridicule*. "Mon coeur trop plein ne put retenir ni ses discours ni ses larmes" (36) and numerous other such evocations are tendencious in that they participate in a rhetoric not of "pure" description but of persuasion, addressed to Mme de Tourvel, and are associated with more recognizable platitudes such as "l'état cruel où vous m'avez réduit." And it is one of the features and functions of this level of discourse to slide gradually towards specifically sexual implications: "je sens que c'est à vous seule qu'il appartient de me rendre heureux" (58)--while avoiding explicitness, to be sure.[29] What can be reasonably inferred from a tendencious phrase like "l'amour véritable, et tel que vous l'inspirez" (68)? Valmont exclaims, "Mais quelle fatalité m'attache à cette femme?" (100), but he does so in a situation where he believes the authentic seduction he was performing is on the rocks, and fears that somehow his own liberty has been compromised ("Je ne supporterai mon sort que du moment où je disposerai du sien"). Love is one explanation, and frustrated vanity another, just as for the despair he advertises at the end, and which the Rédacteur declines to interpret (154, 155). The context, both syntactic and situational, of each such utterance raises doubts about its ultimate meaning. Obviously Valmont has reasons for denying love when writing to Mme de Merteuil, who for her part does not buy his "parfaite indifférence" (138); but where are we to find a Valmont more authentically "himself" than in his letters to her?

Valmont has borrowed from generalized convention a whole range of concepts and expressions which denote and connote "love," and they are perfectly comprehensible to Mme de Tourvel as well, even though it is a language she does not affect to speak. The tragic diction in her letters of intense suffering (102, 114) is of a different register, but is still recognizable to Mme de Rosemonde, in whom it stirs a certain nostalgia, as the continuation of an old discourse: "toujours là le style de l'amour" (103). And although, in her lyrical phase, Tourvel refuses her wise friend's analyses, Rosemonde integrates her effusions immediately into the register of the already known, the "vérités générales" (130).

Despite their cynicism, however, neither Merteuil nor Valmont claims to have invented any new theory about how love is experienced and manifested. When Mme de Merteuil says that desire is transient and insufficient to sustain a liaison, she adds: "C'est une loi de la nature, que l'amour seul peut changer" (131). Thus she subscribes to a notion of love as a superforce, just as she recites the main tenets of the conventional code of femininity: the role of Merteuil and Valmont is not, as actors, to call into question the dominant codes, but to master them and benefit from their protection. Thus we find Merteuil, Danceny, and Valmont all voicing, without apparent irony, the same credence in the proposition that disorder connotes passion because passion produces disorder:

Une remarque que je m'étonne que vous n'ayez pas faite, c'est qu'il n'y a rien de si difficile en amour, que d'écrire ce qu'on ne sent pas. Je dis écrire d'une façon vraisemblable: ce n'est pas qu'on ne se serve des mêmes mots; mais on ne les arrange pas de même, ou plutôt on les arrange, et cela suffit. Relisez votre lettre; il y règne un ordre qui vous décèle à chaque phrase.
[Merteuil, 33]

Si cette lettre a peu d'ordre et de suite, vous devez sentir assez combien ma situation est douloureuse, pour m'accorder quelque indulgence. [Danceny, 64]

J'ai mis beaucoup de soin à ma lettre, et j'ai tâché d'y répandre ce désordre, qui peut seul peindre le sentiment. J'ai enfin déraisonné le plus qu'il m'a été possible: car sans déraisonnement, point de tendresse; et c'est, je crois, par cette raison que les femmes nous sont si supérieures dans les lettres d'amour.
[Valmont, 70]

The protagonists do not fragment conventional discourse; they do not have to invent their medium, but simply manage it. Compare too these two seemingly serious pronouncements by Rosemonde and Merteuil:

> Quand vous devriez un jour avoir le malheur de succomber (ce qu'à Dieu ne plaise!), croyez-moi, ma chère belle, réservez-vous au moins la consolation d'avoir combattu de toute votre puissance. [103]

> La longue défense est le seul mérite qui reste à celles qui ne résistent pas toujours. [121]

Merteuil applies such terms even to herself when, some three weeks later, while denouncing Valmont's "illusion" regarding his own sentiments-- "C'est de l'amour, ou il n'en exista jamais: . . . ce sont là, Vicomte, des symptômes assurés d'amour"--she refers to her own "courage à me défendre" (134). But, really less cagey than Valmont, she has already by this time said, with disarming and perhaps wistful simplicity: "Dans le temps où nous nous aimions, car je crois que c'était de l'amour, j'étais heureuse; et vous, Vicomte?..." (131).

The point is certainly not that Mme de Merteuil's diagnosis of Valmont is "wrong," but that it is not very scientific: she has been saying that he was in love from the very beginning, and for this there are other possible explanations than the necessary accuracy of her diagnostic acumen. At the end too she may be acting principally in view of provoking a certain behavior--in particular, of inciting Valmont to send the famous "ce n'est pas ma faute"[30] missive which, as she says (145), constitutes her victory over him and not over Tourvel. What Merteuil has really done is to insist relentlessly upon one aspect of the love code, one which implicates her at every moment in Valmont's very discourse: namely the uniqueness of the loved one.

Love is the antithesis, the denial of the validity of the libertine code which proclaims interchangeability. "Une femme n'en vaut-elle pas une autre? ce sont vos principes" (152). Love proclaims, on the contrary, that a particular individual is irreplaceable, whether because foredestined or simply because different from all others.[31] Its election is indelible. As Cécile intones, in her best attempt at eloquence, "Ces mots tracés au crayon s'effaceront peut-être, mais jamais les sentiments gravés dans mon coeur"

(69). It thus immediately becomes obvious that there is a conflict in claims: if Merteuil is to be unique among women, for reasons that have nothing to do in her ideological system with love, then Tourvel must be a woman like the rest. It is on this question, seen from their two rather contrasting viewpoints, that much of the contention rides.

Valmont has already been dallying rather lengthily over his new adventure when he doubtless startles his colleague by explicitly rejecting "l'insipide avantage d'avoir eu une femme de plus" (23), which is precisely the yardstick she thought he was applying. Asides such as "cette femme ne fait rien comme une autre" (40, *suite*) and "jamais je n'avais goûté le plaisir que j'éprouve dans ces lenteurs prétendues" (96) meanwhile subtly and implicitly create a qualitative comparison with Merteuil, especially when, as in the latter case, they are accompanied by comments suggesting that Merteuil is a good deal like women in general. As if he dreaded the day when Tourvel would leave her pedestal to join the common lot, he exclaims, "Ah! le temps ne viendra que trop tôt, où, dégradée par sa chute, elle ne sera plus pour moi qu'une femme ordinaire" (96). When she escapes his clutches, he says, "il faut renoncer à connaître les femmes" (100), which suggests that she alone breaks all the standard rules.[32] He is able to claim, conversely, his own exclusivity for Mme de Tourvel: "je n'aurai point de successeur. . . . Elle n'aura existé que pour moi" (115).[33] After her defeat, Tourvel is still on her pedestal, and the terms of his letter of victory, while trumpeting his "savantes manoeuvres," repeat over and again a system of comparison favorable only to Tourvel:

> Dans la foule des femmes auprès desquelles j'ai rempli jusqu'à ce jour le rôle et les fonctions d'amant . . .
> Ici, au contraire, j'ai trouvé . . .
> Ce n'est pas, comme dans mes autres aventures . . . [125]

Although he explicitly denies a place for "telle ou telle femme, exclusivement à toute autre," he overflows with expressions of ecstasy which Mme de Merteuil, when she finally answers him twelve days later, sufficiently underscores. "Ce charme inconnu," though not in itself a notably strong expression, particularly grates because of the implications of the *inconnu*. Merteuil's sarcasms are telling, and so are their revelations of her own reactions: should Valmont now condescend to her, to "chercher des plaisirs, moins vifs à la vérité, mais sans conséquence" (127)? "Mais autrefois, ce me semble . . . vous ne m'aviez pas destinée tout à fait aux troisièmes rôles."

Under this barrage Valmont retreats significantly; he tries to find a way in which the pleasures Merteuil offered him can also be rationalized as "toujours nouveaux" (129), and commutes Tourvel's claim from unicity to mere rarity (133). More still, he laboriously (just for her, or for himself too?) reconstructs Merteuil's own superlative position:

> Je volerai à vos pieds et dans vos bras, et je vous prouverai, mille fois et de mille manières, que vous êtes, que vous serez toujours, la véritable souveraine de mon coeur. [129]

> Ne combattez donc plus l'idée, ou plutôt le sentiment qui vous ramène à moi; et après avoir essayé de tous les plaisirs dans nos courses différentes, jouissons du bonheur de sentir qu'aucun d'eux n'est comparable à celui que nous avions éprouvé, et que nous retrouverons plus délicieux encore! [134]

Yet these terms are subtly unsatisfactory, perhaps because they come too late, and perhaps also because, although they make of the Valmont-Merteuil experience a summit, it is not the *classe à part* which identifies the love she insists he harbors for the Présidente, "non pas, à la vérité, de l'amour bien pur ni bien tendre, mais de celui que vous pouvez avoir; de celui, par exemple, qui fait trouver à une femme les agréments ou les qualités qu'elle n'a pas; qui la place dans une classe à part, et met toutes les autres en second ordre..." (141). Therefore her demands (and she draws attention to the verb *exiger*) center on an unconditional reduction of Mme de Tourvel to just *what she really is* in Merteuil's eyes, an ordinary woman: "J'exigerais donc, voyez la cruauté! que cette rare, cette étonnante Mme de Tourvel ne fût plus pour vous qu'une femme ordinaire, une femme telle qu'elle est seulement" (134).

All the terminological systems we have been looking at are rife with tensions, present at many levels from the start between Valmont and Merteuil and not just between them together and the society they challenge. It takes little more than his suggestion that Merteuil is more lucky than skillful--"plus de bonheur que de bien joué" (76)--to precipitate the Prévan affair, after which Valmont does not write to her again until he has a victory of his own (Cécile) to announce. And when he does, his manner contrasts pointedly with hers: whereas she had begun with a trumpet blast: "J'ai mis à fin mon aventure avec Prévan; *à fin!* entendez-vous bien ce que cela veut dire?" (85), Valmont begins in a roundabout way, decoying her into a discussion of Tourvel for two pages before mentioning Cécile and then dropping, at the *end* of a paragraph, the punch-line, ". . . et le succès a couronné l'entreprise" (96). The one-upmanship is both active and epistolary. It is a way of throwing back at her some of her own words (a game they both play): "mais moi, je n'entends rien à rien, et, comme vous dites, la femme la plus simple, une pensionnaire, me mène comme un enfant." Her infamous letter 81 stakes an outright claim to superiority and treats Valmont like a child devoid of merit even when he succeeds. Relative victories on either side evoke a brooding silence on the other; and the letter which enthusiastically begins, "A merveille, Vicomte, et pour le coup, je vous aime à la fureur!" (106), her first in over a week, is inspired by the rage and humiliation he has suffered over the Présidente's flight. By October 19 he is saying, "nous ne sommes plus de même avis sur rien" (115), and a month later this is expressed as a matter of two systems (141). One could go on and on detailing charge and counter-charge, sarcasm and defense; and even allowing generous discounts for the dosage of salt, which almost always modulates the discourse in some measure, there is no way not to notice symptoms of the progressive tightening of the nerves and muscles. But there is not much margin for reconciliation. "Je ne peux vous laisser sortir de ce cercle étroit" (153) has a predictable effect on the proud woman who reclaimed her liberty earlier by saying that "le caprice qui vous ferait préférer, peut également vous faire exclure" (127). She is almost compelled to receive Valmont only at her own good pleasure, and we never even get around to the *ultimatum* she so sententiously announces.

Meaning is more problematic between these two privileged observers than most critics have thought. They decipher the hidden messages in other people's letters, which connotes control; but the deficiencies of others do not prove their own unfailing accuracy. Their complete reliability to the reader is limited to reporting of events, where they are never contradicted; on all other levels there is always room for doubt. To say that up until the lapse of their correspondence "tous les éléments du récit avaient une interprétation indiscutable"[34] is to neglect signs of the ambiguity which plagues even their vision. Merteuil's announcement of her intention to take on Prévan provokes a bewildered response from Valmont (76): to him, her letter might have almost any meaning but the literal one, which is automatically excluded, and he cannot find a figurative one that makes sense either; the solution he finally hits on--"le mot de l'énigme"--is itself far-fetched. To her, his letter 115 "n'a pas le sens commun" (127). The distinction between *être* and *paraître*, which Todorov uses in the derivation of one of the "action rules" he extracts from the novel, is for schematic purposes greatly oversimplified: it is very difficult to say by what criteria anything passes from *paraître* into the domain of the reliably known. As Jean Rousset writes:

> Chez Laclos, les relations humaines sont des relations de combat ou de représentation, ce qui revient au même dans ce monde où l'on n'est jamais seul, où l'on pense toujours sous le regard d'autrui, que ce soit pour se dérober ou pour se révéler.... Quand Valmont écrit à Mme de Tourvel ou à Cécile, il ne dit jamais ce qu'il pense mais ce qu'il doit paraître penser pour produire l'effet voulu et faire progresser l'entreprise de séduction; et Mme de Merteuil change de masque sous nos yeux selon qu'elle s'adresse à Valmont, à Cécile, ou à Mme de Volanges: un visage par destinataire; grâce aux lettres successives, tous ces visages se dénoncent mutuellement.[35]

This is just what makes impossible any certainty about Valmont and Merteuil themselves (Rousset does not include Valmont's mask for Merteuil): the authenticity of their discourse to each other cannot be verified. There is double (or more) meaning in what the "sincere" characters write because they are blind to its implications, and to what the libertines write because they are deceivers. Subject-consciousness dissolves in a sea of pronouns, and there are only words representing beings.

The reading of Jean Rousset, like that of Georges Poulet, comes down to a schematization of the forces in play which the critic's own metaphors make clearer than does the terminology of the novel itself: "Car les *Liaisons* racontent la destruction du système par la passion, la dissolution du projet volontaire et de la méthode, dont le symbole est la ligne droite, par le sentiment, qui s'exprime dans la ligne sinueuse; à un ordre prémédité se substitue un trouble involontaire, à l'ordre des principes le désordre du caprice."[36] But we have seen that *caprice* in fact has its place in the Valmont-Merteuil system; it is precisely the mark of their freedom on which they insist the most. What then becomes of the neat distinction between the straight and sinewy line? Not to mention the fact that any such interpretation arrogates to itself the right to set aside entirely the one message of the work which is fully explicit, namely its moral one.

Let us recall that the "Avertissement" and the "Préface" both point to parallel but distinct lessons to be drawn from the destruction of Mme de Tourvel on the one hand and of Cécile on the other. This ostensibly makes of them the positively marked characters, and of their attackers the negative ones. A footnote to letter 9 calls Valmont a "scélérat" (Merteuil compares the two of them to "deux fripons" [131]); Mme de Volanges, speaking for the restored order, says the "méchants" are punished (173), and the final footnote pursues even further the demolition of Mme de Merteuil in alluding to "les sinistres événements qui ont comblé les malheurs ou achevé la punition de Mme de Merteuil."[37] This great purgation reinforces the epigraph, suggesting an exemplary scourge which stands as a moral lesson for all and as a pointed warning for some.

But explicit does not mean unambiguous. The commonest objection, from the time of the first publication to the present, has been the unsatisfactory or unconvincing nature of the extrinsic punishment meted out: a duel, a lost suit, and smallpox answer superficially to the moral stricture that vice be punished, but allow such leeway of interpretation that many have considered this moral posture of the book merely ironic if not perfectly cynical. The rehabilitation of Prévan, without intrinsic moral justification, is seen as further proof. There are, however, other, purely textual reasons for insisting on the ambiguity of the end. Several things do not come together quite right. And principal among them, once again, is the perplexing tone of the "Avis de l'éditeur"--perplexing not in that there is any doubt about its irony, but in the uncertainty of what it is directed at: the whole book ("ce n'est qu'un roman")? the validity of its moral? its overly great optimism? The straightforwardness of the book's explicit moral posture cannot but be affected by this subverting, nagging problem. Todorov has pointed out the tidy neutrality of the voice which reigns after the last (159) of the Valmont-Merteuil letters: "l'ordre qui détermine les actions des personnages dans et après le dénouement est simplement d'ordre conventionnel, l'ordre extérieur à l'univers du livre. . . . Le livre peut s'arrêter parce qu'il établit l'ordre qui existe dans la réalité" (Todorov, pp. 75-76).

There are dark secrets too which the text never reveals. What does Merteuil hold to threaten Valmont with, to counterbalance the revelations he can make about her? She implies that whatever it is would suffice to force him into exile (152), nothing more: and thereby, perhaps, that it is in the nature of a criminal offense.[38] But nothing proves that it was her intention at all to destroy Valmont, or that he too did not suppose it was a limited war they were waging. All he in fact does to her is to lure Danceny away to Cécile one night, with insult added to the injury; and all she really does to him is prove to Danceny that Valmont has corrupted Cécile and thus deceived him. There is no telling how far this might go, but at this point they are playing their cards close to their chest. What Merteuil does not expect is that Danceny will challenge Valmont, and what no one expects is that Valmont will lose. Only because of this does Valmont turn over her letters to Danceny, thus insuring himself, in dying, a macabre last laugh. And what still are we to make of the allusion in the final note to "la suite des aventures de Mlle de Volanges" and the hedged promise to "compléter cet ouvrage"? For to believe all the critics, nothing could be more "complet" than *Les Liaisons dangereuses*. It strains the imagination to conceive what the further adventures of Cécile could forebode unless it were something comparable to *Vénus dans le cloître* or worthy of Sade; the very existence of these suggestions at the end is positively destructive of the theoretical tidiness of the novel.

Todorov has insisted on the fact that the text tells the story of its own provenance, via certain indications in the letters and above all this footnote to letter 169: "C'est de cette correspondance [the letters held by Valmont], de celle remise pareillement à la mort de Mme de Tourvel, et des lettres confiées aussi à Mme de Rosemonde par Mme de Volanges, qu'on a formé le présent recueil, dont les originaux subsistent entre les mains des héritiers de Mme de Rosemonde." To this corpus are added too the letters of Cécile which are in Danceny's hands (174). This permits Todorov to bring his analysis full circle:

> L'histoire sous-jacente au roman est précisément celle de sa création; cette histoire est racontée à travers l'autre. . . . Le sens dernier des *Liaisons dangereuses* est un propos sur la littérature. Toute oeuvre, tout roman raconte, à travers la trame événementielle, l'histoire de sa propre création, sa propre histoire . . . . Ainsi apparaît la vanité des recherches du sens dernier de tel roman, de tel drame; le sens d'une oeuvre consiste à se dire, à nous parler de sa propre existence.[39]

Without meaning to invalidate the essential idea, I must point out a simple flaw which neither critic nor editor ever seems to have noticed: *there is no explanation whatever* of how the many letters of Valmont, Cécile,

Mme de Volanges, Danceny, and the Maréchale de ***--forty-two in all--
*held by Mme de Merteuil* found their way into the collection. There is no
mention of their fate in the text, and all we know of Merteuil is that she has
fled to Holland, taking everything of value with her. Ultimately, the story
has "told itself" incompletely, has not resolved its "sense" any more
definitively on this level than on any other. I can think of no better example
of the deviousness of the text, nor of its authoritarian power; for even if it
baits the reader with an assertion easily contradicted by the "facts," it is
likely to be believed. For what other source of facts, after all, do we have at
our disposal? Like Descartes's demon, the text is both the only thing we can
trust and something which may be trying to fool us. Nothing less than
persistent, aggressive reading will keep it "honest."

# NOTES

Pierre Choderlos de Laclos (1741-1803), *Les Liaisons dangereuses*, 1782. Edition: Gallimard, "Folio," 1977. All references will be to letter number. Almost all current editions of this work follow the text of the original edition and can be used equally well for reference purposes here; the exception is the Garnier edition established by Yves Le Hir, which follows instead the manuscript.

[1] Peter Brooks suggests this theme when he refers to them as "novelists" (*The Novel of Worldliness*, Princeton, 1969, p. 179). The desire to be one's own author, as well as that of others--"la volonté de substituer à l'avenir indéterminé, qui est l'oeuvre du hasard, un autre avenir, prédéterminé, qui est l'oeuvre de la volonté"--is, in Georges Poulet's interpretation, the basic subject of the novel (*La Distance intérieure*, Paris: Plon, 1952, p. 71).

[2] *Chef d'oeuvre* appears only once (63), but *ouvrage* occurs often, particularly as an aspect of Valmont's love rhetoric (35, 36, 83, 91, 125) and in relation to a fulfilled project (8, 63, 81, 115, 125, 129).

[3] Parallelism of expression, even in disparate passages, is often striking in *Les Liaisons dangereuses*; cf. Valmont's words to Mme de Tourvel: "L'attachement . . ., la soumission . . .; voilà en deux mots l'histoire de mes sentiments et de ma conduite" (58).

[4] Cf. Cécile: "Mme de Merteuil m'a dit aussi qu'elle me prêterait des livres qui parleraient de tout cela" (29).

[5] Many of these are identified by the Rédacteur in footnotes, but in one instance (early in letter 81) he mystifies instead by pretending not to know whether certain lines are quotes or not; we are to understand that *he* has set them off in italics as if they were, though they may only be "fautes": by this he means that an alexandrin in a prose passage is a stylistic flaw unless it is intended as a quotation.

[6] Merteuil's allusion to "une lettre d'*Héloïse*" (10) could mean the correspondence of Heloise and Abelard or one of its adaptations, but another in letter 33 seems clearly to refer to Rousseau's novel, as does of

course the book's epigraph. Her expression "son *Menechme*" (meaning 'his double') in letter 152 might well be an allusion not to Plautus but to Regnard's *Les Ménechmes, ou les jumeaux* (1705), but no editor seems to have noticed this. The annotation of *Les Liaisons dangereuses* remained in this respect quite incomplete until the recent publication of Laurent Versini's critical edition (*Oeuvres complètes*, Paris: Gallimard, coll. Pléiade, 1979). There still remain ambiguities, however: it is uncertain, for example, whether "Le Sage a bien raison" (145) means "le sage" (Rousseau, according to Versini), or Lesage; Versini does not identify *Pensées chrétiennes* in letter 107, although there apparently were numerous works by that name.

[7] The word *aventure* is more somber in Mme de Volange's style when she refers to Valmont's "scandaleuses aventures," themselves figured as a narrative entity: "Je pourrais vous en raconter qui vous feraient frémir" (9). 9).

[8] *Littérature et signification* (Paris: Larousse, 1967), pp. 47-48. Two objections might be made here: the first, that "imperfection" is a tendenciously judgmental term for an objective analysis, for writing is as much the source of the protagonists' strength as of their weakness; and secondly, that the conclusion about "la création du roman" sounds as if it confuses Laclos as author and Valmont-Merteuil as fictive authors: it would be more accurate to say the fictional materialization of the text (which, though nonidentical, *coincides* with the actual materialization).

[9] Cf. René Pomeau, *Laclos* (Paris: Hatier, "Connaissance des Lettres," 1975), p. 64.

[10] Note another curious echo effect between these two right at the start: the adjectives *jolie* and *gauche* by which Merteuil describes Cécile (2), and which the latter reports as overheard (as if from Merteuil's letter) in letter 3.

[11] Mme de Merteuil italicizes the expression which is, by epistolary convention, a quotation from a previous letter (6). Because such usage is frequent in *Les Liaisons dangereuses*, I will avoid all italics of my own in this chapter's quotations.

[12]I doubt the validity of Pomeau's assertion that the late summer beginning has no symbolic value, "ne renvoie nullement aux ardeurs de la passion" (op. cit., p. 92). The "chaleurs accablantes" (6) have the erotic function of exposing more of Tourvel to Valmont's indiscrete eyes; and cannot *chaleur* suggest the presence too of intense feminine desire? There are two allusions to the *chaleur* with which Tourvel defends Valmont (32, 37); and she says, when she gives him her second letter, "la chaleur est plus vive que je ne croyais" (40).

[13]Op. cit., pp. 73, 75; cf. Jean Rousset: "On assiste donc à un progrès marqué de l'entrelacement et de l'enchevêtrement. L'ordre et la pureté font graduellement place à une fusion et à un foisonnement des relations engagées qui correspondent au développement de la situation romanesque, à l'apparition du trouble et du désordre dans les sentiments" (*Forme et signification*, Paris: José Corti, 1962, p. 97).

[14]Prayer also, as a form of unrequited communication (23), implies the silence of God, particularly noticeable by ironic contrast in the letter where Mme de Rosemonde congratulates Tourvel on the efficacy of divine grace (126).

[15]"Quand [Danceny] n'y est pas, personne ne me parle, et je m'ennuie: au lieu que quand il y est, nous chantons et nous causons ensemble" (7); the harp case serves for the passage of letters between them.

[16]One thing she appropriates through names—and precisely because she has none—is relatives: she invokes Cécile as a sister (8), Valmont as brother (11), and Rosemonde as mother (102), as if she were reaching out with an adoptive nomenclature for human ties. "Aucun personnage ne semble avoir de père," remarks Pomeau (op. cit., p. 95; cf. p. 135). In truth, this is not too unusual in novels, but Mme de Tourvel remains a fairly extreme case, having been married by Mme de Volanges (8) to someone who theoretically exists but is resolutely absent from the (and her) story.

[17]"Surtout, on [=Tourvel] ne veut plus me voir: ce parti pris y est annoncé quatre fois de la manière la plus irrévocable. J'en ai conclu qu'il n'y avait pas un moment à perdre pour me présenter" (Valmont, 138); "si une fois je réponds, ma réponse sera irrévocable" (Merteuil, 141). Cf. Valmont's expression "traits ineffaçables" (151).

[18] An ironical turn in the plot is that the *bulletins* repeated toward the end, also about Tourvel, are the medical ones Mme de Volanges sends to Mme de Rosemonde.

[19] There is an ethnic code involved in this aside too, since the target is a Dutchman.

[20] The Rédacteur scores in his footnote the bad taste of the pun "sauter le fossé" in letter 6, but lets stand others, such as the one on "bois" (ambiguous, moreover) in 59.

[21] Note p. 489 of the ed. cit. Versini notes the "sens grivois" of the verb *écrire* in Valmont's sentence, "Jamais je n'eus tant de plaisir en vous écrivant" (letter 48; see Pléiade ed., p. 1238), but seems oblivious to the thematic implications of such a remark.

[22] Cf. however the ironic footnote to letter 46, which appears nonetheless to valorize Danceny's rhetoric for its earnestness.

[23] There are several allusions to the dullness of others expressed in such ways; Merteuil calls Belleroche "un manoeuvre d'amour" (113); Valmont refers to "les automates près de qui je végète" (100). As regards sex, Merteuil's starkest machine metaphor will suffice: "Ces sortes de femmes [i.e., like Cécile] ne sont absolument que des machines à plaisir. . . . Mais n'oublions pas que de ces machines-là, tout le monde parvient bientôt à en connaître les ressorts et les moteurs" (106).

[24] Whether there is any exit would seem to be one of the questions raised—and begged—by the novel: the "Avertissement" says that "sans doute les mêmes causes ne manqueraient pas de produire les mêmes effets," a notion which Mme de Merteuil parodically echoes: "La même cause produisit le même effet; je fus vaincue une seconde fois" (10). Both of these passages are tinged with irony; cf. also the Rédacteur's note to letter 51.

[25] He adds irony to this letter, as he had done in letter 48, by phrases such as: "[Valmont] fait tout comme vous feriez vous-même" (117). Cf. too the comic substitution of bodily parts in: "La main s'est retirée; mais je ne sais par quel hasard je me suis trouvé moi-même à sa place" (96).

[26]"Après le souper, tour à tour enfant et raisonnable, folâtre et sensible, quelquefois même libertine, je me plaisais à le considérer comme un sultan au milieu de son sérail, dont j'étais tour à tour les favorites différentes. En effet, ses hommages réitérés, quoique toujours reçus par la même femme, le furent toujours par une maîtresse nouvelle" (10).

[27]Merteuil does not appear to share Tourvel's willingness to adopt the (in fact worldly) distinction implied here between "infidélité" and "inconstance" (139).

[28]Besides adducing Valmont's allusions to the somewhat mysterious pact between them--"Que me parlez-vous d'éternelle rupture? J'abjure ce serment, prononcé dans le délire [what kind?]" (15); "notre prétendue rupture ne fut qu'une erreur de notre imagination" (133)--and evocations of "les délicieux plaisirs de notre première liaison" (115), one could argue that the intensity of his effort at the end to renew with her is evidence--but of course it can also be interpreted otherwise.

[29]Cf. Danceny's slightly more obvious "il ne tient qu'à vous de me rendre heureux, parfaitement heureux" (72). It bears noting that Valmont himself, somewhat surprisingly, compares his feelings with those of Danceny in letter 57.

[30]A curiosity: this phrase, which Merteuil imputes to Valmont as characteristic of him, seems to appear only four other times in the novel, twice under the pen of Cécile: "il sentira bien que ce n'est pas ma faute" (18), "Je suis bien fâchée que vous êtes encore triste à présent, mais ce n'est pas ma faute" (30); and twice under Merteuil's own: "ce qui est fait est fait et c'est votre faute" (51), "vous voyez bien qu'il faut encore attendre: et vous conviendrez, sans doute, que ce n'est pas ma faute" (106). Perhaps, like love, it is an instance of an idea she uses purely to get under his skin, something to which she knows him to be sensitive, and therefore capable of provoking a reaction.

[31]In the view of Rosemonde, who speaks for the general rule, the unicity of the loved object is a matter of masculine/feminine differential: "ce goût exclusif, qui caractérise particulièrement l'amour, n'est dans l'homme qu'une préférence . . .; tandis que dans les femmes, c'est un sentiment profond, qui . . . anéantit tout désir étranger" (130).

[32]One way Merteuil has of responding to this is, besides ridiculing the *amoureux*, to declare that he has been unable to carve for himself a special niche in Cécile's heart, who distinguishes Danceny still from all others (113).

[33]As in other instances, she echoes his very words: "je n'aurai vécu que pour lui" (128). For her, of course, Valmont fulfills all the criteria of which it is a question here: he is totally unlike other men ("Valmont est loin de leur ressembler!") and there is a hint of destiny: "Qui sait si nous n'étions pas nés l'un pour l'autre!" (132). Tourvel's letters have the important function at this stage of bearing witness to Valmont's continuing tenderness, on which he himself no longer dares insist.

[34]Todorov, p. 86.

[35]Op. cit., p. 95.

[36]Rousset, p. 97; cf. above, n. 13, and Poulet, p. 77. See Irving Wohlfarth's ingenious deconstruction of the critic's language in "The Irony of Criticism and the Criticism of Irony: A Study of Laclos Criticism," *Studies on Voltaire and the Eighteenth Century*, 120 (1974), pp. 269-317.

[37]Todorov for one suggests that these unstated sinister events might allude to the very publication of the letters, which thus extends Merteuil's moral punishment (p. 47). But how can it punish her when the names have been changed (footnote to "Préface")?

[38]An interesting reading of letter 152 by Peggy Kamuf suggests that Valmont's offense directly concerns the crown and possibly his interference in the royal blood line: see her *Fictions of Feminine Desire* (University of Nebraska Press, 1982), pp. 140-43.

[39]Todorov, p. 49. One could object that this construction of the *sens* of the work still would not preclude a valid inquiry into its *signification*. Similarly, with regard to the action rules Todorov seeks to codify, one could answer to his conclusion—"Savoir que telle succession d'actions relève de cette logique [structurale] permet de ne pas lui chercher une autre justification dans l'oeuvre" (p. 56)—that it applies only on its own level, that of narratology; and that it is perfectly rational all the same to pursue inquiry of other "justifications" (psychological, moral, and so forth).

## Post Scriptum

The need for narrative is so basic to man that it might be said to inhere in our genes.[1] Our notion of literature, however, goes beyond mere fabulation; the text does more than refer, it assumes a stylistic density, a self-conscious opacity, in short a texture. So an attentive act of reading, or at least one of attentive rereading, loses its proccupation with what "happens" as pure sequence of diegetic events, and involves a concern with the substance of language. Once this process begins, it is hard to tell it where to stop, and by what right.

At a minimum, I would hope that this book has demonstrated that the novels it treats are not just stories. It occurs to me, though, that a reader might judge certain word tricks performed by the critic as palpable extravagances. My response is in part disseminated in these pages: the whole text being extant, how can one conclude that particular parts of it (say, a cluster of terms sharing a certain common affinity) are less significant than others? The sometimes strange logic of what might be called "recombinant" semes will not be so easily defeated. The mind is affected by even sub-syntactic bits of language, and meaning is subject to so many influences that they will doubtless never be entirely mapped.

It follows that no "intention" can totally control it, and even that that intention as inferred from the text itself will never be unambiguous. It makes little difference whether patterns in the text are presumed to be willful; it matters only that they are there--or that they are not, which is the only telling refutation. By sticking close to actual, present text, my design has been to avoid pure flights of fancy.

If that much is conceded, then the novels of the period covered here have, I believe, as much power as the fictions of any time and place to enmesh our minds in the play of language and the imaginary--and also, indeed, of language and the real. Originally the genre the least encumbered by canons, free to indulge its own worst temptations, the early novel was also the most available literary form for exploration of themes and figures to be drawn into its literary compass. Its extremes, from facetiousness to preciosity, may be a trap for the unwary--a category which includes both the contemporary for whom they were too plebeian or too insipid, and the reader of the twentieth century who is inclined to view them as something primitive, valid only as reminders of what things were like before progress was invented. They are rich in enigmas and usually reward attention.

I do not think any specific schema will provide the reader with a key equally valuable for all such texts. If keys there be, they must often be coaxed from the text, and sometimes quite in spite of its most overt postures. The text that reveals itself on the surface may be setting a decoy; and even if it isn't, it is likely as not to become tangled in its own rigging. From that standpoint, although conventions may vary over time, the novels of the nineteenth-century heyday are little different from their predecessors or followers. Prose is never a transparent window: it is a prism; and what is seen through it will always depend some on the position(s) of the observer.

## Note

[1] Jacques Monod suggests just that, specifically with regard to a narrative account of human origins and foundation, in *Le Hasard et la nécessité* (Paris: Seuil "Points", 1970), pp. 210-13.

# Index